MEXICO

FROM THE BEGINNING TO THE SPANISH CONQUEST

This book is the first in a three-volume history of Mexico, a major work that conveys the full sweep of Mexican history in all its social, economic, and political diversity, from the first human settlement of Mesoamerica down to the post-PRI politics of our day.

Beginning with the first entry of men and women into the Americas, Volume I charts the development of Mesoamerica from roughly 25,000 B.C. down to the Spanish Conquest in 1519–21. Analysing the principal periods and ethnic groups – Olmec, Zapotec, Maya, Toltec, Teotihuacano, and Aztec – Alan Knight seeks to explain the basic processes of preconquest history: the formation of states and social hierarchies, the rise and fall of empires, the role of religion, "markets," migration and ecology, patterns of settlement and consequent regional differentiation. Clear, comprehensive, and gracefully written, Knight's analysis illustrates the rich diversity of Mesoamerican history, while locating that history within a broader comparative framework of historical change. The book concludes with the trauma of the conquest, the destruction of the Aztec empire, and the birth of colonial New Spain.

Alan Knight is Professor of the History of Latin America at Oxford University. He is the author of the two-volume *The Mexican Revolution* (Cambridge, 1986), which was awarded the Beveridge Prize by the American Historical Association and the Bolton Prize by the Conference on Latin American History.

MEXICO

FROM THE BEGINNING TO THE
SPANISH CONQUEST

ALAN KNIGHT

St. Antony's College, Oxford University

CAMBRIDGE
UNIVERSITY PRESS

PUBLISHED BY THE PRESS SYNDICATE OF THE UNIVERSITY OF CAMBRIDGE
The Pitt Building, Trumpington Street, Cambridge, United Kingdom

CAMBRIDGE UNIVERSITY PRESS
The Edinburgh Building, Cambridge CB2 2RU, UK
40 West 20th Street, New York, NY 10011-4211, USA
477 Williamstown Road, Port Melbourne, VIC 3207, Australia
Ruiz de Alarcón 13, 28014 Madrid, Spain
Dock House, The Waterfront, Cape Town 8001, South Africa

http://www.cambridge.org

© Alan Knight 2002

First published 2002

Printed in the United States

Typeface New Aster 10/13.5 pt.   *System* LaTeX 2$_\varepsilon$ [TB]

A catalog record for this book is available from the British Library.

Library of Congress Cataloging in Publication Data
Knight, Alan, 1946–
Mexico. From the beginning to the Spanish Conquest / Alan Knight.
p.   cm.
Includes bibliographical references and index.
ISBN 0-521-81474-X – ISBN 0-521-89195-7 (pb.)
1. Mexico – History – To 1519.   I. Title.
F1228.98 .K65   2002
972′.01 – dc21   2001052633

ISBN 0 521 81474 X hardback
ISBN 0 521 89195 7 paperback

In memory of Carole

Contents

Preface

I should like to thank the three anonymous readers of this book (then manuscript), who did their job scrupulously, sensitively, and with remarkable speed. I should also like to thank the people of Cambridge University Press – Frank Smith, Alia Winters, Camilla Knapp and Susan Greenberg – who helped bring this book to fruition. Needless to say, any faults are of my making, not theirs.

It is usual in these prefaces to list a roll call of individuals and institutions who made it all possible. In fact, the trend within British higher education – faithfully, even enthusiastically, repeated in my own university, Oxford – has been towards a narrow (and misconceived) utilitarianism, a diminution of real resources dedicated to research, and relentless bureaucratic overload (evident in the endless round of evaluations, assessments, management gimmicks, reforms of 'governance', etc.). All of this – horribly reminiscent of the ill-fated Bourbon Reforms of the late eighteenth century (see Vol. II of this trilogy) – served, certainly in my experience, to impede rather than to advance research and scholarship.

However, I would like to acknowledge the supportive camaraderie of three groups, who in their different ways have all helped counteract this institutional drag: my colleagues in (or associated with) the Oxford Latin American Centre; the handful of Mexican historians based in the U.K. who have kept the flame alight in far from easy times (Professors Brading, Hamnett and Thomson in particular); and, last but not least, the many Mexicans – scholars, students, librarians, archivists and many others – who have helped me along the way, as I have tried to learn about their fascinating country.

Series Introduction

This is one volume in a three-volume series which charts the history of Mexico from the beginning – that is, from the initial human settlements in North America – down to the present. It is, therefore, a sort of 'national' history: it takes what is now – notwithstanding certain internal and external challenges – a clearly constituted nation-state, Mexico, and treats the history of that entity: the geographical space in which Mexico sits and the thousand or so generations of 'Mexicans' who have lived since the first settlers crossed the Bering land bridge from Asia and headed south. Of course, the nation-state of Mexico came into being only in 1821 (the concluding point of my second volume), and, even then, it was a fragile entity, destined for severe mutilation at the hands of the United States some twenty-five years later. Nevertheless, the Mexican nation-state (whose post-1821 history will be the subject of a third volume, now in preparation) was created on the foundations of the colony of New Spain, which in turn had been built on the detritus of the Mesoamerican polities (above all, the Aztec empire) which flourished prior to 1519. 'Mesoamerica' – the cultural-cum-chronological entity which embraced what would later become 'Mexico' (as well as some of Central America) – was, of course, no nation-state; rather, it was a congeries of empires, city-states and stateless peoples. But by virtue of historical processes which involved both deep continuities and sharp ruptures, Mesoamerica metamorphosed into colonial New Spain; and New Spain provided the foundation of the independent republic of Mexico. Those continuities and ruptures form the basis of this study.

National histories are not the staple of historiography that they once were. True, scholars may make a killing with a successful 'national' textbook; but, in doing so, they garner no critical acclaim from their peers. Textbooks, by definition, are succinct and synthetic, uncontentious and undemanding. (That may not stop them being more influential than most works of history, of course.) This book is not a textbook, although it was first conceived as a succinct, synthetic survey of Mexican history, from the beginning to the present (a present that is now quite a few years in the past). With time the survey grew, and I became aware that I was not up to writing a textbook. The result is this three-volume study. Volume I covers the history of Mesoamerica/Mexico from 'the beginning' – that is, from the first human entry into the Americas, c. 20,000 B.C., to the Spanish Conquest in 1519–21. (The first twenty thousand years or so are, however, peremptorily despatched in a matter of pages.) Volume II deals with the colonial period, from Conquest to Independence (1821), and Volume III tells the story of Mexico since Independence.

If national histories are at a discount these days, why hazard this grand and perhaps quixotic survey? A personal justification is that I wanted to educate myself about pre-Independence Mexican history, thus to emancipate myself from the narrowly modernist view I had acquired on the basis of my previous work (which focused on the Mexican Revolution of 1910). Because of the heavy pall of history which hangs over modern Mexico, it seemed to me both necessary and interesting for a historian of modern Mexico to retreat in time, to note the continuities and ruptures previously mentioned and thus to prime oneself against those vendors of historical snake oil who – be they politicians, social scientists, journalists, 'organic intellectuals' or cheapskate historians – exploit and traduce the past in the narrow interests – personal, political or pecuniary – of the present.

While this may offer a (personal) reason for writing these books, it does not justify anyone's reading them. Here, I think, two justifications can be entered. The first is obvious: Mexico, like Mount Everest, is there; hence it is worthy of study, not least by those who may visit the country or who may nurture some nugget of historical information – Cortés's meeting with Moctezuma in 1520; Juan Diego's meeting with the Virgin of Guadalupe eleven years later – which they wish to contextualize. While it would be overly subjective and invidious to compile league tables of national histories, it cannot be denied that Mexico's history is – like the history of Greece or Italy, China or Iran – unusually 'long', rich and culturally diverse, as well as being particularly violent and at times tragic. It is littered with arresting episodes and images (like the two meetings just mentioned). 'May you live in interesting times', says the Chinese curse; the Mexicans/Mesoamericans have had more than their fair share of 'interesting times'. Thus, to the extent that history embodies a genuine 'romantic' appeal – by which I mean the appeal of presenting momentous events and processes, located in radically unfamiliar and intellectually challenging contexts[1] – Mexico/Mesoamerica is a prime candidate for historical study.

The second justification is that Mexico offers ample scope for 'scientific' history, by which I mean history which engages with the social sciences – history which, some would say, is 'nomothetic' as well as 'idiographic', which is concerned with generalities (e.g., processes of religious conversion) as well as with particularities (like the apparition of the Virgin of Guadalupe). 'Scientific' – or, if you prefer, 'analytical' or 'reasoned'[2] – history involves comparing and contrasting, assembling data and marshalling arguments, drawing upon relevant theory for useful explanatory concepts. While narrative, particularist ('idiographic') history and scientific/analytical/reasoned ('nomothetic') history employ different 'rhetorics' and may appeal to different intellects, they are, in my view, complementary and not antithetical. They both depend, for their cogency, on similar rules of evidential inquiry and presentation;[3] and, taken together, they capture

---

[1] Mexico may be, for me, a foreign country; but, as the old adage says, 'the past is a foreign country', hence modern Mexicans, too, face an intellectual challenge when they grapple with their own remote (and maybe not so remote) history.

[2] Stephen Haber, 'Anything Goes: Mexico's "New" Cultural History', *Hispanic American Historical Review*, 79/2 (1999), pp. 310–11, following Fogel and Elton (a decidedly odd couple), contrasts, I think excessively, 'social science' and 'traditional' history; Pierre Vilar, *Iniciación al vocabulario del análisis histórico* (Barcelona, 1980), pp. 9, 11, favours 'reasoned' (*razonada*) history, although he goes on to recall how, when asked 'do you believe that history is a science?', he 'replied, irritated, that if I did not so believe I would not devote myself to teaching it'.

[3] I mention this in part to join together what others might wish to put asunder; in part to rebut, should rebuttal be required, the whimsical notion that history involves free-floating texts, detached from any 'reality', hence incapable of reasoned debate on the basis of empirical evidence: a notion which, if less prevalent than some positivistic scaremongers would have us believe, does nevertheless have its proponents, especially among the Lotophagi of literary criticism: see Richard J. Evans, *In Defence of History* (London, 1997), ch. 4.

two powerful justifications of historical research – the (idiographic) interest in compelling narrative and the (nomothetic) concern for understanding broad processes of social change.

'National' histories, even though they seem *passé* in the eyes of many historical professionals,[4] offer perfectly adequate vehicles for these complementary rhetorics. It is a mistake to believe that a focus on national history precludes comparison or ensures superficiality: not only can 'nations' be compared to each other but also, more importantly, 'nations' (not to mention grand non-national entities like 'Mesoamerica') are themselves composites which have to be disaggregated so that the parts can be analysed comparatively. Thus, historians of Mexico largely agree that there are and always have been 'many Mexicos' and that to understand the loose aggregate 'Mexico' (again, not to mention 'Mesoamerica') we have to disaggregate – not only by region or locality, which, given Mexico's huge size and corrugated landscape, is often crucial, but also by class (e.g., landlord or peasant), ethnicity (Indian, mestizo or creole), ideology (Catholic, 'syncretic' or 'pagan') and sector (market or subsistence; mining, agriculture or manufacturing). Thus, national history requires comparison and – today at least – in no sense implies the contemplation of a flawless national monolith. In this respect, the difference between 'national', 'regional' and 'local' history is purely one of degree and should not be elevated to a ruling shibboleth. Regional and local history, which has rightly proliferated and prospered in recent years, also involves a good deal of aggregation and may, despite its narrower focus, still display superficiality. Furthermore, national history offers a potential context for regional and local histories (plural), hence may help to sort out the typical from the aberrant, just as global or continental history offers a potential context for national studies.

Mexico is also fertile terrain for 'scientific' history. Many of the most weighty questions which historians (and other social scientists) confront have their distinctive Mexican embodiments: the Neolithic revolution and the origins of 'civilization'; the formation of states

---

[4] Hence this argument is directed primarily at the professionals (including budding students of history); the lay reader may see nothing archaic in national history, hence little of relevance in this argument.

and class societies; empire-building, both European and extra-European; the expansion of Europe and the onset of Latin American 'dependency'; the role of religion – again, both European and extra-European; the rationale of ritual practices (including sacrifice) and religious conversion; the dynamics of colonial government, 'native' resistance and accommodation, ethnic miscegenation, migration and cultural syncretism; the genesis of nationalism and the conquest of independence, within the broad context of the 'Atlantic Revolution' of 1776–1821.

Thus, the study of Mexico should shed light on much wider processes of historical change, and therefore without, I hope, losing sight of the specificity of the Mexican experience, I have paid some attention to those processes and to the concepts and explanations which help make sense of them. This has involved some theoretical detours which, in this day and age, may also seem *passé* and even quaint. I have, for example, reprised the old argument about the 'feudal' or 'capitalist' character of Spain and the Spanish empire: an argument which was, in a sense, shelved long before it either achieved resolution or lost all utility. Historians, social scientists and others readily talk about the triumph of capitalism – today more triumphant and triumphalist than ever – and such usage must imply something or (better) somethings (plural) which went before which were not capitalist. Elucidating the difference is therefore a matter of some importance, which cannot be left to mere intuition or common sense. It is particularly important in a broad synthetic study such as this since, as a general rule, the broader the historical sweep is, the more crucial are the 'organizing concepts' used to make sense of the sweep. As Voltaire queried: 'If you have nothing to tell us except that one barbarian succeeded another on the banks of the Oxus and Jaxartes, what is that to us?'[5] Or, we could echo, on the banks of the Lerma and the Usumacinta?[6] Gibbon, of course, told the story of riverside barbarians (*inter alia*), but he linked his magisterial narrative to 'philosophical' inquiries – concerning, for example, the rationale of Christian conversion.[7] Braudel, too, linked specific stories

---

[5] Quoted in E. H. Carr, *What Is History?* (Harmondsworth, 1964), p. 88.

[6] Not that I mean to suggest that those living on the banks of the Lerma and Usumacinta were 'barbarians'.

[7] Peter Burke, *History and Social Theory* (Cambridge, 1992), p. 5.

and other 'idiographic' particularities to a grand vision and quasi-
theory of history. Without claiming to scale the heights of Gibbonian
or Braudelian history, I would plead the legitimacy of asking big
questions and trying to marshal the big concepts necessary to make
sense of them.

Of course, big concepts are a matter of subjective choice. We can
all agree that Cortés made landfall on the Gulf of Mexico in 1519
and entered the smoking ruins of Tenochtitlán as a conqueror in
1521. When it comes to explaining why that happened – why Cortés
overcame Moctezuma and not vice versa[8] – interpretations will differ
and will not be easily adjudicated according to shared criteria. Was
the religious conversion of Mexico's Indians in the sixteenth century a glorious 'spiritual conquest' or a sordid story of oppression,
coercion and dissimulation? Was Mexican independence the result
of endemic social, ethnic and nationalist tensions, or an almost ac-
cidental by-product of the Napoleonic invasion of Spain in 1808 –
without which the colony would have remained in Spanish hands,
content with a modicum of 'home rule'? Did the Aztecs slaughter
prisoners *en masse* because they were avid for protein? Did the Classical Maya cities fall victim to war, revolution, disease or starvation?
Was New Spain feudal or capitalist?

When it comes to asking – and tentatively answering – these big
questions, personal inclinations cannot be avoided. I find these questions interesting, even if they are in some cases old (but nonetheless
unresolved). Some historians find them irrelevant or tedious, and
there is nothing I can do about that. Meanwhile, there are questions –
of a somewhat different sort – which, I concede, are neglected in
these pages. These might be loosely summed up as 'cultural' questions: a catch-all category which includes both traditional historical
themes, such as 'high' culture (e.g., painting, literature, architecture),
and 'new', and certainly fashionable, themes, such as popular culture (religion, ritual, recreation), gender, signs and signifiers. To put
it bluntly, this history may seem overly materialist, concerned more
with the Mexican political economy than with the Mexican psyche.

---

[8] This question is a complex one, involving not only superior Spanish technology, logistics,
morale, or luck but also Spanish motivation – why, in other words, did a Spanish fleet sail
to Mexico, rather than an Aztec fleet to Spain?

Beyond pleading subjective inclination – which is a plea of limited validity[9] – I would enter three modest considerations.

First, it should be recognized that some of the supposedly 'new' cultural history involves a semantic repackaging of older ideas and topics. 'Subalterns', for example, were once called workers and peasants (among other things). I have tried to give a good deal of attention to 'subalterns', even though I have not used the term, at least not systematically. So I think I write 'subaltern history' just as I write prose, but I do not make an issue of it. At any rate, there is a fair amount of 'bottom-up' (popular) history in these pages, not least because 'top-down' (elite) history cannot be understood in isolation; the two are dialectically related. It is true, however, and quite deliberate, that my 'subalterns' are seen more at work than at play, more in acts of protest than in moments of recreation, more on the streets and in the fields than in their own homes. Subjective inclination and constraints of space aside, there are a couple of reasons for this, which have to do with the availablity, status and relevance of the evidence.

Second, some of 'new cultural history' is still incipient (it is contesting for acceptance in the 'market-place of ideas'), and anyone who tries to write a general synthetic history should beware of the dictates of fashion. I have therefore stitched this story together from fairly traditional material, not the latest fashionable fabrics, however eye-catching. Caution is particularly in order when, given the novelty of some themes, there is – as yet – no conclusive evidence, no sign of scholarly consensus. For example, the impact of the Spanish Conquest on Mesoamerican gender relations appears to

---

[9] 'Subjective inclination' is of limited, but not negligible, validity. All historians – irrespective of whether they work on national, regional, local or thematic topics – have to select themes, facts and arguments from a huge range of possibilities. The bigger the topic, roughly speaking, the greater the range of possibilities and the problems of selection. The process of selection, in turn, will reflect the historian's own interests and priorities. The finished work is therefore open to criticism on two fronts: sins of commission (getting the facts, argument or internal logic of the work wrong) and sins of omission (leaving out important topics which deserve attention). The first criticism, being more focused, is more conducive to objective debate; the second is necessarily more subjective. Yet – as readers of academic reviews, regular seminar-goers and doctoral candidates will attest – the second is often the easiest and commonest form of criticism: 'the author/paper/candidate neglected...'. While this criticism can sometimes be substantiated in terms of the overt claims and logic of the book/talk/thesis, it is often just a countersubjective claim: it means, 'if I had written this book/paper/thesis I would have done it differently and would have said more about...'; and, in turn, it begs the question, 'given that time and space are finite, what would you have left out instead?'

be a matter of considerable disagreement, but disagreement based, it seems, on a scarcity, rather than a surfeit, of hard data and mature debate.[10] In comparison, we know a lot about the make-up of the colonial hacienda or the character of the Bourbon Reforms; and, while knowledge does not guarantee consensus, it does provide the national historian with the material with which to attempt an informed synthesis.[11] I do not doubt that, in the years to come, as recent research is consolidated and incorporated into synthetic studies they will mutate accordingly, and for the better.

Finally, the relevance of some 'cultural' themes is not always clear. I work on the assumption that a history of Mexico/Mesoamerica ought to explain the main dynamics of change in a large and complex society. Necessarily, this means heroic (or stupid) aggregation, and the omission of much that might be interesting in itself, but which is of limited relevance to the big story. For example, I have paid relatively little attention to elite culture (literature, 'high' art and architecture), save where it seemed to me that elite culture clearly intertwined with economics or politics, broadly defined. Thus, the lay-out of the sacred city of Teotihuacan or the severe neoclassical architecture of the late Bourbon period clearly carried powerful sociopolitical significance. But this is not true of all products of 'high culture';[12] and I did not want to go the way of some textbooks, which, within the

---

[10] Compare Arthur J. O. Anderson, 'Aztec Wives', pp. 77, 84–5, for whom 'the Aztec world, after the conquest as well as before, was a man's world', hence, 'nothing in the position of Aztec wives had altered much' as result of the Conquest, and Susan Kellogg, 'Tenochca Mexican Women, 1500–1700', pp. 133, 139, who sees an 'eventual and marked decline in the status of Mexican women': both in Susan Schroeder, Stephanie Wood, and Robert Haskett, eds., *Indian Women of Early Mexico* (Norman, Okla., 1997).

[11] Hence, by way of explanation and apology, the colonial volume in this series is heavily footnoted: in order (a) to point the reader to relevant sources and (b) to engage in debates, qualifications and clarifications which would clutter the text but which are important for conveying the scope and complexity of colonial scholarship.

[12] Some might wish to make a tight, even deterministic, conection between high culture and social, political and economic forces, which they see marching in lockstep through defined historical stages or periods. Recent literary criticism (again) inclines to this view; as did Harry Lime (*The Third Man*), with his famous association between, on the one hand, Renaissance political violence and high artistic achievement and, on the other, Swiss sociopolitical stability and – the cuckoo clock. Such a view probably exaggerates Swiss sociopolitical stability and (more important) assumes that high culture is a reflex of social forces, whereas I would see it – as some choose to see the state – as 'relatively autonomous' of those forces. And, since those forces are my chief concern in this book, it follows that high culture need make only an occasional appearance in its pages. A similar argument can be made for popular culture, if narrowly defined to denote *aesthetic* practices (music, dance, textile and ceramic styles) rather than broader *collective* activities (e.g., fiestas, drinking, riots).

grand structure of national history, create tiny token compartments for 'poetry', 'music', 'architecture' and so on. This is not a history of Mexican poetry, music or architecture. The same is true, *mutatis mutandis*, for popular, as opposed to elite, culture: I introduce the industrious Indian potters of Tonalá (Jalisco), or the exalted religious insurgents of Cancuc (Chiapas), both of them exemplary cases of broad trends in colonial society; but I do not claim to present a thorough analysis of, say, popular artisan styles and ritual practices throughout New Spain.

Indeed, critics might say, and they might be right, that this is a mainly materialist history, concerned with forms of economic production and exchange, as well as with the political structures which made those forms possible. Thus, its primary themes are population, agrarian production and labour systems; villages and haciendas, mines and cities; political and clerical authority; state- and empire-building; warfare, rebellion and repression. The Mesoamericans/Mexicans, having lived in 'interesting times' for a good two millennia, have yielded a vast body of evidence under these diverse headings. Hence, in seeking to do them – both the themes and the people – historiographical justice, I have necessarily neglected some other themes, whose omission, whole or partial, may be lamented by those less tarred with the brush of materialism. In conclusion I would ask: given the story told in these pages, what is omitted that is crucial to explaining its course and outcome? There are no doubt plenty of possible answers, and plenty of historians capable of filling the blanks.

ONE. Mesoamerican Origins

I n the year 1518 a report reached the Aztec emperor Moctezuma of a portentous sight: 'a small mountain, floating in the midst of the water' off the Mexican Gulf coast. Moctezuma was troubled. Portents had come thick and fast in recent months. A comet blazed in the heavens; on a calm day the waters of Lake Texcoco boiled; voices wailed in the night, and hunters caught prodigious beasts. Nor was this accumulation of portents altogether surprising (although their failure to explain them cost Moctezuma's astrologers their lives) since, according to Aztec calendrical lore, the impending year 1519 (*Ce Acatl*, One Reed) was one of special significance, associated with both the birth and the death/transfiguration of Quetzalcoatl, the feathered serpent.[1]

The floating mountain was in fact a caravel of the expedition of Juan de Grijalva which had put out from Cuba, made landfall on the Caribbean coast of Yucatán, and then plied up the Gulf as far as the Pánuco River. Grijalva's expedition was not the first to touch the territory of present-day Mexico. In 1517, Francisco Hernández de Córdoba had been routed when he led his men ashore in Campeche; a few shipwrecked Spaniards had already acquainted themselves with the people and terrain of the Yucatán peninsula.[2] Thus when, in

---

[1] Miguel León-Portilla, *The Broken Spears: The Aztec Account of the Conquest of Mexico* (Boston, 1990, first pubd. 1962), pp. 3–11, 16; Nigel Davies, *The Aztecs: A History* (London, 1977), pp. 237, 259; Hugh Thomas, *The Conquest of Mexico* (London, 1993), pp. 46–51.
[2] Inga Clendínnen, *Ambivalent Conquest: Maya and Spaniard in Yucatán, 1517–1570* (Cambridge, 1987), pp. 4–8.

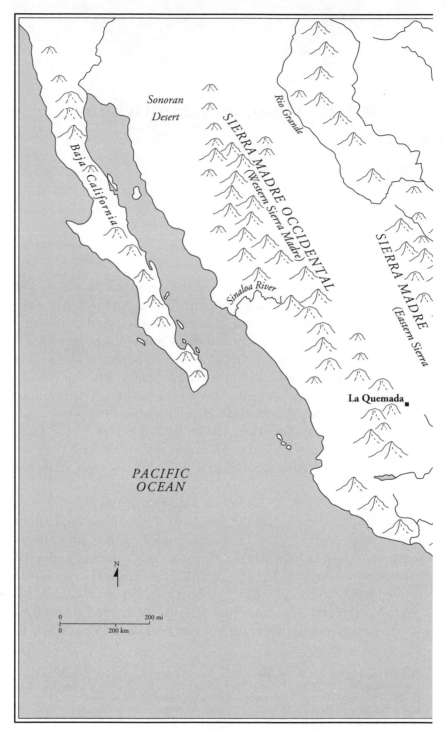

Map 1

Map 1 (continued)

the year One Reed, Hernán Cortés sailed from Cuba with a fleet of eleven ships and, following the now established route, made landfall in Yucatán before beating his way up the Gulf coast, his arrival was no sudden revelation; indeed, Aztec intelligence was swift and efficient, and Moctezuma's envoys soon made contact with the newcomers. But if Moctezuma and his generals, priests and soothsayers were apprised of Cortés's approach, they could not have been aware of the threat it posed. Nor did Cortés and the Spaniards, with their vague but seductive notions of a rich empire lying inland from the Gulf, anticipate the sheer scale, wealth and complexity of the Mesoamerican civilization they were about to plunder. Thus two great empires, mutually ignorant, confronted one another. They were empires, too, which displayed a strange historical kinship. Both were of recent creation: Ferdinand and Isabella, displaying statecraft which Machiavelli applauded, had united Aragon and Castile in 1469, thus converting two minor kingdoms into the core of an empire. Their grandson, Charles of Ghent, succeeded to an enlarged inheritance, to which he added his own Burgundian possessions (1517); and, in the year of Cortés's expedition, he was elected Holy Roman Emperor with the title Charles V. The Aztecs likewise had risen from the status of a minor, mercenary people in the late fourteenth century to create what has been called – with only a degree of hyperbole – 'the greatest empire of all times on the North American Continent'.[3]

Both empires were possessed of a certain missionary zeal and martial self-confidence, the product, for the Spaniards, of the Reconquista and, for the Aztecs, of their brisk expansion from the Valley of Mexico east to the Gulf and west to the Pacific. To contemporary Europeans the Spaniards seemed a particularly fortunate and dynamic people; the Aztecs, too, conceived of themselves as a kind of chosen people – and, like other chosen peoples, they rewrote their history to prove it. Yet both empires also faced internal schisms and conflicts, the results of too rapid recent expansion. In Spain, the Comunero revolt was brewing as Cortés set sail; in Mexico, the Aztecs enjoyed only partial control of Oaxaca (where a bloody campaign had been fought in 1511), they faced resolute neighbouring

---

[3] Jerome Offner, *Law and Politics in Aztec Texcoco* (Cambridge, 1983), p. 46. Offner overlooks the 'Imperial Republic' of the United States.

enemies in the Tarascans and Tlaxcalans (most recent campaign 1518), and many formally subdued peoples remained unreconciled to Aztec rule. Since the impending conflict with the Spanish invaders was to be fought on Aztec territory, however, it was the fissiparous tendencies of the Aztec empire which would prove decisive to the outcome.

But the confrontation was more than one of rival empires. It also pitted civilization against civilization, culture against culture, in an historically unique clash of faiths, societies and regimes which had hitherto lived hermetically sealed one from another. Christians and Moslems had fought, traded and polemicized for centuries. Sino-European contacts, though more tenuous (and necessarily peaceful), had a long history. Trade routes spanned the Sahara long before Portuguese ships rounded the Cape. Africa and Eurasia were therefore accustomed to exchanging goods, blows, ideas and diseases. And, when the Spaniards crossed the Atlantic, they first encountered – and conquered – not civilized states, but the primitive chiefdoms of the Antilles. Now, in Middle America, rival civilizations confronted each other, in a moment of unique historical discovery. Two branches of the human race, sundered some twenty millennia earlier, were suddenly, traumatically, reunited. The world was made whole.

I. The First Mesoamericans

For the real 'discovery' of America, of course, preceded all this by as much as forty thousand years. Columbus merely rediscovered it, using a different route. The first discoverers came from the east, crossing the broad land bridge which linked Siberia and Alaska during periods when, because of glacial advance, the sea level was lower. Such periods existed between 70,000 and 40,000 B.C. and again between 25,000 and 10,000 B.C. (the possibility that people also crossed outside these periods, by means of boat or sheet ice, seems unlikely).[4]

---

[4] H. H. Lamb, *Climate, History and the Modern World* (London, 1982), p. 105; Mark Nathan Cohen, *La crisis alimentaria de la prehistoria* (Madrid, 1984), pp. 170–2; Brian Fagen, *The Great Journey* (London, 1987), pp. 101–18, which forms part of a good general introduction to early New World settlement. The date of that settlement is a matter of continued controversy: the current consensus seems to favour a 'late' crossing (c. 15,000 B.C.), in the face of tenuous evidence, which I mention, of earlier peopling of the Americas: see Jared Diamond, *Guns, Germs, and Steel: A Short History of Everybody for the Last 13,000 Years* (London, 1997), pp. 44–50.

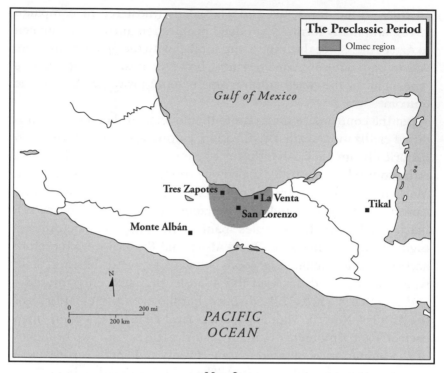

Map 2

Radiocarbon dating of finds in North America suggest – but scarcely prove – the existence of humans between 40,000 and 30,000 B.C., which implies an early crossing by Paleolithic people, (relatively) recently equipped with the more sophisticated hunting weaponry and cold-resistant fur garments which their Neanderthal counterparts had lacked. Weaponry expanded the scope of the hunt (traps became less necessary), and fur garments made possible the arduous migration through eastern Siberia (Beringia), then, probably, down the ice-free corridor east of the Rocky Mountains, whence the migrants debouched on to the game-rich Great Plains. For these Asian migrants were hunters and gatherers, whose crossing of the so-called land bridge represented a simple and gradual extension of their Siberian existence, probably stimulated by their constant quest for prey which, in the shape of mammoth, bison, horse and camel, had long preceded man in this eastbound odyssey.

Thereafter, human progress south through the New World was rapid, more rapid than it had been in the Old. The inexorable pressures which acted upon such hunting people, as their numbers grew, did not abate; while in the New World they encountered an animal population unprepared for the onslaught of hunters who had honed their skills for millennia in Eurasia. The result was the rapid spread of people and the progressive elimination – sometimes accelerated by climatic factors – of entire species, including mammoth and mastodon, and of species, such as the horse and camel, which in the Old World managed to survive. In consequence, the New World lacked the domesticated animals of the Old: its only unique asset was the giant sloth. The absence of sheep, cattle, camels and horses was particularly crucial for American social development. There could be no widespread transhumance of flocks and herds, hence no nomadic societies possessed of swift mobility and military capacity: no Scythians, Tartars, Mongols. The Old World battles between pastoral and arable peoples would not be replicated in the New. There would also be no resistance to certain animal-related diseases, and there would be no functional wheel. If no wheel then, it has been suggested, no pulleys, gears, cogs and screws: the technological advances achieved in the Old World were premised upon animal resources which the New World lacked. The hunting to death of Pleistocene big game ultimately explains 'why it was that Columbus "discovered" America and Powhatan did not "discover" Europe, that Cortés conquered Moctezuma rather than the other way around'.[5] The argument is arresting, if exaggerated. Certainly, of the great triad of prehistoric societies – hunter-gatherers, pastoralists

---

[5] Marvin Harris, *Cannibals and Kings: The Origins of Cultures* (New York, 1978), p. 42. Diamond, *Guns, Germs, and Steel*, ch. 3, discusses a variant on this theme: 'why the Inca Emperor Atahuallpa did not capture King Charles I of Spain'. It is not clear why Diamond chooses to focus on the second of these European-Amerindian encounters [Pizarro and Atahuallpa] rather than the first [Cortés and Moctezuma]; nor is it clear why he qualifies it as 'the most dramatic moment in . . . European-Native American relations' since 1492, thus overlooking certain previous, pretty dramatic events in Mexico. This is something of a quibble; Diamond's general analysis of the encounter, stressing a kind of epochal, ecological causality, is highly suggestive and largely convincing. However, such analysis is much better at explaining *how* the Spaniards conquered the Amerindians than *why*; that is, it explains *capabilities* better than it explains *motives*. Analysis of the latter requires a shorter-term perspective, which I try to develop in the following pages.

and sedentary farmers – only the first and third developed in Mexico. Both depended entirely on human motive power. Thus, when the Spaniards came, the native Mesoamericans faced two novel threats: that of armed cavalry and (less spectacular, but more significant) that of sheep and cattle, which would ravage their fields and population.[6]

As skilled hunters met vulnerable prey, human numbers grew and spread over the face of the continent. People reached the stormy tip of Tierra del Fuego around 9000 B.C. Meanwhile, population growth began to prompt fundamental changes in human society. These changes have often been summarized under the title of the 'Neolithic revolution', alias the dawn of civilization. Since Mesoamerica was to become one of the first great cradles of civilization (one of the 'seven regions of primary urban generation') in the world, and since this early development stamped Mexican society in an indelible fashion, it is important – though not easy – to explain how this 'revolution' came about.[7] It is, in a sense, the first crucial question facing the historian of Mexico.

The Neolithic revolution embraced two related elements: the establishment of sedentary farming communities and the birth of cities. The first fed the second, and the second engaged in 'civilized' activities: political, religious, aesthetic, architectural. The relationship involved some necessary social stratification and political subordination. In the Mesoamerican case a large maize- and manioc-producing peasantry supported a non-agricultural population which devoted itself to art, artisanry, statecraft, religion and war. We will consider these aspects of Mesoamerican civilization shortly. But we should first ponder their origins. We should, in other words, disaggregate the catch-all 'Neolithic revolution'.

---

[6] Forms of pastoralism developed in highland South America, thanks to the llama; but the llama, for obvious reasons, could not perform the military or socioeconomic role of the Eurasian horse, and even Genghis Khan could not have built an empire on sheepback. Diamond, *Guns, Germs, and Steel*, pp. 92, 195–7, 212–13 further argues that it was exposure to animals that generated Eurasian 'crowd diseases' – smallpox, influenza, measles, plague. Hence, in the animal-deficient New World, such diseases were absent; their advent after 1492 brought a terrible mortality among the Native Americans.

[7] Gordon Childe, *What Happened in History* (Harmondsworth, 1982, first pubd. 1942), pp. 30, 55; Paul Wheatley, *The Pivot of the Four Quarters. A Preliminary Inquiry into the Origins and Character of the Ancient Chinese City* (Edinburgh, 1971), pp. 225–6, 234–5, 273ff.

Such an exercise is of more than antiquarian interest; it is not a question of the historian – chiefly interested in the later, luxuriant foliage – digging up roots 'because they are there' and because historians of nations are, like Beatrix Potter's Tommy Brock, driven by some inner compulsion to go around 'digging things up'. On the contrary, the issue may be as lively and contentious as any to be found in contemporary history. It relates to the fundamental origins of class society and of the state; and it raises questions concerning social conflict and cohesion which are central to any broad historical inquiry. It is also very relevant to an understanding of Mesoamerican *history*, as opposed to *pre*history. Sedentary agriculture and states developed early in central and southern Mesoamerica; thence they were exported to the north. In social science jargon, Mesoamerica produced 'pristine' states, which in turn encouraged state-formation elsewhere. But the Neolithic revolution was never complete and enveloping. Down to the Spanish conquest – and beyond – the settled civilizations of central Mexico confronted a population to the north which retained many of the characteristics of the original hunting and gathering peoples. Conversely, they (often loosely and collectively termed the Chichimecs) lacked the attributes of civilization: classes, states, hieratic religion. They had never been 'revolutionized' (in Neolithic terms); or, in some suggestive cases which we will touch upon, they had been 'revolutionized' and then relapsed. It was from the barbarian north, too, that migrants – and invaders – regularly entered central Mesoamerica, the most famous being the Aztecs themselves.

One scholar has attributed the supposed Aztec character – belligerent, messianic, obsessed with the need to placate a relentlessly hostile environment – to the Aztecs' harsh hunting-and-gathering prehistory.[8] But this interpretation (like a good deal written about the Aztecs) is fanciful and based upon a crude, mistaken, evolutionary view of human development; a view which took root in the nineteenth century and which accorded well with 'Western' notions of hard work, civilization and progress. It is now clear that the hunting-and-gathering bands which first populated America were, like similar bands in other times and places, viable, successful social entities; indeed, for some 90 per cent of their existence on earth

---

[8] Christian Duverger, *La fleur létale: Economie du sacrifice aztèque* (Paris, 1978).

humans have lived in such bands. Hunters and gatherers did not chronically hover on the brink of subsistence: their diet, health and life-style were often superior to those of more 'advanced' agricultural peoples. They worked less, ate well, suffered less endemic disease and were quite likely bigger.[9] The Stone Age, it has been said, produced 'the original affluent society'.[10] Fit and well-fed, Stone Age man also reproduced with vigour; and here lay the problem. The curse upon this prehistoric Cain was the injunction to go forth and multiply; having complied, Cain had to forsake the garden and its hanging fruits in favour of a life of arable toil: 'in the sweat of thy face thou shalt eat bread' – or, in this case, maize-cakes. Prehistoric societies grew slowly, not least because growth conferred few collective benefits (hunting-and-gathering bands usually number fewer than fifty members) and because their members engaged in practices which limited population growth: abortion, prolonged lactation, warfare and infanticide, especially female infanticide. The latter 'lurks in the background of prehistory as an ugly blight in what otherwise might be mistaken for a Garden of Eden'.[11] The affluent society depended upon the regular culling of female infants – by neglect, abandonment or outright murder – and of young males by recurrent inter-band skirmishing.

Nevertheless, population inched up, perhaps at the rate of 0.1 per cent per year during the Neolithic period.[12] Thus, by around 9000 B.C., all the Americas were populated, albeit at the low population densities characteristic of hunters and gatherers. Now the transition to sedentary agriculture began: not as a sudden technological breakthrough, nor as a joyful conquest of 'civilization', but as a necessary, even reluctant, response to inexorable demographic pressure acting upon nomadic bands whose sustenance required broad tracts of land and abundant game. Given the gradual nature of this pressure – and its mitigation by the culling methods just mentioned – the transition

---

[9] Harris, *Cannibals, and Kings*, pp. 11–14, 19; Tony Dingle, *Aboriginal Economy: Patterns of Experience* (Melbourne, 1988), pp. 4–5ff. Diamond, *Guns, Germs, and Steel*, pp. 20–2, even argues that, given natural selection and life-style, hunters and gatherers may be more intelligent than the population of high–mass-consumption 'Western' society.

[10] Marshall Sahlins, *Stone Age Economics* (London, 1974), ch. 1.

[11] Harris, *Cannibals and Kings*, pp. 22–5; Dingle, *Aboriginal Economy*, pp. 23–6; Diamond, *Guns, Germs, and Steel*, p. 89.

[12] Cohen, *La crisis alimentaria*, p. 65.

was slow, patchy and selective. The idea of a 'Neolithic revolution' – if that implies a rapid shift from one mode to another – is misleading. A revolution it was, in terms of sociohistorical significance; but the sheer longevity of the transition makes talk of 'revolution' (with its connotations of rapidity) inappropriate. For, just as the origins of the industrial revolution are now discerned in preceding, pre-industrial centuries, so the roots of the Neolithic revolution must be traced back through millennia. Hunters and gatherers, it is clear, made necessary incremental adjustments in their quest for subsistence: they exploited new plants (again, as necessity demanded rather than as discovery permitted: we must assume that their knowledge of available plants was compendious, their use thereof selective); they began to accumulate stocks, to plant and to harvest, and to control plant reproduction to their own advantage, capitalizing on random mutations. It was a long process, spanning millennia, perhaps seven millennia in the New World. During this long transition, hunting and gathering coexisted with incipient agriculture. Diet became more diverse, as the proportion of big-game meat declined (it may never have been that large: 'they probably found one mammoth in a lifetime and never got over talking about it'), and as the consumption of small game, fish, shellfish, grubs and insects increased.[13] Major prey died out, regionally, continentally, even globally; the more thorough extinction of species in the Americas may have partly reflected climatic factors (glacial retreat signalled a warming trend about 13,000 years ago), but it also attested to the success of American hunters, prompting them to diversify and assure their threatened means of subsistence.

The demographic pressure making for this gradual move towards plant consumption and cultivation did not imply a general Malthusian crisis. Pressure was selective, by region and season, inducing a 'slow shift in subsistence strategies', which forestalled any Malthusian crisis.[14] Agriculture thus developed partly as a form of insurance, before the 'carrying capacity' of a region – its ability to support a human population – was subjected to chronic strain. But

---

[13] MacNeish, quoted in Barbara Stark, 'The Rise of Sedentary Life', in Jeremy Sabloff, ed., *Supplement to the Handbook of Middle American Indians* (Austin, 1981), p. 349.

[14] Stark, 'Rise of Sedentary Life', p. 365; note also Dingle, *Aboriginal Economy*, p. 8.

the pressure was necessarily greatest in regions such as the arid highlands of Middle America, where fauna were rarer, and, conversely, weaker in game-rich regions like the Great Plains to the north. Roughly, therefore, the New World Neolithic revolution occurred in zones which were suitable for agriculture but (no less important) unsuitable for continued hunting and gathering – zones which, in somewhat Toynbeean fashion, faced subsistence challenges but were capable of creative responses. And it was particularly evident in regions – river valleys or lacustrine basins – where the newly sedentary population began to cluster within defined ecological boundaries. Here, nucleation (the concentration of settled population) made possible – though it did not require – the development of early civilization: in the Valley of Mexico, as in the valleys of the Indus, Nile, and Yellow Rivers, or of coastal Peru. Yet, if this 'revolution' was compelled rather than chosen, it was also reversible. In appropriate circumstances – demographic, climatic, even political – agricultural peoples returned to hunting and gathering: ostensible regressions which, for the people themselves, were no regressions at all, but relaxations induced by new, less exigent circumstances. For some, the expulsion from Eden was temporary.[15]

If change was neither uniform nor unilinear, nevertheless the trend over millennia was towards sedentary agriculture. In Mesoamerica the trend can be plotted over a wide area (in other words, there was no single centre from which agriculture diffused). Evidence of human habitation dates back some twenty thousand years. But for over half this time hunting and gathering prevailed, with a marked emphasis on hunting: meat formed between one-half and two-thirds of the diet in both Tamaulipas (in northeastern Mexico) and Tehuacan (in the central highlands) around 7000 B.C., and these were probably typical examples. But with the growth of population and the diminution of supply – more pronounced in Middle than in North America – meat consumption fell, such that it afforded only 10–20 per cent of diet by 4000 B.C. The shortfall was met primarily by collected,

[15] Richard A. Diehl, 'Prehispanic Relationships between the Basin of Mexico and North and West-Mexico', in Eric R. Wolf, ed., *The Valley of Mexico: Studies in Preshispanic Ecology and Society* (Albuquerque, 1976), pp. 269, 273. For comparable cases of 'regression', see Diamond, *Guns, Germs, and Steel*, pp. 55–6, 109.

not cultivated, plants: nuts, fruit, maguey, wild beans and grains.[16] Gradually, some of these wild plants came under human control: the process is evident as early as 5000 B.C., and, by 4000–2000 B.C., cultivated crops provided half of total consumption. The most important of these early cultigens – maize, beans and, in the warm lowlands, squash – were selected less because of their innate desirability or convenience (maize, the staff of life and basis of agrarian civilization in highland Mesoamerica, requires labour-intensive preparation before it can be eaten) than because of their familiarity, their suitablity for storage and their genetic flexibility. Necessity, rather than choice, determined a maize-based civilization. And the transition was a long one: the first maize cobs, grown five millennia before Christ, measured less than one centimetre; during the fourth and third millennia B.C., as maize became established as a staple, the cob quadrupled in size; by 1000 A.D., it had attained ten centimetres.[17]

Thus, we need posit no great conceptual leap, no 'forgotten genius' who made 'an epoch-making discovery when he learned that by dropping back into the soil some of the seeds he had gathered to eat he could make a plant grow'.[18] Since need was the spur (people became farmers because they had to, not because farming beckoned with its easy bounty), agriculture developed fastest in regions, like central Mesoamerica, where hunting and gathering faced diminishing returns. If hunting had originally spread from the northern Great Plains to the mountains and valleys of Mexico, maize cultivation now followed a reverse path. Settled agriculture flourished in parts of Mesoamerica as early as the fifth millennium B.C., while its appearance in the American southwest (with the Mogollon and related traditions) awaited the period 500 B.C.–A.D. 500.[19]

With settled agriculture came a range of social changes which culminated – in some cases – in fully fledged states and cities: the 'urban revolution', made possible by the prior Neolithic revolution. But the

---

[16] The pioneering work was done by R. S. MacNeish and others in the Tehuacan Valley: for a useful resumé, see Stuart J. Fiedel, *Prehistory of the Americas* (Cambridge, 2nd ed., 1992), pp. 171–86.

[17] Joyce Marcus, 'The Size of the Early Mesoamerican Village', in Kent V. Flannery, ed., *The Early Mesoamerican Village* (New York, 1976), p. 93.

[18] Nigel Davies, *The Ancient Kingdoms of Mexico* (Harmondsworth, 1983), p. 16; cf. Fiedel, *Prehistory of the Americas*, p. 168.

[19] Thomas D. Hall, *Social Change in the Southwest, 1350–1880* (Lawrence, Kans., 1989), p. 41.

causal sequence was neither straightforward nor inevitable. Like any evolutionary scheme, this one embodied elements which, for very good reasons, declined to evolve, or which evolved only partially. Some groups remained hunters and gatherers, spurning agriculture; some established settled yet egalitarian farming societies, lacking states and social classes; some acquired the full panoply of cities, dynasties and empires. However 'civilization' is defined – and wherever on this continuum from band to empire it is deemed to have arrived – it is clear that sedentary agriculture was a necessary prerequisite. All the world's examples of pristine state-formation are to be found in areas of early agricultural settlement: Egypt, Mesopotamia, Northern China, the Indus Valley, coastal Peru, Mesoamerica. But there were also agricultural populations which remained happily unacquainted with kings and cities. Agriculture made civilization possible but not inevitable.[20] A key task, therefore, is to try to explain the process of state-formation in Mesoamerica.

We must first return to the variable which has so far been stressed, that of population. Population growth offers the best general explanation of the slow transition from hunting and gathering to settled agriculture (it can explain the remarkable worldwide regularities in this process in a way that neither diffusionist theories nor appeals to human nature – the 'assumption that human beings naturally want to "settle down"' – possibly can).[21] But, even under conditions of nomadism, population growth was not an independent variable: it was subject to indirect vicissitudes (climatic change, disease) as well as to direct human control (war, abortion, infanticide). With settlement and farming, new conditions and pressures came into play. Agriculture demanded a greater input of labour per unit of area (hunting and gathering, in contrast, was land- rather than labour-intensive). Effort now had to compensate for reduced living space. The difference – and an important one when considering the human implications of social 'progress' – is well captured by Richard Diehl: 'new demands on time for agricultural activities and construction must have caused

[20] Ronald Cohen, 'State Origins: A Reappraisal', in Henri J. Claessen and Peter Skalnik, *The Early State* (The Hague, 1978), pp. 38, 41. For a vigorous rebuttal of economic and ecological explanations of state-formation, see Pierre Clastres, *Society against the State* (New York, 1989), pp. 201–2.
[21] Harris, *Cannibals and Kings*, p. 15.

more than one old-timer to look back wistfully to the days when a man could go up into the mountains to collect wild millet whenever he pleased'.[22]

With the development of agriculture, larger, denser populations could be supported. In addition, larger population was often functional to agricultural success, for both household and community. Parents saw advantages in increasing family size; no doubt they also welcomed some relaxation of the old constraints – the need to abort and kill their offspring – which nomadism had imposed. Communities also derived benefit from numbers: first, for defence, and second, by mobilizing collective labour, for example, for forest clearance or irrigation works. Over and above these benefits, however, important social repercussions followed. In simple terms, larger populations made division of labour and social stratification feasible; and – even if population growth was not the sole or even the primary cause of social stratification (that we will address shortly) – social stratification, once under way, tended to reinforce population growth, since the power and prestige of emergent elites were directly related to the size of the population they dominated. If population encouraged agriculture, agriculture in turn encouraged population growth.

Within this sequence, however, there is an obvious and crucial gap, both causal and chronological. Between the development of agriculture and the onset of civilization (social classes, states, cities) a range of historical factors came into play, determining whether the sequence was to advance, halt or regress. For regression was common, the birth of civilization rare.[23] Some analysts interpret such sequences in terms of a demographic and ecological determinism; their approach is favoured by the 'strong materialist bias' of archaeology, which relies heavily on the analysis of material remains.[24] Others stress either political processes ('it is the political break ... that is decisive, not the economic transformation') or cultural and ideological factors ('the environment does not determine man's culture;

[22] Diehl, 'Prehispanic Relationships', pp. 268–9.
[23] Charles S. Spencer, 'Rethinking the Chiefdom', in Robert D. Drennan and Carlos A. Uribe, eds., *Chiefdoms in the Americas* (Lanham, Md., 1987), p. 378; Michael Mann, *The Sources of Social Power*, vol. 1, *A History of Power from the Beginning to 1760 AD* (Cambridge, 1986), pp. 63–9.
[24] Kenneth G. Hirth, 'The Analysis of Prehistoric Economic Systems: A Look to the Future', in Kenneth G. Hirth, ed., *Trade and Exchange in Early Mesoamerica* (Albuquerque, 1984), pp. 282–3.

it merely sets the outer limits and, at the same time, offers opportunities').[25] It is hardly possible for an inexpert historian to adjudicate between these grand theories; all that can be done is to review the evidence and – as far as is possible – to tell it like it was, in particular cases. The analysis of those cases will inevitably be influenced by the use of theories which seem to be fruitful and appropriate (here, a certain eclecticism may be permitted); but the purpose of the analysis is to illuminate the cases, not to pronounce upon the general theories, which belong to a higher ontological realm.

According to a well-known and elegant schema, derived from extensive ethnohistorical and anthropological research, the path to civilization involves four progressive steps, each bringing enhanced social complexity and integration: the band, the tribe, the chiefdom and the state.[26] This typology, as one of its principal exponents points out, may be inferred, but cannot be proven, for prehistoric societies.[27] The presumed progressions are not easily established archaeologically, hence there can be considerable disagreement as to the status within the schema of a particular society. Were the Olmecs and Maya of Mesoamerica constituted in chiefdoms or states? 'Chiefdom' would imply smaller units ('states' connote populations roughly in excess of 10,000), more fissile communities prone to dispersion, and social ranking without clear class stratification. 'Chiefs' lack the enduring, centralized, coercive powers of states.[28] These distinctions,

---

[25] Clastres, *Society against the State*, p. 202; Peter Farb, *Man's Rise to Civilization as Shown by the Indians of North America from Primeval Times to the Coming of the Industrial State* (New York, 1968), p. 38; note also Olivier de Montmollin, *The Archaeology of Political Structure: Settlement Analysis in a Classic Maya Polity* (Cambridge, 1989), pp. 8–9ff. Diamond, *Guns, Germs, and Steel*, p. 277, offers a schematic review of four mechanisms which have been advanced to explain the rise of 'kleptocrats' (roughly, privileged, power-holding elites): top-down coercion; material redistribution; the maintenance of peace and order; the construction of a persuasive 'ideology or religion'.

[26] Ellman R. Service, *Primitive Social Organization: An Evolutionary Perspective* (New York, 2nd ed., 1971); William T. Sanders and Barbara J. Price, *Mesoamerica: The Evolution of a Civilization* (New York, 1968), pp. 37–44; Diamond, *Guns, Germs, and Steel*, pp. 267ff.

[27] Ellman R. Service, *Origins of the State and Civilization: The Process of Cultural Evolution* (New York, 1975), pp. 303–4.

[28] Clastres, *Society against the State*, ch. 2, makes the point forcefully; Drennan and Uribe, *Chiefdoms in the Americas*, offer several contrasting perspectives; note also Robert L. Carneiro, 'The Chiefdom: Precursor of the State', in Grant D. Jones and Robert R. Kautz, eds., *The Transition to Statehood in the New World* (Cambridge, 1981), pp. 37–79. In contrast to Clastres, Diamond, *Guns, Germs, and Steel*, pp. 273–4, depicts quasi-Weberian chiefs enjoying a 'monopoly on the right to use force [and] . . . on critical information', making 'all critical decisions', and enacting them by means of 'one or two levels of bureaucrats'. I suspect that these discrepancies are

useful in theory, are difficult to make in practice, particularly on the basis of archaeological evidence. Similar problems arise when we try to detect the earlier transition from 'band' to 'tribe' – the latter being both archaeologically inaccessible and analytically questionable. It is therefore preferable to collapse these two forms ('band' and 'tribe') into a single, broad category, characterized by limited population, egalitarian social organization, fissile tendencies and the predominance of kin groups (households, extended families and larger tribal lineages).[29]

Within this typology, it is the successive transitions from band or tribe to chiefdom, then from chiefdom to state, which command historical attention and require explanation. What did these transitions entail? We will deal with the first in general terms (specific evidence is lacking; we are flying by the seat of our theoretical pants) and with the second within the context of specific Mesoamerican cases. For millennia, Mesoamerica was populated by hunting-and-gathering bands – loose, egalitarian groups, united by bonds of kinship and probably numbering fewer than one hundred members apiece. Each band roamed a roughly defined area which lacked any clear political boundaries; inter-band skirmishing culled the male population and, for a time, preserved a degree of ecological balance.[30] Although some modest surplus might be realized and stockpiled, it was necessarily limited. Such groups were highly mobile, living in caves and temporary camp sites, travelling light. They enjoyed (as already suggested) a comfortable margin of subsistence and did not have to toil endlessly to survive. A modern parallel would be the Yurok Indians

---

inevitable whenever a broad continuum – in this case, from egalitarian bands to full-fledged states – is sliced into sections; experts, differing as to their precise criteria, then make their respective incisions at different points along the continuum, and one expert's chief becomes another's paramount chief and yet another's petty king.

[29] On the problems of the 'tribe' as a concept: Hall, *Social Change in the Southwest*, pp. 28–9; Diamond, *Guns, Germs, and Steel*, p. 270. I return to this theme later.

[30] Ellman R. Service, *The Hunters* (Englewood Cliffs, 1966), sets out the model; cf. Diehl, 'Prehispanic Relationships', pp. 251–2, for the Chichimec example. Diamond, *Guns, Germs, and Steel*, pp. 265–6, 277, stresses the endemic violence of 'noncentralized' societies (which in turn becomes a potential rationale for the establishment of political authority in prehistory); however, there is a whiff of ethnographic upstreaming here (that is, the restrospective application of contemporary evidence – derived from New Guinea – to the remote past); and, as Diamond makes clear (e.g., pp. 53–4), some hunter-gatherers, like the Moriori of the Chatham Islands, were 'entirely inexperienced at war', hence utterly vulnerable to the marauding Maori who descended on them in 1835. Levels of violence, in other words, may have been highly variable.

of California, who, in more recent times, lived comfortably off the bounty of nature.[31] The very process of hunting and gathering, which involved the immediate gratification rather than the civilized deferral of wants, made accumulation, especially accumulation by an elite, difficult to sustain. Why accumulate? Food was better left on the branch or in the burrow. Political authority – the social superego, disciplining wants and imposing order – was superfluous.

In the absence of material accumulation – including, of course, the accumulation of landed property – social classes, based on differential access to property, could not develop. The hunting-and-gathering band might defer to the wisdom of shamans or the skill of veteran hunters; it might accept the temporary and conditional leadership of 'big men' (e.g., to resolve intra-band disputes); but such leadership did not crystallize into political authority, nor did deference form the basis for class differentiation.[32] Indeed, the very fluidity of hunting and gathering militated against the emergence of social class or political authority. Bands moved, migrated, clashed, skirmished and intermarried (given their small size, exogamy was important). The imposition of centralized social control was impossible: disaffected people could too easily vote with their feet.

The advent of agriculture did not bring any immediate – nor, in some cases, any long-term – change. Sedentary farming villages were clearly established during the third millennium B.C. Yet, for a further two millennia, the typical Mesoamerican community remained a small hamlet, usually less than two hectares (five acres) in area and comprising perhaps a dozen households, or sixty individuals.[33] A minority of communities (no more than 10 per cent) exceeded these norms, but in most instances population growth led to segmentation (splitting-off) rather than nucleation. In the Maya zone of southeastern Mexico, farming was well under way by 1000 B.C.; as population grew, people quit their hospitable riverine niches and carved out new communities – the archetypal hamlets – in the forest.

---

[31] Farb, *Man's Rise to Civilization*, p. 12.

[32] Clastres, *Society against the State*, ch. 2, goes furthest, depicting even (contemporary) chiefs as weak, dependent and subject to 'continuous looting' by their peoples; chieftaincy is 'more than a duty: it is a bondage'. Similarly, Spencer, 'Rethinking the Chiefdom', p. 370, describes the 'ephemeral, context-dependent nature of egalitarian leadership' in certain chiefdoms.

[33] Marcus, 'The Size of the Early Mesoamerican Village', p. 82.

Hence it was not until the fourth century B.C. that chiefdoms emerged and not until the first Christian millennium that they became standard.[34] Similar egalitarian forms endured in the Bajío, the rolling plain northwest of the Valley of Mexico, throughout the same period: 'the people were sedentary farmers living in small villages, but indications of social stratification, urbanism, or complex religion are absent'.[35] The same would be true of many northern Mexican Indian peoples right through the colonial period.[36] Farming was compatible with an egalitarian, stateless existence throughout centuries, in Mesoamerica as in the Neolithic Old World.[37] Such farming communities of course yielded a surplus over and above daily needs; but this surplus represented peasant insurance rather than the rewards of a priestly or secular elite.

Furthermore (and here we enter the debate between 'materialists' and 'idealists' concerning the origins of the state), it is not at all obvious that these egalitarian farming communities inevitably expanded, by natural reproduction, to the point where population pressure called forth political authorities and social classes.[38] Population growth was a powerful but not wholly independent variable; it could be socially checked (as it had been in the past), just as it could be socially encouraged. Thus, many communities remained in an egalitarian, pre-political stasis for centuries, even millennia, and their belated acquisition of ruling elites and structural social inequalities often ultimately depended upon external pressures rather than internal dynamics. These communities, in other words, suffered either direct conquest or the indirect consequences of 'secondary' (imitative) state-formation. Competition and imitation eventually made states and classes the norm (although not the uniform norm). However,

---

34 Joseph W. Ball, 'The Rise of the Northern Maya Chiefdoms', in Richard E. W. Adams, ed., *The Origins of Maya Civilization* (Albuquerque, 1977), pp. 107–9, 111, 125.

35 Diehl, 'Prehispanic Relationships', p. 271.

36 Hall, *Social Change in the Southwest*, pp. 63–5, 103–4; Edward E. Spicer, *Cycles of Conquest: The Impact of Spain, Mexico and the United States on the Indians of the Southwest, 1553–1960* (Tucson, 1962), pp. 12–15ff.

37 Cohen, 'State Origins', pp. 40–2, 55; Colin Renfrew, *Before Civilization: The Radiocarbon Revolution* (Harmondsworth, 1990, first pubd. 1974), ch. 7.

38 Robert D. Drennan, 'Regional Demography in Chiefdoms', in Drennan and Uribe, *Chiefdoms in the Americas*, pp. 308, 320; Clastres, *Society against the State*, pp. 200–1; Elizabeth Brumfiel, 'Regional Growth in the Eastern Valley of Mexico: A Test Case of the "Population Pressure" Hypothesis', in Flannery, *The Early Mesoamerican Village*, pp. 234–6.

states and classes were not invariably and inexorably predetermined by social needs, still less by human nature.

Incipient political authority and social stratification developed through the medium of the chiefdom (a concept which is open to criticism, but which we will retain).[39] It may be hypothesized how chiefdoms came about, but the process cannot be confidently, empirically, described: 'no-one has observed the actual origin of a chiefdom'.[40] The Mesoamerican archaeological record makes clear that during the latter part of the second millennium B.C. certain communities stood out from the common ruck of small hamlets: these 'monsters' covered areas of 40–50 hectares (100–125 acres) and embraced populations of between one and four thousand: the Olmec site of San Lorenzo; San José Mogote in Oaxaca; Chimalhuacan in Veracruz.[41] The presence of ceramic figurines and early ceremonial architecture indicates that these communities were centres of religion, artisanry and trade; burial practices also reveal an emergent social hierarchy. It is plausible to infer from these material findings that these larger communities were constituted as chiefdoms, in which religiously sanctioned 'big men' were responsible for collective ritual, for defence and for the redistribution of goods, whose (relative) abundance derived from trade and agriculture. Such chiefs came to enjoy a measure of decision-making authority. Their authority derived from their office rather than from any personal characteristics or charisma; yet their coercive powers were limited, and such chiefs were not set dramatically apart from or above the community which they (loosely) governed.[42] Perhaps the eighteenth-century Cherokee offer a parallel: the communal chief 'associates with the people as a common man, converses with them, and they with him in perfect ease and familiarity'.[43] Most chiefdoms were probably confined to single communities (hence we may posit a network of coexisting chiefdoms, Polynesian-style), but some extended their influence and linked dominant centres to subordinate satellites: at San Lorenzo, for

---

[39] Note the contrasting views concerning the utility and application of the concept of the chiefdom put forward by Steadman Upham, 'A Theoretical Consideration of Middle Range Societies', and Spencer, 'Rethinking the Chiefdom', in Drennan and Uribe, *Chiefdoms in the Americas*, chs. 18, 19.

[40] Service, *Primitive Social Organization*, p. 135.

[41] Marcus, 'The Size of the Early Mesoamerican Village', pp. 88–9.

[42] Cf. Harris, *Cannibals and Kings*, pp. 105, 109; Clastres, *Society against the State*, ch. 2.

[43] Harris, *Cannibals and Kings*, pp. 110–11, quoting William Bartram.

example, or in the Valley of Mexico.[44] Such 'paramount chiefs' exercised a broader control, which was the preamble, in some cases, to state authority; indeed, the distinctive form of the primitive state may be discerned in the evolution of a three-tiered system which linked local villages to local chiefs, and the latter to paramount chiefs – potential kings.[45]

None of this explains *how* chiefdoms came into being. Population growth and farming made them possible, but not inevitable. Hence the staggered inception of chiefdoms: pre-1000 B.C. on the Gulf coast and in Oaxaca; in the middle of the first millennium B.C. in much of the central highlands; towards the end of the millennium in Yucatán and highland Jalisco; later still in northwestern Mesoamerica.[46] This sequence does not suggest a correlation between chiefdoms and natural resources. Early chiefdoms were not endowed with superior resources either in Mesoamerica or, it would seem, in other parts of the world.[47] A more convincing ecological and economic explanation of chiefdom-formation stresses the redistributive aspects of chiefly rule. Historically, chiefs have often served as economic managers, responsible for the collection and redistribution of goods, both those produced within the community and (sometimes more important) those acquired by long-distance exchange. Such a role was stimulated, but not necessitated, by enhanced agricultural production and inter-community exchange. Chiefs organized the collection and storage of goods; they distributed goods to favoured clients (notably warriors); they alleviated shortages; and they monitored the entry and exit of long-distance exchange goods. Chiefs were also able to organize their people for war and for collective labour, and possibly – as in Africa – they controlled access to wives and women. According to this explanation of chiefly rule, which derives heavily from ethnographic sources, it is logical that chiefdoms in Mesoamerica – as in the Andes – should appear to correlate with exchange networks rather than with agriculturally privileged zones

---

[44] David L. Rossman, 'A Site Catchment Analysis of San Lorenzo, Veracruz', in Flannery, *The Early Mesoamerican Village*, pp. 100–2; Brumfiel, 'Regional Growth', p. 247.

[45] Carneiro, 'The Chiefdom', p. 69.

[46] Ball, 'Rise of the Northern Maya Chiefdoms'; Phil C. Weigand, 'Evidence for Complex Societies during the Western Mesoamerican Classic Period', in Michael S. Foster and Phil C. Weigand, eds., *The Archaeology of West and Northwest Mesoamerica* (Boulder, 1985), pp. 63–9.

[47] Hirth, 'The Analysis of Prehistoric Economic Systems', p. 292; Mann, *Sources of Social Power*, p. 67, citing Friedman.

and that the formation of chiefdoms should have been somewhat slower in the Maya lowlands than in the central highlands.[48]

Chiefdoms, however, were not states. Chiefs enjoyed limited powers: they established themselves – if the ethnographic examples can be generalized – by dint of their hard work, personal sacrifice and example; their people ('subjects' would be wrong) voluntarily accepted their loose chiefly authority, not least because it brought benefits. And they lived among their people: the *mico* (supreme chief) of the Cherokee, we have noted, mixed with his people and did not lurk in some sheltered regal precinct; nor did the chiefs of the Pueblo, Mojave, Papago or Comanche Indians.[49] The same was probably true of the early Mesoamerican chiefs. Over time, however, some chiefdoms developed into embryonic states. It seems likely that this process occurred as chiefs gave way to 'superchiefs' or 'paramount' chiefs, whose authority spanned several communities, and who, as that authority thickened, acquired coercive powers, bolstered by religious sanctions. For some analysts, the transition from chiefdoms to states was progressive, linear and unproblematic. Yet, as they also recognize, it was a profound transition: consent gave way to coercion, voluntary contributions of goods became obligatory tribute, natural resources – fields, forest and water – ceased to be 'elements of rightful access' and, instead, became 'dispensations' of the king.[50]

Why would the local population submit to this process, which turned chiefs into kings and people into subject peasants? We will discuss this crucial, but difficult, question in the next section, which deals with the early Mesoamerican states. However, it is worth briefly anticipating the argument. Two standard and related explanations are frequently put forward: stronger centralized political authority (1) offered advantages in warfare and (2) occurred in regions of 'impaction', where population grew within 'markedly circumscribed zones of production' which inhibited the out-migration

[48] Service, *Primitive Social Organization*, pp. 135–43; but note the doubts of Upham, 'A Theoretical Consideration', pp. 346, 349, and Spencer, 'Rethinking the Chiefdom', pp. 375–6, 378–9.

[49] Harris, *Cannibals and Kings*, p. 111; Hall, *Social Change in the Southwest*, p. 29; Spicer, *Cycles of Conquest*, pp. 153–5.

[50] Harris, *Cannibals and Kings*, p. 113.

of disgruntled subjects.[51] Because escape was too difficult 'caged' populations had to submit to the emergent state; furthermore, the emergent state offered greater protection against enemies. State formation obeyed a Hobbesian rationale.

These explanations, however, are not wholly convincing. In many cases, escape was not so difficult and enemies were not so threatening. A rational cost-benefit calculation would not necessarily have induced free cultivators to become subject peasants; the advantages offered by states over simple chiefdoms hardly justified the extra costs in terms of lost liberty and equality. Perhaps the process of subordination and state-formation was insidiously incremental: political 'caging' crept up on an unsuspecting people, who awoke to their subjugation too late. But it is hard to square this interpretation with the historical incidence of segmentation, migration and rebellion, which recurrently eroded unpopular authority and demonstrated the efficacy of collective protest. For a weak chiefdom to mutate into a strong state required a political transformation which could not be accomplished by coercion alone, since coercion was initially lacking (or weak). Coercion was a consequence, not a cause of the process, which – we may hypothesize – required some additional catalyst, some means of generating legitimacy which went beyond mere coercion but which did not necessarily represent rational collective self-interest. It may therefore help to introduce the element of religion which, arguably, offered a powerful ideological resource for emergent states.

Religion, broadly defined, was as old as human communities. Evidence of ritual burials, very likely involving sacrifice and cannibalism, dates back to at least 5000 B.C.[52] During the second millennium B.C., as the early chiefdoms evolved, burials became more lavish, ceremonial centres and ceramic figurines began to proliferate. It is likely that the brisk trade evident during this period also carried strong religious connotations. Meanwhile, the growth of agriculture made possible a more lavish ritual, eventually conducted by religious

---

51 Harris, *Cannibals and Kings*, p. 117; Carneiro, 'The Chiefdom', p. 64, and Robert Carneiro, 'A Theory of the Origin of the State', *Science*, 169 (1970), pp. 737–8; Diamond, *Guns, Germs, and Steel*, p. 277, also stresses 'maintaining public order and curbing violence'.
52 Robert D. Drennan, 'Religion and Social Evolution in Formative Mesoamerica', in Flannery, *The Early Mesoamerican Village*, p. 351.

specialists: professional shamans and sanctified chiefs. Though, in more recent times, chiefs have often been designated as either theocratic or secular, it does not follow that this dichotomy applied in prehistoric Mesoamerica; certainly, subsequent Mesoamerican development suggests an intimate confusion of sacred and secular authorities. Subsequent development also attests to the pervasive power of Mesoamerican religion and its capacity to cement an otherwise tenuous 'social bond'.[53] Anticipating the argument which follows, it seems plausible to suggest that religious sentiments, perhaps evolving from some sort of ancestor cult, underwrote chiefly rule, reinforced the cohesion of the growing community, inhibited fission, bolstered morale against external enemies, and thus played a vital role in the progressive accumulation of chiefly power which, in turn, mutated into coercive kingship: 'the rise of stratified society and the evolution of the visibly expressed Mesoamerican pantheon happened at an extraordinarily fast rate and went hand-in-hand'.[54] Gods and kings, earthly and unearthly powers, nurtured one another in sacred symbiosis. For chiefs and chiefly lineages were no doubt keen to exploit this advantageous sanction: religion joined war, exchange and redistribution as pillars of chiefly power.

Chiefs were also keen to boost and retain population, which was their glory, defence and livelihood. More people meant more (emergent) subjects, soldiers, worshippers and labourers. Eventually, super-chiefdoms – incipient states – emerged, such as the Olmec San Lorenzo or Tlatilco in the Valley of Mexico, which acquired dependent communities scattered over a wider area, thus forming the characteristic three-tier hierarchy of the primitive state. The

---

[53] Nancy M. Farriss, *Maya Society under Colonial Rule: The Collective Enterprise of Survival* (Princeton, 1984), pp. 117, 142–5; note also Montmollin, *Archaeology of Political Structure*, pp. 89, 141; and, from the other end of Mesoamerica, Ramón A. Gutiérrez, *When Jesus Came the Corn Mothers Went Away: Marriage, Sexuality and Power in New Mexico, 1500–1856* (Stanford, 1991), p. 22: 'the forces of dispersion that could destroy Pueblo society were centrifugal. The political discourse that religion made possible was centripetal'.

[54] Michael D. Coe, 'Religion and the Rise of Mesoamerican States', in Jones and Kautz, *Transition to Statehood*, p. 166; Drennan, 'Religion and Social Evolution', pp. 349–50. David Horrobin, *The Madness of Adam and Eve: How Schizophrenia Shaped Humanity* (London, 2001), puts forward the intriguing argument that the advance of civilization – including religion, state-building and organized violence – is linked to the schizophrenic genome, which was in turn affected by nutritional changes associated with sedentary agriculture (specifically, a decrease in the consumption of fatty acids). The result: more exuberant art and religion, but also 'paranoid violence and psychopathic tendencies': p. 191. I am endebted to Katharine Winkley for this reference.

restraints on population growth which had afflicted hunters and gatherers were now relaxed. Population growth and nucleation thus *followed* as much as they *caused* the establishment of early political authority and social stratification. That is to say, while a given level of population was a necessary condition of early state-formation, it was not sufficient. There were plenty of examples of population growth which did not produce chiefdoms, still less states; on the other hand, further population growth and attendant nucleation followed logically from the establishment of political authority. Thus, the era of the chiefdom was one of rapid demographic growth compared with the preceding era, for the imperatives of population now went into reverse. Adam's instructions – 'go forth and multiply' – were no longer a divine curse but a secular order. Restraint gave way to prodigality (populations are more easily boosted than restrained, so long as Malthusian crises and major epidemics are avoided); the cull of infants, especially female infants, was curtailed; and, as swelling endogamous populations abstracted themselves from the great Neolithic melting pot, so cultural differentiation accelerated, and loose linguistic frontiers began to parallel the political. Discrete cultures came into being; some, over time, built cities and empires.

II. Dates and Places

The analysis of state- and empire-building requires both a chronological and a geographical perspective. Mesoamerican history has been conventionally divided into three periods, following the Archaic period of prehistory (7000–2000/1500 B.C.), which has been briefly covered. These periods, with rough dates, are (1) the Formative, or Preclassic (2000/1500 B.C.–A.D. 1/100); (2) the Classic (A.D. 1/100–A.D. 750/900); and (3) the Postclassic (A.D. 750/900–A.D. 1519). There are numerous objections to this, as there are to most broad historical periodizations. It appears to equate cultural/aesthetic phases ('Classic') with levels of sociopolitical development; it tends to homogenize wide ranges of cultures and regions; and it carries certain normative and teleological connotations. More complex alternative schemes, utilizing the concept of 'horizons' derived from Peruvian chronology, have been propounded, while the original scheme has also been amended, subdivided and debated by a number of scholars (hence the ambivalence in the time periods just listed).[55] Some scholars have opted for value-free but jaw-breaking labels derived from ceramic sequences: Tzacualli, Tlamimilolpa, Tezoyuca-Patlachique. But there is a danger – certainly for our humble purposes – of an excess of sophistication.[56] For the sake of brevity and simplicity, we will adhere to the conventional periodization, while stressing that its application must be flexible (e.g., the Classic period ended at different times in different regions) and free from normative judgements ('Classic' serves as a purely descriptive label and does not imply cultural or sociopolitical superiority).[57]

Similar problems arise when geographical generalizations are hazarded, as they must be. Mesoamerica may best be defined as 'a culture-area-with-time-depth': it was, in other words, a historical and cultural entity; it was not, like Metternich's Italy, a 'geographical expression'.[58] Mesoamerica's spatial parimeters changed over time and never conformed to the borders of modern Mexico: roughly, Mesoamerica stretched from within northern Mexico to far beyond Mexico's southern frontier, where it encompassed Guatemala, El Salvador and parts of Honduras, Nicaragua and Costa Rica. Governed by the somewhat arbitrary outcome of recent history, we will devote attention almost exclusively to that (greater) part of Mesoamerica which falls within Mexico's present national territory, largely ignoring Central America; on the other hand, we will discuss, where appropriate, those vast but underpopulated regions which lay to the north of the loose Mesoamerican cultural frontier, and which would later comprise the northern reaches of colonial New Spain and the disputed borderlands where the Republic of Mexico faced the expanding United States of America.

Mesoamerica embraced a multitude of ecological subregions, defined chiefly by degrees of altitude and aridity. Any regional generalization therefore suffers from numerous exceptions. Nevertheless, it

---

[55] Sanders and Price, *Mesoamerica*, pp. 23–32; Richard E. Blanton, Stephen A. Kowalewski, Gary Feinman and Jill Appel, eds., *Ancient Mesoamerica: A Comparison of Change in Three Regions* (Cambridge, 1981), pp. 50, 115; Gordon R. Willey, 'Recent Researches and Perspectives in Mesoamerican Archaeology: An Introductory Commentary', in Sabloff, *Supplement to the Handbook of Middle American Indians*, pp. 4, 10–11.

[56] Note the pertinent observations of Kent V. Flannery in his review of Wolf, ed., *The Valley of Mexico*, in *Science*, 196 (1977), p. 761.

[57] Robert J. Sharer, *The Ancient Maya* (Stanford, 5th ed., 1995), p. 49.

[58] Willey, 'Recent Researches', p. 4. See also Blanton *et al.*, *Ancient Mesoamerica*, pp. 6, 245–6.

is possible and useful to generalize that Mesoamerica/Mexico contains three principal regions, which possess a certain ecological and historical unity: the north, the central highlands (which particularly demand further subdivision), and the southeast.[59] The north comprises the huge zone stretching from the American southwest down to a line drawn roughly between Tampico and Tepic. Here, a broad arid plateau lies between the arms of two mountain ranges: the Sierra Madre Oriental to the east and the mightier Sierra Madre Occidental, an extension of the Rocky Mountains, to the west. Historically underpopulated, the north has provided a pathway for migrants and invaders since humans first entered Mesoamerica: no major obstacles confront the traveller heading south; in fact, the mountains, marching north-south, act as a kind of funnel, converging on the central highlands – or, to adopt a more contemporary image, Mexico resembles a cornucopia, with its generous, gaping mouth pointing north. Open and arid, the north – the Gran Chichimec of colonial times – could support only patches of sedentary agriculture in favoured river valleys (those of the Río Grande and Río Yaqui, for example); sedentary agriculturalists were perennially threatened by dessication and by the depredations of nomadic bands which retained their ancient hunting, gathering and raiding way of life, in some cases down to the nineteenth century. Farming communities, established during the first Christian millennium, formed a tenuous archipelago, linking the dense civilized populations of central Mexico to the Anasazi, Mogollon, Hohokam and other cultures of the American southwest. The frontier which demarcated northern from central Mexico, though it was permeable and shifting, remained a 'hard' frontier in the sense that insurmountable ecological barriers barred the way to extensive northward migration and settlement. Colonists and conquerors – Mesoamerican and Spanish – penetrated the hostile north only in response to specific incentives, such as precious minerals or trade goods; but northern invaders and migrants periodically descended on the civilized centre, where, like the Mongols of East Asia, they settled and merged with an ancient civilized culture.

---

[59] Eric Wolf, *Sons of the Shaking Earth* (Chicago, 1972, first pubd. 1959), pp. 1–20, offers a good overview; a more complex – ecological – breakdown is offered by Sanders and Price, *Mesoamerica*, pp. 102–4, which proposes eight Mesoamerican regions, six of them confined to modern Mexico.

If, in the north, sedentary farmers were the exception, in the central highlands they formed the basis of an old and complex agrarian society. Here, a concatenation of mountain ranges, some actively volcanic, created a swath of rugged uplands, some arid and chill, interspersed with more hospitable valleys, watered and possessed of temperate or subtropical climates. Suitable for cereals, as well as other crops, many of the temperate valleys were nevertheless prone to frosts and droughts which threatened farmers' livelihoods and encouraged them to devise labour-intensive forms of agriculture, including terraces, irrigation systems and, as we shall see, the so-called *chinampas* – 'floating gardens' – of the Valley of Mexico. The latter – more strictly titled the Basin of Mexico – was an area of some 70 by 120 kilometres, standing at an altitude of 2,000 metres, which provided the location for two of Mesoamerica's most powerful and populous states: Teotihuacan and Tenochtitlán. But the fragmented terrain, carved up by mountains and bereft of navigable rivers, favoured multiple settlements and the growth of rival centres in the Valleys of Toluca to the west, Cuernavaca to the south and Puebla to the west, all of which lay within a 100-kilometre radius of the Valley of Mexico.[60]

If this region constituted the heart of the central highlands, two important outlying zones – the centre-west and Oaxaca – also deserve mention. These zones shared many of the broad ecological features of the central plateau and therefore merit inclusion in the central highlands, but they were also, to a degree, historically and culturally distinct. The centre-west, stretching from present-day Querétaro through Guanajuato to Jalisco and Michoacan, formed a rough plateau at an elevation of around 1,500 metres – lower, more open and more undulating than the region around the Valley of Mexico. Within Mesoamerica it marked the shifting boundary between the nomads of the northwest and the sedentary civilizations of the centre; but it also embraced agrarian kingdoms, like those of the Tarascans or of highland Jalisco, which resisted Aztec domination down to the Conquest. Once the Spaniards had defeated Aztecs and Tarascans alike, the centre-west was transformed from a frontier zone into a nexus of commerce and settlement linking the colonial capital and the mining north; as a major centre of cereal-farming and

[60] Wolf, *Sons of the Shaking Earth*, pp. 7–10.

silver-mining, it eventually became the economic pacemaker of the late colony.

South of the central plateau lies a roughly parallel, though smaller and less geopolitically strategic, complex, that of Oaxaca: a region of rugged mountains cradling temperate, cereal-growing valleys, which stretches down to the hot lowlands of the Isthmus of Tehuantepec. Within the three 'arms' of the chief of these valleys, the Valley of Oaxaca, the Zapotec culture flourished, centred on the great city of Monte Albán, which throughout centuries co-existed and contested with the states of the central plateau.

The third main zone – the southeast, beyond the Isthmus – is chiefly characterized by its lowland tropical climate. It embraces the broad, flat Yucatán peninsula (arid in the north, lush and forested farther south in the Petén), and, ecologically and culturally, it also includes the hot Gulf lowlands, which curve northward from Campeche and Tabasco through Veracruz as far as the Pánuco River. True, the southeast also contains the Chiapas highlands, ecologically akin to the central plateau. But the basic character of the southeast reflected a form of lowland agriculture which was more diversified, less dependent on maize (manioc offered an alternative, especially in hard times), and, thanks to its hotter and wetter climate, suitable for swidden (slash-and-burn) farming, which tended to be land- rather than labour-intensive. On this ecological basis, distinct from that of highland Mexico, arose the main lowland civilizations, those of the Olmec and the Maya.

As we have said, Mesoamerica did not stop at the current Mexico-Guatemala border (though, it is interesting to note, the Aztec empire did). The Maya of Belize and Guatemala – as these regions would later be called – were inseparably linked to the Maya of southeastern Mexico; trade, migration and invasion routes criss-crossed current national boundaries. However, the Spaniards demarcated New Spain from Guatemala, sundering the old Maya territory; Mexico and its southern neighbour, briefly united in 1821, definitively split apart in 1824. While the Aztec empire remained the unitary heartland of first New Spain and then Mexico, the Maya zone was dismembered into discrete colonies, later republics.

Within this rough geographical matrix, the central highlands and southeastern lowlands – both individually and by their diverse interactions – moulded the history of Mesoamerica. The north, in contrast, remained peripheral; some would term it a 'periphery' in the specific sense propounded by Wallerstein – that is, it enjoyed a dependent, reflexive relationship vis-à-vis the Mesoamerican 'centre'.[61] The north received cultural imprints and mounted military threats, but, even when those threats were realized, northern conquerors were assimilated into mainstream Mesoamerican culture, just as China's northern invaders were recurrently Sinified. Civilization had its attractions as well as its discontents, especially from the conqueror's elevated point of view. Not until the twentieth century did the old pattern change and the north – now dynamic and more populous – impose its will on the historically hegemonic centre. Three millennia earlier, when the north counted for little, Mesoamerica was a fundamentally 'two-faced, Janus' civilization, divided between centre and southeast, highland and lowland, plateau and forest.[62]

Thus the principal Mesoamerican cultures, to which we now turn, may be schematically placed within their geographical as well as their chronological locations:

	c. 1500 B.C. → PRECLASSIC/FORMATIVE	c. A.D. 1 → CLASSIC	c. A.D. 900 → POSTCLASSIC	1519 CONQUEST
H				
I	VALLEY OF MEXICO:	TEOTIHUACAN	TOLTECS AZTECS	
G		Teotihuacan	Tula Tenochtitlán	
H				
L				
A	OAXACA: ZAPOTECS		MIXTECS	
N	Monte Albán i,ii	Monte Albán iii	Monte Albán iv,v	
D				
············				
L				
O	GULF: OLMECS			
W	San Lorenzo,			
L	La Venta			
A				
N	YUCATÁN: MAYA	CLASSIC MAYA	TOLTEC MAYA	
D		Tikal, Palenque	Chichén Itzá	

---

[61] Richard A. Pailes and Joseph W. Whitecotton, 'The Greater Southwest and the Mesoamerican "World" System: An Exploratory Model of Frontier Relationships', in William W. Savage and Stephen I. Thompson, eds., The Frontier: Comparative Studies, vol. 2 (Norman, Okla., 1979), pp. 105–21.

[62] Ignacio Bernal, 'Views of Olmec Culture', in E. P. Benson, ed., Dumbarton Oaks Conference on the Olmec (Washington, 1968), p. 138. The highland/lowland, (later) Aztec/Maya, dichotomy has generated some fanciful parallels: Rome/Athens, Germanic/Latin. These are not pursued in this book.

(*Key:* time line runs left to right [see top] and is matched with conventional Mesoamerican periodization. Left margin gives broad highland/lowland distinction. *GULF* denotes geographical region; OLMECS refers to major civilization; San Lorenzo indicates principal centre).

Despite the enduring differences imposed by climate, ecology and geopolitical location, these varied cultures, highland and lowland, all belonged to the generic type termed Mesoamerican. Interaction between different cultures or states was the rule rather than the exception: at times, particular centres achieved a form of regional, sometimes even areawide dominance (though whether such dominance was political, military, economic or cultural is a difficult question, to be raised in specific contexts): the Olmecs during the Preclassic, Teotihuacan during the Classic, the Toltecs and Aztecs in the Postclassic. These were periods when, by various means and to various extents, centripetal forces pulled together the different regions of Mesoamerica, reinforcing the communality of their history. Yet, even when centrifugal forces prevailed (as often they did) and the area was Balkanized, the common features of Mesoamerican culture were individually retained: a productive, sedentary agriculture, permitting marked social stratification and state-formation; military and priestly elites; grandiose ceremonial centres, usually possessing pyramidal temples and ballcourts; an elaborate pantheon and calendar; glyphic forms of 'writing'; and a ubiquitous, though not uniform, penchant for war, tribute and sacrifice.[63] This complex of features can first be discerned – if not in their full maturity – in the Olmec culture, the 'mother culture', as it has been termed, of Mesoamerica. It is here that the analysis of state-formation and early civilization must begin.

III. The Olmecs

The Olmec culture developed on the Gulf coast, in what is today southern Veracruz and western Tabasco. Here, from about 1500 B.C., the Olmecs (their name, signifying 'dweller in the land of rubber',

---

[63] Kenneth G. Hirth, 'Early Exchange in Mesoamerica: An Introduction', in Hirth, *Trade and Exchange*, pp. 7–8, following Kirchhoff.

refers to a key export of the Gulf lowlands) created a culture embracing most of the elementary features of Mesoamerican civilization: a degree of (as yet limited) social stratification; large ceremonial centres, characterized by massive earth pyramids, carved stone stelae (monoliths), mosaic floors and the famous giant Olmec heads; glyphic 'writing'; calendrical knowledge; and probably human sacrifice. The archaeological record, derived from the principal Olmec centres of San Lorenzo, La Venta and Tres Zapotes, indicates a marked degree of economic specialization: Olmec pottery, although aesthetically undistinguished, was produced in large quantities and, as we shall note, was exported; jadework and stone-carving, especially the distinctive 'jaguar' child and 'Uncle Sam' types, were both skilful and voluminous.[64]

Compared to both their Mesoamerican forerunners and their contemporary rivals, the Olmecs were clearly able to mobilize a large labour force. Pits have been found containing tons of quarried green serpentine blocks; San Lorenzo's ceremonial centre constitutes a kind of man-made mesa: 'an artefact on a gigantic scale'.[65] The massive basalt heads of La Venta (up to nine feet in height and forty tons in weight) are formed of a stone which, in a manner reminiscent of the making of Stonehenge, was quarried, floated, perhaps on balsa wood rafts, and logrolled over fifty miles from the Tuxtla mountains.[66] Consonant with this evidence, it is reckoned that the population of the entire Olmec zone may have reached between a third and a quarter of a million, which in turn implies a productive sedentary agriculture. For some, this has been perplexing, since in more recent times the Gulf lowlands have been sparsely populated and would-be colonizers have had to face the trials of heat, floods, insects, disease and poor tropical soils. Furthermore, the traditional swidden agriculture of the Gulf was thought to be inefficient and unproductive, incapable of supporting so large and dense a Mesoamerican population.

---

[64] On the basis of these two types, Ignacio Bernal, *The Olmec World* (Berkeley, 1969), pp. 26–8, infers a bi-ethnic community. Both the origins and the language of the Olmec remain mysterious: Richard A. Diehl, 'Olmec Archaeology: What We Know and What We Wish We Knew', in Robert J. Sharer and David C. Grove, eds., *Regional Perspectives on the Olmec* (Cambridge, 1989), pp. 17–32.

[65] Robert H. Heizer, 'New Observations on La Venta', and Michael Coe, 'San Lorenzo and the Olmec Civilization', in Benson, *Dumbarton Oaks Conference*, pp. 10, 44.

[66] Bernal, *The Olmec World*, pp. 68–9.

It is now recognized, however, that swidden farming is not quite the exercise in feckless prodigality it was once thought to be; it may be ecologically appropriate and, when combined with more limited intense cultivation, it can be suitably productive. In addition, conditions were different three thousand years ago: the association of the lowland tropics with disease and debilitation derives from the post-Conquest introduction of malaria and cattle, the latter inimical to the health of humans and the environment alike. In the Olmec region, as in Yucatán, life was healthier then than now, while farming ravaged the environment less. Slash-and-burn agriculture, though inefficient in terms of output per unit area, was correspondingly efficient in its use of labour, it conserved the environment, and it could sustain a sizeable population. True, the Olmec centres were not true cities. San Lorenzo, covering an area of about 50 hectares, had a permanent population of maybe one thousand; thus, it served as a ceremonial centre for a large rural hinterland, dotted with farming hamlets, where population density probably corresponded to the 'compact low-density village' model, or about twenty persons per square kilometre. Possibly intermediate centres, as yet undiscovered, also existed: Mayan analogies would suggest that they did, thus creating a linked three-tier hierarchy of settlement, ranging from the numerous scattered hamlets up to the pre-eminent centre.[67] Whatever the precise distribution, population was sufficiently large to presuppose some forms of intensive cultivation, supplementing the standard slash-and-burn techniques. Apart from some limited hunting and (rather more) fishing, the Olmecs exploited the fertile river levees of the flood plain. San Lorenzo boasted an 'elaborate system' of water control, designed to channel flood-water and, perhaps, to irrigate farmlands; a system, it has been suggested, requiring 'an incredible expenditure of labour' and 'a highly advanced knowledge of hydraulic engineering'.[68] Very likely, the early 'take-off' of Mesoamerican civilization in the Gulf lowlands partly derived from the ecological peculiarities of the region: here, a population originally dependent on hunting, gathering and fishing rapidly acquired

[67] Heizer, 'New Observations', p. 23; Bernal, *The Olmec World*, pp. 53–4; cf. William T. Sanders, 'The Cultural Ecology of the Lowland Maya: A Re-evaluation', in T. Patrick Culbert, ed., *The Classic Maya Collapse* (Albuquerque, 1973), pp. 327–8.
[68] Coe, 'San Lorenzo and the Olmec Civilization', pp. 57, 64–5.

enhanced productive powers – and, in consequence, enhanced numbers – as crops and farming methods originally developed, out of necessity, in the central highlands were now introduced alongside the traditional methods of the region.[69]

Such an ecological argument may help explain lowland population growth. But it does not readily explain how and why that population cohered, nor how cohesion was retained in the face of incipient social stratification. The problem is the more taxing given the prevalence of slash-and-burn agriculture, which did not require a complex state or social organization for the people to wrest a living from the prolific soil. Water was abundant (too abundant in some cases), and both flora and fauna were diverse. Households could probably exist on what they produced in autonomous decentralized fashion: no central direction, no 'hydraulic' authority, was needed. To the extent that hydraulic works developed, here and, more grandiosely, in the Valley of Mexico, they followed and did not precede the establishment of the state. Of course, the relationship between state-formation and hydraulic public works was a dialectical one: state power could be enhanced by undertaking ambitious and socially necessary public works (a later Aztec example would be Nezahualcóyotl's dike, which inhibited the chronic flooding of the Valley towns). However, the chronological record strongly suggests that state power *antedated* such hydraulic projects, which in turn served to bolster, rather than to create *de novo,* such power. This would suggest that the mobilization of labour required for hydraulic projects usually demanded the pre-existence of the state, and it is hardly plausible to argue that populations submitted to state authority out of a prescient awareness of future hydraulic projects.

In addition, the resource endowment of the Olmec region was fairly uniform and did not foster forms of local economic specialization which might in turn lead to a regional integration based on exchange. Neither the 'hydraulic' nor the 'exchange' theory of state-building looks particularly appropriate for the Olmec – or the Maya – lowlands. It seems likely that, if soils deteriorated, if population pressure grew and if incipient social stratification proved oppressive,

---

[69] Comments of MacNeish in Kent V. Flannery, 'The Olmec and the Valley of Oaxaca', in Benson, *Dumbarton Oaks Conference*, p. 115.

there was ample opportunity for the fissure of communities, for emigration and colonization in new regions of the tropical lowlands.
True, there were geographical barriers to movement: the sea to the
north, swamps to east and west. But these did not form a ferrous
ring around the Olmec zone, which consequently lacked the ecological constraints and demographic concentration of the highland
valleys, such as those of Oaxaca and Mexico.[70] Relatively speaking,
the Olmec region remained ample and open; its population was not
'caged'. The question therefore remains, in the context of the Olmecs
and later of the Maya, of how society cohered, of why populations
submitted to the emergent power of the state.

For Olmec society certainly cohered; something like an Olmec
state emerged. Abundant labour was needed to raise the giant Olmec
heads and pyramids, and surplus production was required to feed the
priests, stonemasons, artisans and traders of the major centres. Coercion and state-formation offer one answer. Coe sees San Lorenzo
as 'the center of a coercive state of grandiose proportions', embracing secular rulers, organized armies, laws, a state religion, marked
social stratification and even a 'national bureaucracy'.[71] This seems
excessive. A military establishment is likely to leave clear archaeological and pictorial evidence, but none is to be found; the presumed
forces of the Olmec state are, according to one critic, mere 'ghostly
armies'.[72] Conversely, it can be argued by analogy that even stateless
tribal peoples have raised up impressive monuments, ceremonial
and mortuary (European megaliths would be an example).[73] Such
projects require cooperative labour, collective organization and social integration; but coercion was not the only means to achieve
them. Big buildings *per se* do not prove the existence of big states.
In the Olmec case, the buildings are big, arguing a significant level
of social integration, but we should hesitate before inferring from
this the existence of a mighty Olmec state. Nor should we resort to

---

[70] Bernal, *The Olmec World*, pp. 68–9; Michael D. Coe, 'San Lorenzo Tenochtitlan', in Sabloff,
Supplement to the Handbook of Middle American Indians, pp. 143–4; cf. Mann, *Sources of
Social Power*, p. 118.

[71] Coe, 'San Lorenzo and the Olmec Civilization', p. 60.

[72] Comments of Paddock in Coe, 'San Lorenzo and the Olmec Civilization', p. 72; Bernal, *The
Olmec World*, p. 88, notes the absence of pictorial militarism.

[73] Comments of Furst in Coe, 'San Lorenzo and the Olmec Civilization', p. 72; cf. Renshaw, *Before
Civilization*, ch. 7.

that recurrent fallback, state-formation by conquest and imitation. This argument is regularly sustained by those who, failing to discern the ecological preconditions presumed to be appropriate for state-formation in a given case, maintain that the incipient state in question was a 'secondary' (as opposed to a 'pristine') state, that is, that it arose out of a Darwinian struggle with more precocious neighbouring (perhaps pristine) states.[74] This is an overworked, and often an *ex post facto*, argument, introduced to salvage awkward exceptions. It smacks of diffusionism (the notion that innovations – in this instance the state – spread around the world like tumbling dominoes); it leads to lengthy and arbitrary causal regressions (ultimately, one New World state could be held responsible for initiating the process of continental state-formation; which prompts one to ask how this pristine pioneer managed to develop); and, in the crucial Olmec case, there is no obvious candidate for prior, exemplary, state-building in Mesoamerica. The Olmecs were the pioneers of state-formation, or something close to it. They do not seem to have been frightened or cajoled into it by powerful rivals. It does not appear, as I have said, that their ecological 'caging' compelled them to accept state authority. Whence, then, the origins of Olmec social stratification and political authority?

I have already suggested that Mesoamerican chiefdoms developed on the basis of the economic redistribution of goods (and, perhaps, wives), coupled with powerful religious sanctions. It may further be suggested that the Olmec 'state' (or 'super-chiefdom' or 'paramount chiefdom') was grafted upon such conventional chiefdoms, scattered throughout the Olmec region. This was the recurrent pattern in Mesoamerica (to some extent, in colonial New Spain too), as greater, more complex, ultimately 'imperial' units incorporated and governed through the medium of lesser, simpler units. Similar patterns have been discerned in Africa too.[75] Only by means of such 'indirect rule' could the principal authorities (of state or paramount

---

[74] M. Webb, 'The Peten Maya Decline Viewed in the Perspective of State Formation', in Culbert, *Classic Maya Collapse*, pp. 370–82, seems to approach a circular argument, whereby any political unit lacking obvious military traits is reduced to 'chiefdom' status and cannot aspire to statehood. Note also Mann, *Sources of Social Power*, pp. 54–8.

[75] Mann, *Sources of Social Power*, p. 69. Like Webb (n. 74), Mann does not wish to accord 'statehood' to units which lack obvious coercive apparatuses.

chiefdom) exercise a measure of control over scattered subordinate communities; and, often, control was partial, or precarious, even when the state – such as the Aztec state – possessed sizeable military forces. Lacking such forces, the Olmec 'state' could only loosely – we might even say 'consensually' – integrate subordinate communities. Hence the debate as to whether it deserves the title 'state' at all, or whether it may be better seen as located at a midpoint along the continuum from chiefdom to state.[76] San Lorenzo, for example, may have directly controlled two neighbouring, quite likely tributary, communities: to that limited extent, chiefly rule could achieve some modest coercive control. But beyond, in the great rural hinterland, San Lorenzo's authority was indirect, non-coercive and exercised in conjunction with – perhaps also in opposition to – the authority of local chiefs (such an ambivalence being a hallmark of systems of indirect rule). A limited radius of coercive power was therefore surrounded by a larger, looser radius of cultural influence.

What was the nature of this loose, non-coercive, but integrative influence? There is scant evidence of a pre-eminent secular or dynastic ruler, lodged in a recognizable palace (as there is elsewhere in Mesoamerica).[77] There is, however, ample evidence of religious activity, from which we may infer a form of ideological integration of the Olmec 'state'/'paramount chiefdom'. Ceremonial centres like La Venta were modestly populated and, like later Maya centres, served to attract large visiting populations which gathered at (astronomically?) determined times of the year, presumably during pauses in the agricultural cycle. For, if these lowland peasants worked longer hours, according to a more rigorous schedule, than their hunting-and-gathering ancestors, they were still far from being the ceaselessly active human cogs of modern industrial society. The agricultural year contained large lacunae; as already noted, slash-and-burn agriculture was a land- rather than labour-intensive system of cultivation. Recurrent visits to ceremonial centres were therefore feasible and, presumably, rewarding, in that they offered recreation, markets, religious and aesthetic satisfaction and human company on a scale which small communities could not afford (they may also

[76] Webb, 'The Peten Maya Decline', p. 382; cf. Bernal, *The Olmec World*, p. 91.
[77] Bernal, *The Olmec World*, pp. 48–9.

have facilitated exogamous marriage, which contested the authority of matchmaking local chiefs). The ceremonial centre could thus
minister to a range of human wants over and above the basic subsistence needs which were met within the household and local community. Such needs, as Eric Wolf reminds us, are (and were) powerful
and pervasive: 'no human society restricts its purposes to the pursuit of the food quest; as soon as this basic need is met, it raises its
sights and strives to transcend its earth-bound limitations'.[78] Indeed,
it is arguable that Mesoamerican people both enjoyed more opportunity and felt more need for such transcendental activity than their
modern, urban, industrial counterparts, whose place on the economic treadmill – while it may assure their basic subsistence – also
tends to monopolize individual effort and dictate mental horizons.
Modern people are constituted according to their place in a complex
technological order, which determines many aspects of life, culture
and identity; early Mesoamericans enjoyed (or suffered) less occupational determinism and were constituted according to alternative
influences – customary, familial and religious – which filled great
areas of life. The satisfaction of non-material wants clearly generated
powerful symbolic allegiances: 'men seem to be impelled to far more
strenuous and sustained action by the idea of two-headed eagle[s],
immortality, or freedom than by the most succulent bananas'.[79]

   Here the argument from analogy is powerful. Historically, the
ceremonial centre has played a primary role in the genesis of urban settlement; and this applies to centres which, like those of the
Olmec, existed amid a dispersed population as well as those which
constituted true cities. Even allowing for the possible bias of the archaeological evidence, it can be shown that religious cults – rather
than, say, primordial markets or fortresses – often provided the rationale and even the structural principles upon which the world's
first cities were built.[80] This is borne out not only by the evident
religious function of such major centres but also by the absence
of clear ecological rationales: initial nucleation – the breakthrough
from village to urban community – while it necessarily occurred in

[78] Wolf, *Sons of the Shaking Earth*, p. 69.
[79] Childe, *What Happened in History*, p. 20.
[80] Wheatley, *Pivot of the Four Quarters*, pp. 225, 318–19 and *passim*.

regions of dense population, did not take place in ecologically privileged niches (a classic Mesoamerican example, which will follow,
is Oaxaca's Monte Albán). Ecological 'caging' cannot, as a general
rule, explain pioneer city- and state-formation. On the contrary, pioneer urban centres were often privileged less as regards their earthly
than their spiritual resources (their inhabitants, of course, did not
recognize this modern distinction). As Fustel de Coulanges put it,
over-generalizing as French intellectuals are wont to do, 'ce qui
faisait le lien de toute société, c'était une culte'.[81]

As a complement and counterpoint to local, community and
chiefly authorities, therefore, the peasantry formed an allegiance to
ceremonial centres and their priests, rulers and rituals. Possibly this
allegiance was fortified – and even the priesthood recruited – by a
forerunner of the cargo system, whereby villagers vied to partici-
pate in religious rituals, thus enhancing their social status.[82] And we
need not interpret this tendency in terms of a detached, mystical
religiosity. Mesoamerican religion, like any dominant ideology, was
intimately associated with social organization and political authority
(many later examples will be given). Religion offered solace amid the
routines and vagaries of the agricultural cycle. It also bolstered rival
forms of authority: that of head of family, chief, paramount chief,
priestly elite. Here, religion entered the early tug-of-war between
emergent political rivals. So long as families coexisted in egalitarian groups, religion remained (inevitably) apolitical, linked to the
hunt, the harvest and the veneration of ancestors. As stratification
began and forms of authority (chiefdoms) evolved, religion acquired
proto-political significance. It was enlisted to further – perhaps,
sometimes, to resist – these evolutionary processes. Ecological explanations, while helpful in explaining the genesis and rationale
of chiefly rule, are less helpful in explaining why subject populations allowed this rule to consolidate, expand and transmute into
fully-fledged state authority: an incremental explanation (the piece-
by-piece accumulation of chiefly, eventually state, power) cannot

---

[81] 'The bond of every society has been afforded by a cult' ('society' meaning a supra-kin, supra-village, community): quoted in Wheatley, *Pivot of the Four Quarters*, p. 302.

[82] Sharer, *The Ancient Maya*, p. 509; D. Webster, 'War and the Evolution of Maya Civilization', in Adams, *Origins of Maya Civilization*, p. 353. Frank Cancian, *Economía y prestigio en una comunidad maya* (Mexico, 1976), offers a contemporary analysis.

explain why, at given moments, the increasingly subjected population did not break away, migrate or rebel. Sometimes (as we will see)
they did and incipient political authority collapsed. But sometimes
they did not and state-building forged ahead.

Was this because the mass of subjects rationally perceived benefits (e.g., those of centralized economic management) that would
accrue from state-building? In many cases this is untenable: either
the economic benefits were scant, or they were compatible with egalitarian social organization. Were the people coerced? It seems unlikely that Neolithic military technology and communications would
permit a weak, primordial state to control a scattered rural population by means of outright coercion. Were subjects 'caged', that is,
incapable of escape? That, too, is a shaky generalization, especially
when applied to lowland Mesoamerica. Or were the incipient subjects merely stupid, unaware of their progressive subjection: 'by im-
perceptible shifts in the redistributive balance from one generation
to the next, the human species bound itself over into a form of social
life in which the many debased themselves on behalf of the exaltation of the few'.[83] Descriptively valid, this account remains weak
in terms of causal explanation. However gradual and incremental
the process of state-formation, its victims had every opportunity to
perceive its consequences and contest its advancement. That they
did not necessarily do this suggests to me that there were countervailing forces of cohesion, which justified increasing subjection. In
part these were religious, or psychological: ceremonial centres exercised a genuine appeal to the people of the rural hinterland. But
such centres also played a political role, offsetting the emergent – or
emerged – power of local chiefs. As the latter augmented their redistributive powers, their subjects may well have looked to the power
of the ceremonial centre (and its paramount chief) to seek a counter-
weight, a patron, a source of goods (and perhaps of wives). The potentially irksome power of the local chief was thus offset by the more
distant power and influence of the ceremonial centre/paramount
chief. Incipient subjects remained subjects; but they played rival
authorities off against each other to their own advantage. (Of
course, the local chiefs also tried to capitalize on their relationship

83 Harris, *Cannibals and Kings*, p. 122.

with the ceremonial centre/paramount chief: this was a three-way contest.)

Such a hypothesis cannot, of course, be empirically demonstrated. But it receives powerful corroboration by analogy, in that 'traditional' states regularly govern indirectly and, in doing so, alternatively reinforce and undermine the lower tier of indirect rulers (in this case chiefs), who stand between them and the mass of their subjects. So it was with the Spanish authorities and Indian *caciques* in New Spain; with China's dynastic rulers and the local scholar-gentry; with the British colonial state and the chiefs and emirs of West Africa. These analogous cases were the product of conquest, but they nonetheless reflect a systemic political pattern. Central states (even paramount chiefdoms which preceded them) can acquire legitimacy by offsetting and constraining the authority of pre-existing local authorities. Paradoxically, central states may thus become legitimate in part by cannibalizing an alternative political authority and by capitalizing on the common people's resistance to local bigwigs. States thus emerged from a process of three-way, three-tier, contestation, whereby power, sanctified by religion, ascended to the newest, topmost tier (the state), at the expense, first, of middling chiefs, then of the peasant communities at the base.

In the Olmec case, the ceremononial centre offered a new, numinous centre of influence. Eventually it boasted a powerful priesthood and elaborate ritual, whose influence radiated through the rustic hinterland. The priesthood may have been the first occupationally specific stratum to emancipate itself from subsistence labour and constitute itself as a distinct, self-recruiting body.[84] Certainly the Olmecs possessed such a priestly caste, and Olmec religion, like subsequent Mesoamerican religion, was potent and encompassing, confounding the conventional modern distinction between sacred and secular. The principal Olmec religious symbol – whether, as usually interpreted, a jaguar or 'were-jaguar', or, alternatively, an earth-serpent – was a deity of the earth and of fertility, as befitted a peasant people largely dependent on rainfed farming.[85] Jaguars (or serpents) appear

---

[84] Bernal, *The Olmec World*, p. 90; Wheatley, *Pivot of the Four Corners*, p. 303.

[85] Karl W. Luckert, *Olmec Religion: A Key to Middle America and Beyond* (Norman, Okla., 1976), pp. 24ff., sees the jaguar cult usurping an older popular serpent cult, before itself giving way to a neo-serpentine revivalism, led by the 'Green Reformer' (pp. 98–9).

on axes and altars, pots, masks, and the outstanding Olmec jade carvings. The existence of 'were-jaguars' – quasi-human jaguars or, if you prefer, feline humans – lends support to the notion that Olmec religion, at least in its formative origins, represented 'a half-way stage between tribal shamanism and the complex religious system of late times'; certainly there are many South American parallels which tend to corroborate this evolutionary thesis.[86] Certainly, too, the crowded pantheon of later Mesoamerica had not yet developed ('I don't see in the metropolitan Olmec any clear appearances of recognisable gods', Bernal states; though others have claimed to identify ten gods and nearly two hundred constituent elements within Olmec iconography). At any rate, deities of war were happily absent, reinforcing the hypotheses that Olmec social integration was not fundamentally coercive and that Olmec state-formation was not the 'secondary' consequence of external military threats.[87] Rather, the Olmec ceremonial centres – pioneering a role that would become central to Mesoamerican civilization – served as religious cynosures of the rural hinterland, their aesthetic splendour and inspiring ritual helping to bind together a sprawling fissiparous peasant population, while, at the same time, both legitimizing and counteracting the power of local chiefs (legitimizing those who deferred to the centre, counteracting those who resisted). Thus Olmec influence encouraged both centralization and stratification: local chiefly lineages might benefit from the imprimatur of Olmec 'civilization', but only at the cost of relinquishing part of their local chiefly power; thus occurred the political transformation which turned chiefdoms into paramount chiefdoms, and the latter into states.

As a prepotent culture, the Olmecs spread their influence widely throughout – and even beyond – Mesoamerica, especially in the period c. 1300–500 B.C. The Olmec influence is to be found particularly clearly in Guerrero, Morelos and Puebla, thus in a wide arc stretching from the southwest to the southeast of the central plateau; it is also evident in the Valley of Mexico itself, at Tlatilco; in Oaxaca (to degrees that are debated), in Chiapas, and even as far south as Guatemala

---

[86] Nigel Davies, *The Ancient Kingdoms of Mexico* (Harmondsworth, 1983), p. 51; Bernal, *The Olmec World*, pp. 101–3; Peter T. Furst, 'The Olmec Were-Jaguar Motif in the Light of Ethnographic Reality', in Benson, *Dumbarton Oaks Conference*, pp. 143–78.

[87] Bernal, 'Views of Olmec Culture', p. 142; Luckert, *Olmec Religion*, p. 23.

and El Salvador, over a thousand kilometres, as the crow flies, from the Olmec heartland.[88] Nor was this necessarily the limit of Olmec influence. Olmec-style figurines and massive temple mounds, aligned with the equinoctial sunrise, are to be found 600 kilometres up the Mississippi at Poverty Point in northern Louisiana.[89] The nature of such influence and the means of its transmission over these huge distances are subjects of insoluble debate; and it is a debate which will be repeated, *mutatis mutandis*, when discussing other prepotent cultures: Teotihuacano, Toltec, Aztec. 'Influence' – a favourite term of archaeologists – is notoriously vague and capable of quite different implications. Does it denote 'cultural' (i.e., aesthetic or technological) borrowing? Religious proselytization (if that is not too Eurocentric a concept: we will return to this theme too)? Outright conquest and colonization? A dependent, tributary, imperial relationship? In the case of the Olmecs, for which written sources are unavailable and the evidence is necessarily archaeological, the analysis consists of discerning Olmec – or 'Olmecoid' – styles, chiefly in carving, pottery, wall-painting and architecture, and measuring their fidelity to the original: close in the cases of Tlatilco, Chalcatzingo (Morelos) and Juxtlahuaca (Guerrero); more tenuous elsewhere. On this basis, Bernal boldly terms Tlatilco an Olmec 'colony' and posits a loose colonial empire, a 'clearly imperialistic endeavour', involving a 'war-tribute-commerce' network of subordination.[90] Coe likewise conceives of an Olmec empire embracing 'Puebla, Morelos and perhaps Guerrero'.[91]

But to infer political control from aesthetic style – however faithful – is surely risky. As Nigel Davies points out, the vogue for chinoiserie in Regency England did not reflect England's dependency upon Manchu China.[92] Furthermore, similarities in aesthetic style may reflect not simply diffusion from a single (in this case, Olmec) source, nor yet, at the other extreme, separate, spontaneous and

[88] Bernal, *The Olmec World*, pp. 121–73; Flannery, 'The Olmec and the Valley of Oaxaca', p. 101; see also Sharer and Grove, *Regional Perspectives on the Olmec*, chs. 6–10.

[89] Dean Snow, *The Archaeology of North America* (New York, 1976), pp. 39–42; Luckert, *Olmec Religion*, p. 142; but note the caution of Fiedel, *The Prehistory of the Americas*, pp. 114–15.

[90] Bernal, 'Views of Olmec Culture', pp. 137, 141; Bernal, *The Olmec World*, p. 188.

[91] Coe, 'San Lorenzo and the Olmec Civilization', p. 63.

[92] Davies, *Ancient Kingdoms of Mexico*, p. 95.

coincidental development (which is more plausible in respect of technological than of aesthetic overlap), but rather common influences
stemming from a neglected third party: in this case, the Preclassic
cultures of highland Guatemala and the Pacific coast, which were coeval with the Olmec and which may have influenced both the Olmecs
and their supposed 'colonies'.[93] In other words, 'Olmec' influence
may not always have been of strictly Olmec origin. Moreover, the
notion of imperial conquest and control does not conform all that
well to the archaeological evidence (here, and later, I will tend to deflate Mesoamerican empires, stressing their political and territorial
limitations). The 'metropolitan' Olmec centres, we have seen, were
modest in size and probably did not exercise strict coercive control over their hinterlands. It is even less likely that they could directly control far-flung provinces, possessed of sizeable populations
capable of self-defence.[94] As even the Aztecs found, the odds were
stacked against effective, unitary empire-building. What is more,
where later hegemonic cultures transmitted their influence from a
single large metropolis which brooked no local rival (Teotihuacan,
Tula, Tenochtitlán), successive Olmec centres ('cities' would be risky)
rose and fell: San Lorenzo, La Venta, Tres Zapotes; and their broader
Mesoamerican influence tended to reflect this succession. This does
not look like a system of centralized imperial rule; rather, it suggests a pattern within the Olmec heartland whereby rival communities (city-states or paramount chiefdoms) jostled for power, formed
loose federations and rose and fell. Indeed, such a pattern appears
to be characteristic of the Mesoamerican lowlands, as well as of
some of the highlands, during many periods. Meanwhile, Olmec influence (not conquest and control) radiated out from the heartland,
its intensity, direction and precise origin varying over the long sweep
of time – perhaps 800 years – under consideration. The medium of
this influence might be religion, migration, trade, or some combination of all three. In some instances, Olmec artisans may have carried
faithful Olmec styles – for example, of wall-painting – to Guerrero; or,

[93] Tatiana Proskouriakoff, 'Olmec and Maya Art: Problems of Their Stylistic Relation', in Benson, *Dumbarton Oaks Conference*, pp. 119–34.

[94] Flannery, 'The Olmec and the Valley of Oaxaca', p. 80; Arthur Demarest, 'The Olmec and the Rise of Civilization in Eastern Mesoamerica', in Sharer and Grove, *Regional Perspectives on the Olmec*, pp. 307–12, 316–17, 323, 343.

perhaps, Olmec architects gave help and inspiration in the construction of 'Olmecoid' pyramids at Cuicuilco, in the Valley of Mexico, or even at Poverty Point.[95]

Clearly, similarities in wall-paintings and pyramids imply migration and face-to-face contact. But trade, evidenced in the diffusion of Olmec artefacts, was probably the more common and effective medium of Olmec influence (there is, of course, no antithesis between the two: we may presume that migrants, artisans and architects tramped the same trade routes). Research on Mesoamerican prehistory increasingly stresses the role of trade as an integrating force which transcended, or infiltrated, political boundaries (such as they were). Dense concentrations of population, characterized by a more marked division of labour and possibly organized by local elites, would tend to produce more (and perhaps better) artefacts which could be dispersed along extended trade routes; craftsmen, builders and even priests might follow these routes, placing their sophisticated and coveted skills at the service of grateful masters – at Chalcatzingo, for example, where reliefs, executed in the Olmec style, depict warlike scenes untypical of the Olmec heartland.[96] Trade goods also offered bankable surpluses, which a community could save and turn to in times of dearth.[97] The resulting patterns of trade, determined in part by the resource endowments of different regions and communities, appear to offer the best general explanation of the varied incidence of Olmec influence: for example, its strong impact in the highlands, its relative weakness in the Maya lowlands.[98]

As regards the export of goods, the Olmec trade inventory was typical of an advanced (i.e., stratified and productive) culture, working out of a lowland base: pottery, jade, ceramic figures, probably feathers and, of course, the rubber which gave the Olmecs their name and which was needed, above all, for the ubiquitous Mesoamerican ballgame. In the eyes of the recipients, Olmec trade goods not only

---

[95] Davies, *Ancient Kingdoms of Mexico*, pp. 60–1; Sanders and Price, *Mesoamerica*, pp. 119–20.

[96] Bernal, *The Olmec World*, pp. 138–9; Davd C. Grove, 'Chalcatzingo and Its Olmec connection', in Sharer and Grove, *Regional Perspectives on the Olmec*, pp. 122–47.

[97] Hirth, 'The Analysis of Prehistoric Economic Systems', pp. 292–3.

[98] David C. Grove, 'The Pre-Classic Olmec in Central Mexico: Site Distribution and Inferences', in Benson, *Dumbarton Oaks Conference*, p. 182; Michael D. Coe, 'Olmec and Maya: A Study in Relationships', in Adams, *Origins of Maya Civilization*, p. 195.

possessed a practical use-value and, perhaps, represented an insurance against hard times, they also carried a certain social cachet, which might reinforce the prestige of emergent elites; and – notably with the jade artefacts – such goods probably embodied supernatural powers. Sacred, symbolic values, rather than any quantified commercial value, underwrote this form of 'trade' (thus we must be careful not to equate this form of exchange with the strictly mercantile trade of later times): 'the Olmec and the Valley of Oaxaca', for example, 'interacted most strongly on the level of shared concepts about religion, symbolism and status paraphernalia'; hence the significance and *modus operandi* of such trade were very different from free market commerce. This was an administered, ritualized and possibly redistributive trade, comparable to that which developed in many ancient societies around the world.[99] It depended on chiefs and states more than on freelance merchants. And it tended to favour communities strategically located at the nodal points of emergent trade networks. Again, therefore, simple agricultural resources – such as rich alluvial land – did not prove the prime determinants of nucleation and stratification.

Redistribution occurred both between and within regions. Highland obsidian and magnetite were exchanged for lowland jade and rubber. Within 'trading' communities, emergent chiefs controlled the exchange network, monopolizing or redistributing imported goods to the advantage of their prestige and authority. By serving as the pointmen in such networks, chiefs could justify their role as 'great providers' and, quite likely, cloak their chiefly lineage in a certain sacred aura. Thus, Wolf sees 'the Olmec art style as the outward manifestation of a religious cult which also possessed strong political overtones', and which, achieving purchase within incipiently stratified communities, 'underlined the new lines of cleavage within the social order'.[100] Again, there are global parallels for this association

---

[99] Demarest, 'The Olmec and the Rise of Civilization in Eastern Mesoamerica', p. 309, warns against equating Olmec trade with the 'militaristic, fiercely competitive market [*sic*] economies of Postclassic times'. On the character of early trade, note also Bernal, *The Olmec World*, p. 100; Flannery, 'The Olmec and the Valley of Oaxaca', pp. 101, 105; Jane W. Pires-Ferreira and Kent V. Flannery, 'Ethnographic Models for Formative Exchange', in Flannery, *The Early Mesoamerican Village*, pp. 287–92; and cf. Wheatley, *Pivot of the Four Quarters*, pp. 226, 264.

[100] Wolf, *Sons of the Shaking Earth*, p. 73; note also Flannery, 'The Olmec and the Valley of Oaxaca', pp. 100–2.

of trade with stratification and state-building. It is therefore logical that the spread of Olmec influence – responding to local demands rather than following some random pattern of gaseous diffusion – was most marked in communities like Tlatilco which were experiencing early stratification. The Olmec influence at Tlatilco – or at San José Mogote in the Valley of Oaxaca – did not initiate this evolution; rather, it was selected, internalized and utilized by already evolving societies, especially by their elites.[101] It therefore accelerated incipient stratification and political centralization, while lending both processes a sacred aura.

If the idea of a broad integrated empire of conquest is rejected in favour of this picture of a selectively ramified, sacralized network of exchange, there still remains the problem of the internal evolution of the Olmec heartland. Here, I have suggested, pre-eminent centres exercised some loose, local supremacy in roughly sequential fashion. San Lorenzo, for example, flourished between 1200 and 900 B.C. and was then supplanted by La Venta (900–600 B.C.); Tres Zapotes (about which less is known) dates to 500–100 B.C. But no massive primate cities like Teotihuacan – or even Tikal – emerged. Like both these metropolises, however, the Olmec centres eventually suffered sudden, if not terminal, collapse. San Lorenzo came to an end as a ceremonial centre around 900 B.C.; La Venta was abandoned some three centuries later, about the time that Olmec influence in the highlands faded. In both instances, the end was dramatic and deliberate: the altars and carved basalt heads were systematically defaced and ceremoniously interred.[102] If, elsewhere in the Olmec zone, decline was more gradual, the outcome was still the abandonment of long-established centres.

Various explanations of this phenomenon – by no means unique in Mesoamerican history – have been put forward, some of which may be productively permutated: peasant revolt, disease, invasion (perhaps from the Pacific coast of Chiapas), agricultural exhaustion, religious revivalism. None can be supported with great confidence:

---

[101] Flannery, 'The Olmec and the Valley of Oaxaca', pp. 96, 106; Joyce Marcus, 'Zapotec Chiefdoms and Formative Religion', in Sharer and Grove, *Regional Perspectives on the Olmec*, pp. 193–4, presents an even more skeptical evaluation of Olmec influence in Oaxaca, stressing instead local evolutionary dynamics.

[102] Bernal, *The Olmec World*, p. 116; Coe, 'San Lorenzo and the Olmec Civilization', p. 63.

the evidence does not exist. But the nature of the collapse can be hypothesized. Since the Olmec centres were, precisely, ceremonial centres and not substantial cities, their collapse was less consequential than that of Teotihuacan a millennium later. Nor does it seem that a massive demographic collapse ensued, as it did with the Classic Maya of the Petén. The rural hinterland continued to support a sizeable and vigorous population; San Lorenzo was revived as an inhabited centre; Tres Zapotes flourished (and developed glyphic writing) in the half millennium before Christ. The Olmec region of Tabasco went on to figure as a key political and cultural pivot within Mesoamerica: it is likely that the Nonoalca, co-founders of the Postclassic Toltec empire, carried elements of the Olmec Great Tradition (such as astronomical knowledge) to their new highland metropolis.[103]

So we are dealing with major sociopolitical crises, but not a collapse of civilization. It may be suggested, therefore, that crises came with a sundering of centre-hinterland ties, as sacred rulers lost their legitimacy, because of either natural disasters, external invasions or (perhaps most likely) local disaffection conceivably brought on by excessive demands for labour and manifested in a kind of rampaging religious revivalism.[104] An interpretation consonant with the ecological approach favoured by many scholars of Mesoamerica would posit a build-up of demographic pressure (the result of an overly successful period of settlement and growth, encouraged by ambitious elites), diminishing returns to swidden farming and recurrent food shortages, hence an erosion of politico-religious authority. The result may have been less a wild tropical *jacquerie* than a progressive withdrawal of peasant allegiances, a retreat into local communities, a quest for fresh frontier land and a spurning of ancient revered shrines. Local chiefs remained: perhaps they even connived at and benefited from the fall of their theocratic overlords, which enabled them to reassert control over local goods and people. The transition from chiefdom through super-chiefdom to state, always vulnerable to reversal, was aborted.

---

[103] Bernal, *The Olmec World*, pp. 112–15; Coe, 'San Lorenzo and the Olmec Civilization', p. 46; Nigel Davies, *The Toltecs until the Fall of Tula* (Norman, Okla., 1977), pp. 141–2, 158, 176–7.
[104] Luckert, *Olmec Religion*, pp. 91–9.

This failure at the topmost tier of social integration – a tier which we may see as ideologically moulded and temple-oriented – had implications for the far-flung sacralized trading network which carried Olmec influence throughout Mesoamerica. In its heyday, San Lorenzo strongly influenced the Valley of Mexico and Morelos; La Venta, in turn, transmitted Olmec styles to Guerrero and Chiapas. Shifts in local pre-eminence, associated with the rise and fall of centres and their theocratic elites, thus sent waves throughout Mesoamerica. The fall of the priestly elite is most clearly revealed at San Lorenzo, whose systematic desecration appears to have been the work not of barbarian invaders, nor even of irate peasant rebels (although Coe envisions 'stupendous... emotional fury' vented against San Lorenzo's 'symbols of authority'), but very likely of the deposed, disillusioned hierarchs themselves – or of fervent religious reformers, dedicated to a new order – who presided over a concerted ritual of desecration.[105] For political crisis and repudiation logically indicated the end of supernatural privilege, which the sacred elite of the Olmec had claimed and, one assumes, in which they genuinely believed. Destruction thus signalled the demise of the belief system upon which Olmec hegemony had been based; it was also, perhaps, the necessary preliminary to religious rebirth, according to the cyclical pattern embedded in Mesoamerican thought.[106] In a sense, San Lorenzo – the site itself – was ritually sacrificed.[107] Or, in the terminology of another ancient, cyclical *Weltanschauung*, the mandate of heaven was withdrawn and conferred on new beneficiaries: La Venta after the fall of San Lorenzo; the Valley of Mexico following the decline of Olmec civilization itself.

[105] Coe, 'San Lorenzo and the Olmec Civilization', p. 72.
[106] Drennan, 'Religion and Social Evolution', pp. 362–3.
[107] Coe, 'San Lorenzo and the Olmec Civilization', pp. 74–5.

TWO. Classic Mesoamerica

T he Classic period in Mesoamerica (at least if the 'protoclassic' is included) roughly spans the first Christian millennium. It was a period of widespread population growth, made possible by the preceding and concurrent development of agriculture; a period when population began to cohere in sizeable concentrations – genuine cities – under the authority of complex organized states, which now emerged from the ruck of petty chiefdoms. State-building occurred in three principal regions: the Valley of Mexico (where the city of Teotihuacan led the way); the Valley of Oaxaca (Monte Albán); and the Maya lowlands (Tikal, Seibal, Palenque and others). The first two were highland cultures, essentially maize-based; the third, which developed in comparative isolation, resembled the Olmec heartland in terms of its tropical ecology. Both Teotihuacan and the Maya cities ultimately experienced collapse around the eighth century, but Monte Albán displayed greater durability, thanks in part to its capacity for flexible response, allied to its more favourable environment and geopolitical location. Of the three, Teotihuacan represented the greatest concentration of population and power hitherto in Mesoamerica, and its influence pervaded the entire region, stamping the Classic era with its distinctive character; Monte Albán, in contrast, merely dabbled in distant imperialism, while Maya expansionism was confined to the transisthmian southeast. Teotihuacan was neither the oldest nor the most long-lived of the Classic centres. But, given its cultural pre-eminence and pivotal role within Mesoamerica

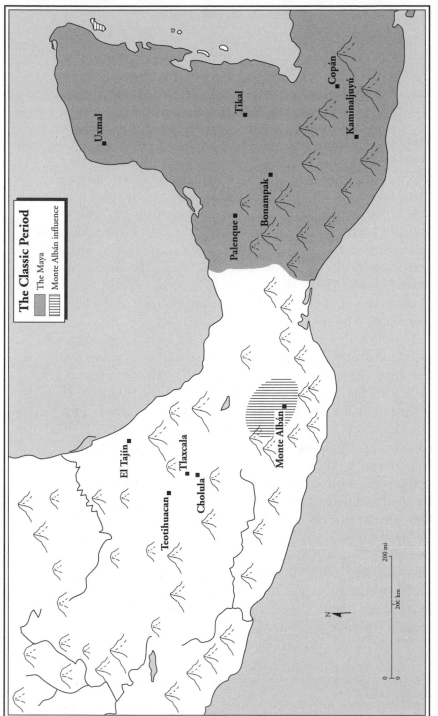

The Classic Period
■ The Maya
▥ Monte Albán influence

Uxmal ■

Tikal ■

Copán ■

Kaminaljuyú ■

Palenque ■

Bonampak ■

El Tajín ■

Teotihuacan ■

Tlaxcala ■

Cholula ■

Monte Albán ■

N

0   200 mi
0   20C km

Map 3

as a whole, it is logical to begin this discussion of the Classic era with this, its greatest civilization.

I. Teotihuacan

Teotihuacan, located at the northern end of the Valley of Mexico, bears comparison with any of the great pre-industrial cities of the Old World. The city's area alone comprised some 20 square kilometres (greater than that of imperial Rome), and its rural hinterland, devoted to the supply of the voracious metropolis, embraced the Valley of Mexico and more. At its peak, the city's population stood at some two hundred thousand, perhaps more. It boasted 'an unbelievable quantity of civic architecture', including the famous Pyramids of the Sun and Moon, the first of which covers an area equal to that of the Pyramid of Cheops.[1] It is not surprising that the later Aztecs took these to be the works of gods.

The rise of this great metropolis was, by archaeological standards, rapid, ultimately precipitate. The first settled farming communities appeared in the southern part of the Valley of Mexico around 2000 B.C. The original settlers may have been migrants from the warmer, smaller Valley of Morelos, who were already grouped in chiefdoms; by 1000 B.C., one Valley of Mexico centre, Tlatilco, the site of marked Olmec influence, may have exercised a loose local supremacy.[2] By then, substantial villages existed, and pottery (some of it Olmec-inspired) was in widespread use. Evidence of social stratification and political authority, however, remains patchy: as late as 800–600 B.C. (the floruit of La Venta) there were communities in the Valley of Mexico which numbered between one and two thousand, but which lacked public architecture (which, we will note, was now well advanced in the Valley of Oaxaca). Furthermore, the process of social stratification was not smooth and linear: social ranking appears to have been more pronounced in some of the earlier than in some of the later sites.[3] Assumed correlations of population growth,

---

[1] Diehl, 'Prehispanic Relationships', p. 259.

[2] Jeffrey R. Parsons, 'Settlement and Population History of the Basin of Mexico', in Wolf, *Valley of Mexico*, pp. 74–6.

[3] William T. Sanders, Jeffrey R. Parsons and Michael H. Logan, 'Summary and Conclusions', in Wolf, *Valley of Mexico*, p. 163; Brumfiel, 'Regional Growth', p. 236.

nucleation, stratification and state-building may therefore be misleading.

The general trend, however, throughout the first millennium B.C. was one of population growth which reached 'massive' proportions ('massive', that is, by previous standards) at the beginning of the Christian era; with this growth came demonstrable – though not generalized – population pressure and increased differentiation between communities.[4] Some of the more populous centres, experiencing a relative shrinking of their arable resources, probably began to exact tribute from less crowded communities (it is impossible to establish causal priority in the population-tribute relationship, to say, in other words, whether population growth initially spurred demands for tribute, or whether the successful exaction of tribute spurred population growth; at any rate, a system of positive feedback eventually obtained). By now the first major public works had been constructed, towns of several thousand people were well established, and two incipient cities, Teotihuacan and Cuicuilco, standing to the north and south of the Valley respectively, boasted some twenty thousand inhabitants each, out of a total Valley population of around one hundred seventy five thousand (a density already greater than that of the Olmec region at its demographic peak).

More than the Olmec heartland, therefore, the Valley of Mexico combined favourable ecological resources with marked ecological restrictions; here, in other words, the case for 'caging' (or 'impaction') as the primary motor of state-building is more compelling.[5] Formidable mountains fenced in the Valley on three sides, and arid hills marched to the north. Such an environment was particularly conducive to stratification and incipient state-building since growing communities, reluctant to fissure and decamp from their choice ecological niches, preferred to intensify arable farming and to organize for self-defence, even for expansion, under the aegis of centralizing chiefdoms.[6] Economic integration at the supra-community level was encouraged by the relative diversity of such niches, which, deriving from the Valley's particular combination of mountain slope,

---

[4] Sanders, Parsons and Logan, 'Summary and Conclusions', p. 165; Brumfiel, 'Regional Growth', pp. 246–7.

[5] Harris, *Cannibals and Kings*, pp. 115–16, 140–3.

[6] Webb, 'The Peten Maya Decline', p. 372.

forest, hillside and lakeshore, contrasted with the relative uniformity of the Olmec or Maya lowlands.

Such ecological factors help explain the trend towards nucleation and political centralization, but they cannot explain the unprecedented *degree* of centralization – the 'extreme primacy' – which Teotihuacan achieved.[7] For the city's growth was exceptional. By A.D. 100 its population had swollen to eighty thousand; its rational, gridlike groundplan covered some 20 square kilometres; and huge ceremonial works, including the two major pyramids, had been erected. At its peak in the middle of the first millennium, Teotihuacan's population of some two hundred thousand, grouped in distinctive residential compounds within the city, dwarfed the lesser communities of the Valley, whose numbers shrank as migrants were drawn into the maw of the great metropolis, or as they were denied access to the Valley's varied but circumscribed resources. Teotihuacan thus became a classic primate city, sucking goods and labour from the entire Valley – and beyond. Soon, its influence pervaded Mesoamerica, even penetrating Guatemala and – more remarkably – the hostile fastnesses of the far north.

So dramatic a phenomenon demands careful analysis. The kind of ecological argument now (rightly) favoured by many experts is, again, suggestive but incomplete. It cannot explain such a prodigy. The ecology of the Valley made Teotihuacan's development feasible (in both the weak sense of affording the necessary resources and in the strong sense of encouraging certain culturally appropriate responses, e.g., the intensification of agriculture, warfare and tribute). The Valley offered good land, well-watered by springs and lakes; and the latter, in turn, facilitated transport for a people lacking draught animals. Around A.D. 250 it seems, increased rainfall enhanced these advantages. The Valley also enjoyed a reasonably equable climate (although maize grown at 2,000 metres ran the perennial risk of frost), and it possessed certain key resources, notably obsidian. It was also strategically located, capable of acting as an entrepôt for north-south, highland-lowland trade; in particular, Teotihuacan commanded the chief route east to the Valley of Puebla and the Gulf. It was hardly coincidental that Teotihuacan, Tenochtitlán and finally

[7] Richard E. Blanton, 'The Rise of Cities', in Sabloff, *Supplement to the Handbook of Middle American Indians*, p. 394.

Mexico City should all capitalize on these advantages in order to dominate first the central highlands, then parts of the lowland periphery. But the pre-eminence of Teotihuacan was unusual, even for a Valley of Mexico metropolis. Teotihuacan not only commanded its local rivals it eclipsed and annihilated them. Other metropolises faced local challenges and needed local confederates: Tenochtitlán built its power on the basis of the famous Triple Alliance. Elsewhere in Mesoamerica the tendency towards city-state conflict and Balkanization was endemic – and in many respects materially determined. The greater a city grew, the wider it spread its power and influence and the more effort it had to exert to feed its people, contain its enemies and communicate its imperial will. The logistics of pre-industrial empires were always faulty; in Mesoamerica all the more because of the lack of animal and river transport. Imperial expansion soon incurred diminishing returns, and once-burgeoning powers had to retrench, curtail their ambitions and rest content with a reduced, local hegemony. Such was the recurrent pattern in Oaxaca, the Maya lowlands and, at times, the Valley of Mexico. Teotihuacan departed from this cyclical pattern. Why?

The infant city certainly enjoyed certain ecological advantages. It was founded in the northern part of the Valley, close to an important water supply and two major obsidian sources (obsidian has been found in the early levels of Teotihuacan, dating from a time when it constituted no more than a 'very large village').[8] Here, a canal network was dug, harnessing the waters of natural springs and of the San Juan River; possibly, *chinampa*-style irrigated fields were constructed too.[9] Some scholars have therefore chosen to see Teotihuacan as an example of Wittfogel's 'hydraulic' theory of state-building: roughly, a complex, centralized bureaucratic authority was required to 'manage' this water system.[10] It is true that hydraulic works formed part of the Teotihuacan complex, as they did of lesser Maya sites and, on a grander scale, of Aztec Tenochtitlán; they helped make possible these unusual concentrations of population. But Wittfogel's thesis cannot explain the rise of Teotihuacan. In general terms, the theory

---

[8] Davies, *Ancient Kingdoms of Mexico*, p. 66.

[9] William T. Sanders, 'The Agricultural History of the Basin of Mexico', in Wolf, *Valley of Mexico*, p. 117.

[10] Karl Wittfogel, *Oriental Despotism* (New Haven, 1957); cf. Harris, *Cannibals and Kings*, p. 245.

is vulnerable to serious objections.[11] And, in this particular case, the scale of Teotihuacan's hydraulic system is quite insufficient to carry the chief explanatory burden of the city's greatness.[12] The reasons for this greatness must be sought elsewhere, in non-hydraulic factors. Finally, to the extent that hydraulic works made a significant contribution to the city's sustenance, it can be argued that they were less cause than effect of Teotihuacan's size and power. Centrally directed irrigation, in other words, was called into being by a populous state, not vice versa. Teotihuacanos, like their hunting-and-gathering ancestors, learned to organize, innovate, graft and specialize because they had to.

What, then, encouraged the population growth and concentration, and the concomitant state-formation, which in turn facilitated (modest) hydraulic works? We may hypothesize two structural factors (roughly, trade and religion) and one conjunctural factor (volcanic activity). Teotihuacan combined vital commercial and religious activities. While it intensively exploited its immediate rural hinterland, its commercial network spread far wider. It controlled the crucial supply of obsidian from the Valley itself and from the Pachuca region, 50 kilometres to the northeast, and it elevated the processing and export of obsidian – Mesoamerica's steel – to an unequalled level of specialization and monopoly. Perhaps a third of the city's working population were non-agricultural specialists, and a third of these (i.e., over 10 per cent of Teotihuacan's labour force) were obsidian workers. Thus, the four obsidian workshops of early Teotihuacan (200 B.C.) grew to several hundred, perhaps as many as six hundred; there were well over one hundred ceramic workshops; and the city's distinctive residential system appears to have developed in order to accommodate this manufacturing boom.[13] Rival obsidian centres in the Valley, which might have challenged the city's monopoly, were, it

[11] Wheatley, *Pivot of the Four Quarters*, pp. 357–60; Mann, *Sources of Social Power*, pp. 94–8; Diamond, *Guns, Germs, and Steel*, p. 283. Harris, *Cannibals and Kings*, pp. 237–47, is more sympathetic.

[12] René Millon, 'Social Relations in Ancient Teotihuacan', in Wolf, *Valley of Mexico*, p. 245; Davies, *The Toltecs until the Fall of Tula* (Norman, Okla., 1977), pp. 273–4. Mann, *Sources of Social Power*, p. 119, overdoes the hydraulic argument.

[13] Millon, 'Social Relations', p. 215; Robert S. Santley, Janet M. Kerley and Ronald R. Kneebone, 'Obsidian working, Long-Distance Exchange, and the Political-Economic Organization of Early States in Central Mexico', in Barry L. Isaac, ed., *Economic Aspects of Prehispanic Highland Mexico: Research in Economic Anthropology*, suppl. 2 (1986), pp. 101–2.

seems, deliberately suppressed, and their artisans congregated – out of choice or compulsion – in the teeming warrens of Teotihuacan. Indeed, artisans were recruited from as far afield as Oaxaca, which supplied the population of an entire district of the city. Obsidian, vital to Mesoamerican civilization, formed Teotihuacan's export staple: ample evidence has been unearthed at Monte Albán, in southern Veracruz, at Tikal and even in the far north. But the city also churned out clay figurines, mass-produced in specialized moulds, as well as abundant pottery (as the famous Fine Orange ceramics show, large-scale production did not necessarily mean a sacrifice of quality to quantity). It is very probable, too, that textiles, wood and leather goods also figured in Teotihuacan's manufacturing inventory, but, given the less durable nature of these products, the archaeological record remains inconclusive. The importance of manufacturing and mercantile activity is further suggested by the scale of the Great Compound, the city's biggest construction, which is plausibly supposed to have been the central market-place. And, we shall note, Teotihuacan came to dominate the trade routes of Mesoamerica, achieving a remarkable and unprecedented degree of regional commercial and integration.

Thus, following but far outstripping Olmec precedent, Teotihuacan became a great entrepôt and commercial and manufacturing centre. From its rural hinterland (where the form of land tenure, unfortunately, remains obscure) the city extracted a surplus sufficient to maintain a huge non-agricultural population, many of whom were productive craftsmen. Exports of manufactures were offset by the import of 'foreign' goods, the result of trade and, very likely, tribute; in particular, Teotihuacan imported the lowland goods which highland societies, especially highland elites, coveted: feathers, cacao, cotton and rubber (although no ballcourt has been found at Teotihuacan, the ubiquitous Mesoamerican ballgame was almost certainly played in the city).[14] Quantities of Veracruz and Maya pottery have also been recovered. Although consumption of these luxury

---

[14] Esther Pasztory, *The Murals of Tepantitla, Teotihuacan* (New York, 1976), pp. 191–2, 201–7; Robert S. Santley, Michael J. Berman and Rani T. Alexander, 'The Politicization of the Mesoamerican Ballgame and Its Implications for the Interpretation of the Distribution of Ballcourts in Central Mexico', in Vernon L. Scarborough and David R. Wilcox, eds., *The Mesoamerican Ballgame* (Tucson, 1991), p. 11.

imports was clearly skewed in favour of the city's elite, the urban masses no doubt enjoyed some benefits from their membership of this teeming metropolitan community: possibly by their private appropriation of such goods and certainly from their enjoyment of public goods (e.g., the aesthetic display and collective ritual which, compared to those of the Olmecs, were open, lavish and geared to a mass audience). This conclusion must reinforce the supposition that Teotihuacan's large-scale artisan production, often of quality goods, could not have been based on outright coercion. If coercion existed, it was ancillary to some more pervasive and effective organizing principle.

This brings us to the second structural consideration (religion). Teotihuacan achieved an unprecedented combination of urbanization and stability: it survived and prospered, a genuine metropolis, for some eight centuries. What brought these myriad Stone Age city-dwellers together and – no less remarkable – held them together for twenty-five generations? What, to repeat an earlier question, constituted the 'social bond' which enabled Teotihuacan to cohere, as a city, a state, an empire? Coercion no doubt played a part, not least in reducing rival centres of economic and political power within the Valley. But its role should not be exaggerated. Size alone cannot be taken as indicative of coercive authority, even if it may suggest coercive capacity. Rather, as Eric Wolf and others have suggested, ideology, closely linked to the production and circulation of goods, offers a better explanatory principle for understanding the growth and florescence of Teotihuacan.[15] The city does not seem to have been a particularly martial polity. Its lavish representative art – its murals especially – display few scenes of war, and such as there are date from the city's final years.[16] Nor is the city's record of concentration and stability evidence of a purely, or even a primarily, coercive state. Economic self-interest, rather than coercion, may have impelled people to the city, which acted as a magnet to traders, artisans, landless workers, thieves and whores. The depopulation of the Valley,

[15] Wolf, *Sons of the Shaking Earth*, pp. 79–83; Davies, *Ancient Kingdoms of Mexico*, pp. 98–9; Millon, 'Social Relations', pp. 229–30.

[16] Pasztory, *Murals of Tepantitla*, pp. 248–9, 253, 255.

paralleling the city's boom, suggests powerful centripetal forces of a non-coercive character. However, to call these forces 'economic' and to impute motives of 'economic self-interest' (loaded terms, derivative of classical political economy) is to beg some crucial questions.

The problem, recurrent in Mesoamerican studies, may be roughly summarized as follows. The exchange of goods was ubiquitous throughout Mesoamerica. Centres like Teotihuacan served as the pivots of complex and extensive systems of exchange, which operated at different levels (local, regional, 'continental') and which arguably followed contrasting patterns of organization (e.g., 'solar' as against 'dendritic').[17] Trade has therefore been accorded major importance in recent analyses of Mesoamerican state-formation.[18] There is sometimes a related assumption, however, that Mesoamerican trade and markets obeyed much the same principles as trade and markets in other, more recent, more 'modern' societies. Implicitly or explicitly, Mesoamerica is seen to be populated by rational economic actors; rational not simply in their quest for subsistence (which involves a basic rationality common to both market and non-market societies), but rational also in their response to market signals. To varying degrees, it is assumed that profit-maximization and the law of supply and demand played significant roles in Mesoamerican society, at least in its sizeable 'market' sector. In the terms of a well-known anthropological debate, this 'formalist' position stresses the timelessness of market principles and practices; it echoes Adam Smith's belief in 'a certain propensity of human nature ... to truck, barter, and exchange one thing for another', which in turn gave rise to the division of labour and to economic progress.[19]

---

[17] For a general discussion of market systems in Central Mexico see Ross Hassig, *Trade, Tribute and Transportation: The Sixteenth-Century Political Economy of the Valley of Mexico* (Norman, Okla., 1985), ch. 4. Teotihuacan's 'dendritic' (treelike) structure of trade implied a marked degree of 'commercial' centralization. Rival centres of trade and production were by-passed or eliminated: Santley, Kerley and Kneebone, 'Obsidian working'.

[18] Blanton *et al.*, *Ancient Mesoamerica*, pp. 36–8, 234–42; William L. Rathje, 'The Tikal Connection', in Adams, *Origins of Maya Civilization*, pp. 373–82.

[19] Adam Smith, *An Enquiry into the Nature and Causes of the Wealth of Nations* (Harmondsworth, 1986, first pubd. 1776), p. 117. The inspiration of classical political economy (e.g., Ricardo) is sometimes recognized: D. Phillips and W. Rathje, 'Exchange Values and the Rise of the Classic Maya', in Norman Hammond, ed., *Social Process in Maya Prehistory: Essays in Honour of Sir J. Eric S. Thompson* (New York, 1977), pp. 104–5.

The 'substantivist' alternative – which owes a good deal to Polanyi's work[20] – emphasizes the time-bounded and relatively recent genesis of the (Smithian, profit-maximizing) market and conceives of earlier exchange as embodying quite different principles, notably those of reciprocity and redistribution. For 'substantivists' the economy is defined as 'the instituted process through which humans in society interact with nature to supply the material means of livelihood'; this process is integral to any society but does not require (and usually has not required) market relations; rather, the economic processes of production and consumption have obeyed a different rationale and – in a manner distinct from classic 'market society' – have been embedded in ostensibly – or formalistically – 'non-economic' relations: political, familial, religious, magical.[21]

The approach taken here is basically substantivist. It is assumed that even on a grand scale the movement of goods – and people – does not necessarily presuppose markets, the law of supply and demand, or the rational pursuit of profit, as nowadays understood. Exchange may occur and markets – in the sense of physical market-places – may exist. Both may involve the pursuit of 'gain' (which is a much broader category than 'profit'). But this is, in a sense, tautologically true for all human activities. Ascetics scourge themselves for spiritual gain; North American or Polynesian chiefs amass, distribute and destroy quantities of goods and animals (such as canoes and pigs) in order to register gains in status and prestige.[22] But these gains are not monetary, they do not derive from profit-maximizing transactions, they cannot be calibrated according to the law of supply and demand, and they are not geared to the accumulation and reinvestment of capital. To assume that all (physical) markets and all forms of extensive exchange embody profit-maximizing market behaviour

---

[20] Karl Polanyi, *The Great Transformation* (New York, 1957, first pubd. 1944). On the formalist/substantivist debate, compare Marvin Harris, *Cultural Materialism* (New York, 1979), pp. 233–4, who believes that 'both [sides]...are stuck in a single metaphysical tar pit'; Philip D. Curtin, *Cross-cultural Trade in World History* (Cambridge, 1984), p. 14, who summarizes and then dismisses both approaches; and Montmollin, *Archaeology of Political Structure*, pp. 5, 36, 89, 94, who – in my view rightly – regards the debate as important and the substantivist position as correct.

[21] Rhoda Halperin, 'Introduction: The Substantive Economy in Peasant Societies', in Rhoda Halperin and James Dow, *Peasant Livelihood: Studies in Economic Anthropology and Cultural Ecology* (New York, 1977), pp. 1–13.

[22] Farb, *Man's Rise to Civilization*, pp. 138–9, 148–9.

is to impose anachronistic categories upon ostensibly similar but in fact quite distinct phenomena; it is like seeing the Mesoamerican ballgame as a prototype of Wimbledon, though with the added bonus of regular decapitation of the losers.

Mesoamerican exchange, being both ancient and extensive, embraced many forms.[23] It involved both subsistence and 'exotic' goods; it was dictated by ecological endowment and local craft specialization; and it was governed by principles of both reciprocity – whereby groups exchanged mutually desired goods, sometimes along chains of actual or fictive kin – and redistribution, whereby chiefs and elites, enjoying privileged access to the supply of goods, were responsible for collecting and distributing them among their people. Such forms of exchange were not premised on considerations of profit-maximization or capital accumulation. 'Use-values' rather than 'exchange-values' predominated.[24] There was no profit motive to serve as a spur to greater production. To the extent that (modest) accumulation occurred, it did so for reasons of insurance: agricultural surpluses could not be banked, but they could, to a limited extent, be converted into durable exchange goods which, when times were hard, could be traded for consumption goods. Pots or jade were the Mesoamerican equivalent of the French peasant's cache of *louis d'or* hidden under the floor. Exchange goods were therefore accumulated not according to rational market principles, but with a view to subsistence and biological reproduction; they correspond to what Wolf terms the peasant's 'replacement fund'.[25] Nor, when exchanged, did these goods conform to a rigorous law of supply and demand. Transactions were governed by principles of reciprocity and redistribution, which were sociopolitically determined and sanctioned.

Similar substantivist arguments can be put forward in respect of major centres, where manufacture, accumulation and exchange were conducted on a more grandiose scale. Cities may have built up stocks of 'trade goods' as insurance against hard times; such goods served to regulate the flow of subsistence goods between regions and

---

[23] Pires-Ferreira and Flannery, 'Ethnographic Models', pp. 287–9.
[24] G. A. Cohen, *Karl Marx's Theory of History: A Defence* (Oxford, 1978), p. 81, is helpful.
[25] Eric R. Wolf, *Peasants* (Englewood Cliffs, 1966), pp. 5–6.

communities. Luxury imports also played a major role in defining social differences. Chiefdoms, we have noted, functioned as mechanisms of redistribution. Cities – like the later Tenochtitlán – were governed by strict sumptuary laws which regulated the consumption of exotic goods to the advantage of social elites and in defiance of market principles. Commoners did not flaunt themselves in cotton cloth, but wore rough clothes of maguey fibre: the prestige of cotton cloth depended precisely upon this limited and privileged access. Other forms of circulation and consumption were public and tributary. Tribute denoted subordination, hence it possessed a political and symbolic significance (like the canoe-load of obsidian which three subject towns owed to Texcoco in Postclassic times); but tribute also put goods into circulation and enabled recipient chiefs or states to reward their peoples, in which respect it formed an integral part of economic life (Polanyi's 'material-means provisioning process'), without remotely conforming to market principles.[26]

Finally, we must recall the ancient presumed liaison between 'trade' and religion – between goods and gods. Items like jade were invested with a ritualistic and supernatural significance, hence they were coveted for their own sake (they possessed, as it were, a use-value, albeit one that we today might fail to recognize). By the same token, participation in 'trade', in artisanry, or in temple-building may have conferred psychic benefits – and therefore attracted participants – in ways we can hardly fathom. Numinous as well as numerical values prevailed; as they did, analogously, for the anonymous stonemasons of Europe's Gothic cathedrals. Thus, an extensive production and circulation of goods, readily apparent in the archaeological record, could respond to a variety of motives, of which profit-maximization (i.e., orthodox market behaviour) was probably among the least important. In Classic Mesoamerica, as in most human societies down to the fairly recent present, the role of the price-determining, profit-maximizing market 'was no more than incidental to economic life', which, insofar as exchange was concerned, was instead organized according to principles of reciprocity, redistribution and ritual, hence was irretrievably embedded in ostensibly

[26] Offner, *Law and Politics*, p. 91; Halperin and Dow, *Peasant Livelihood*, p. 2; Montmollin, *Archaeology of Political Structure*, pp. 26, 36.

'non-economic' institutions and relations.[27] We shall return to this
argument when we shift the focus to Postclassic, especially Aztec,
society.

Teotihuacan's pre-eminence as a centre of exchange and manufacture may therefore have lured people to its crowded precincts; but
the lure was not necessarily material, nor were the motives those of a
nineteenth-century Manchesterite. The alliance of trade and religion,
just mentioned, also suggests the second salient characteristic of the
city. It was steeped in religiosity. Although major secular buildings
are extant, the great pyramids are clearly religious in concept and
ritualistic in purpose (they are not, like the Egyptian pyramids, mau-
soleums for secular or semi-secular dynasts). Their lay-out is clearly
planned and related to solar and astral alignments, which have been
the subject of extensive and ingenious analysis.[28] The 'Street of the
Dead', the central axis of the city, which runs from the Pyramid of
the Moon to the Citadel, has been plausibly described as a massive
via sacra, designed for maximum ritualistic effect.[29] Temples proliferated at Teotihuacan: as early as the first century A.D., when the
city contained some forty-five thousand inhabitants, it boasted at
least twenty-three temples.[30] Beneath one, the Pyramid of the Sun,
archaeologists have located a multichambered cave, very likely a
shrine and perhaps even the basis of an early cult which drew pilgrims and gave a religious imprimatur to the emergent metropolis.[31]
Like other great cities, therefore, Teotihuacan's growth, though made
possible by local ecological potential, was stimulated by strong non-
material factors. Bearing in mind the capacity of religious centres
(Mecca, Compostela, Mexico's own Villa de Guadalupe) to catalyse a
phase of secondary, secular growth, linked to trade, construction and
government, it may be hypothesized that Teotihuacan acquired a dis-
tinctively religious reputation, that it was constituted as a 'sacralized'
community, and that the urban growth thus set in motion eventually

[27] Polanyi, *Great Transformation*, p. 43.
[28] Pasztory, *Murals of Tepantitla*, p. 25; Anthony F. Aveni, *Skywatchers of Ancient Mexico* (Austin,
1980), pp. 222–34.
[29] Millon, 'Social Relations', p. 226; George Kubler, *The Art and Architecture of Ancient America*
(New York, 1984), pp. 51–4.
[30] Davies, *Ancient Kingdoms of Mexico*, p. 69; Pasztory, *Murals of Tepantitla*, p. 28.
[31] Millon, 'Social Relations', p. 246; Aveni, *Skywatchers*, p. 234.

became self-sustaining, while remaining premised on the city's religious *raison d'être*.

Teotihuacan's priests, accordingly, were numerous and powerful, their imposing temples proof of divine favour and terrestrial pre-eminence. Murals, scattered throughout the city, display a host of religious motifs, mixed with naturalistic representations. Military scenes are relatively rare and appear to date from the city's final years. Dynastic, commemorative art – common among the Maya city-states – is notably absent.[32] And, amid a varied pantheon – more complex and populated than the Olmecs' – one god stands out: Tlaloc, who stares, goggle-eyed, from numerous reliefs and murals, dispensing showers of raindrops (or drops of blood? or jade counters?), amid riotous scenes of jaguars, owls, butterflies and foliage. If the sophistication is greater, the kinship – in terms of style and substance – with Olmec art is notable; and there are clear signs of Maya influence, regarding both motifs and astral configurations.[33] Lowland images – shells, jaguars, cacao – abound. Tlaloc thus appears to represent a translation of the ill-defined Olmec god (or symbol) of fertility to the harsher altiplano, where his attributes of growth, vegetation and, above all, water exercised a powerful appeal. Like most Mesoamerican deities, however, Tlaloc was a shifting, evolving deity, a symbolic hybrid (like the were-jaguars/earth-serpents of the Olmec); different aspects of his Protean being might be emphasized by different peoples at different times. At Teotihuacan, Tlaloc still figures as the central deity, incorporating a range of attributes, of which fertility is the common denominator (the etymology of 'Tlaloc' probably traces to 'earth'). But on the altiplano, more than in the lowlands, fertility implied water, and Tlaloc evolved, as a highland deity, towards a more limited, specific and ultimately secondary aquatic role. But, like the primal gods of the Graeco-Roman pantheon (Chronos, Saturn), Tlaloc first managed to sire his chief successor and supplanter: Quetzalcóatl, the 'Feathered Serpent', whose image blends inextricably with Tlaloc's at Teotihuacan, but who later emancipated,

---

[32] Pasztory, *Murals of Tepantitla*, pp. 32, 41, 248–9, 253; this compares sharply with the Classic Maya pattern: Linda Schele and David Freidel, *A Forest of Kings: The Untold Story of the Ancient Maya* (New York, 1990), pp. 86–8.

[33] Pasztory, *Murals of Tepantitla*, pp. 101, 131–2, 136; Aveni, *Skywatchers*, pp. 222–37.

defined and established himself as the principal deity of highland civilization. It was as if the old Olmec earth-serpent had acquired wings and raised his earthbound body – represented by the Olmecs' earthen mounds and ridges – in order to adorn the steeper stone pyramids of Teotihuacan.

Teotihuacan religion, therefore, seems to exemplify an original cult of telluric fertility, developed to grand proportions, celebrated and codified by professional priests, and hence tending towards more complex, abstract symbols – even primitive glyphic writing.[34] Thus it has been suggested that the city's priestly power, manifested in art, building and ritual, eventually became obsessive and hypertrophied, outgrowing its original role – which had been functional to the growth and maintenance of the city – like some grotesque, overexercised, religious limb. Theocratic integration gave way to priestly tyranny (characterized, in the fractured jargon of information theory, by 'the hypertrophy of the apparatus concerned with the issuance of meta-messages').[35] Teotihuacan, in other words, became a priestridden society. Ultimately, perhaps, the people rose up in protest.

But before this happened – if it happened at all – it was the integrating and organizing role of religion which predominated, making possible the transition from incipient city to sacred metropolis. Religion drew migrants and awed them with its ritual; the very lay-out of the city, astronomically aligned like comparable cities, was calculated 'to overwhelm the viewer, to impress upon him the power and glory of the gods of Teotihuacan and their earthly representatives'.[36] To outsiders, inhabitants of wattle-and-daub peasant huts, the city's temples, murals and pyramids surely excited wonder, just as the associated ritual, promising a harmonious relation of vulnerable humans to threatening cosmos, elicited a powerful allegiance. Again, it is possible that this allegiance was cemented by an early variant of the cargo system, whereby commoners enhanced their social status by periods of service to the gods. At any rate, ritual religious activity, which mediated between men and gods, making sense of and offering some control over an uncertain universe, represented a *quid pro quo*

[34] Pasztory, *Murals of Tepantitla*, p. 42.
[35] Wolf, *The Valley of Mexico*, 'Introduction', p. 8, quoting Rappaport.
[36] Millon, 'Social Relations', p. 226; Pasztory, *Murals of Tepantitla*, p. 25.

for tax, labour and tribute, and thus underwrote Teotihuacan's social contract. Logically, a breakdown in theocratic legitimacy would
jeopardize that contract and with it the social bond which held the
great city and its subjects together.

Although it would be rash to label Teotihuacan a theocracy *tout
court* (the lack of empirical data and the sheer conceptual uncertainty of the term together inspire caution), it is likely that priests
exercised a major role within the city. A secular elite (i.e., an elite
which did not perform primarily religious functions) certainly existed; there was a developed class structure and several apparent
'palaces', distinct from the temples, where this elite was presumably
lodged. But it was the priestly caste which legitimized Teotihuacan's
power, making the city, in Millon's phrase, a 'sacralized polity', hence
a polity which did not engage in the crude terrorism of later Postclassic states. Priestly authority, it seems likely, was also deployed
in more mundane tasks: managing the vast city, its integrated agricultural system, its supplies, markets, tributaries and far-flung trade
routes. True, Teotihuacan's specific economic system is impossible
to reconstruct (we can discern what Braudel calls the 'basis of material life' – fields, buildings, artefacts, even an excellent drainage
system – but we can do little more than speculate about the relations of production which brought them into being). Nevertheless,
it is clear that the system required the large-scale acquisition and
transmission of information: about crops, taxes, tribute, food supply, raw materials, trade, ritual, education, construction, astronomy,
the measurement of time and space, the reproduction of the political
and religious order and the organization of soldiers and priests, of
artisans and peasants. All this endured, it should be remembered,
for rather longer than the western Roman empire.

The priests of Teotihuacan, like the priests of medieval Europe,
were the clerks and administrators of their day, although at Teotihuacan their tasks were greater, their role central rather than ancillary to
a feudal aristocracy. There could be no doctrine of the 'two swords',
no investitures dispute, at Teotihuacan. The intimate association of
(what we choose to dichotomize as) sacred and secular has already
been mentioned in regard to trade and artisanry. Workshops and
temples stood cheek by jowl, and they were probably functionally
as well as spatially related. Religious sanctions probably bolstered

the 'peace of the market', upon which much of the city's prosperity depended.[37] Calendrical knowledge affords another example of the union – or osmosis – of categories, such as sacred and secular, which modern Western thought has tended to segregate. Following Olmec precedent, the literati of Teotihuacan showed a lively interest in astronomy and the study of calendrical cycles; indeed, Teotihuacan's astronomically aligned plan reveals notable parallels with other Mesoamerican sites, north and south, and attests to the rich tradition of astronomy, numerology and calendrical lore which characterized Mesoamerican culture from Preclassic to Postclassic. Such ostensibly abstract knowledge – an example, very likely, of 'art for art's sake' – nevertheless came to acquire practical significance, as abstract knowledge is wont to do. Calendrical knowledge influenced decision-making, public and private (so, at any rate, we might infer back from proven Aztec practice). It governed the great decisions of state and the naming of newborn babies. As in Europe, China or Mesopotamia, astronomy was inseparable from astrology. But, more practically (at least from a modern standpoint), astronomical knowledge also developed in tandem with geometrical knowledge, facilitating large-scale construction and town planning (evident in the city's lay-out and, even, in its vital drainage system, which is in places still capable of practical renovation).[38]

The practical significance of such astronomical and mathematical arcana was not confined to divination and construction. A capacity to count, date and record was clearly essential for the successful ordering of this – as for any – populous city and empire (writing, after all, originated in Mesopotamian tribute rolls). Heads, taxes, tribute and trade goods all had to be enumerated. Calendrical knowledge – the ability to record the passage of time, to locate the present within a temporal continuum – was also functional for other practical, non-ceremonial activities. The suggestion is often made that 'by virtue of their knowledge of calendrics, the priests were able to direct the

---

[37] Millon, 'Social Relations', pp. 236, 241–2. Comparisons with ancient Mesopotamian 'temple trade' may be drawn; but Curtin, *Cross-cultural Trade*, pp. 61–7, strongly argues that such trade was, in fact, less temple-controlled than previously thought (e.g., by Polanyi).

[38] Pasztory, *Murals of Tepantitla*, p 25; Davies, *Ancient Kingdoms of Mexico*, p. 67; Lindsay Jones, *Twin City Tales: A Hermeneutical Reassessment of Tula and Chichén Itzá* (Niwot, Colo., 1995), pp. 224–7, notes the recurrent astronomical alignments of Mesoamerican metropolises, Teotihuacan included.

economy, telling the people when to sow and when to reap'.[39] This
seems unlikely or, at least, exaggerated. First, such an argument assumes a high degree of state control of agriculture: it is more likely
that the peasant household and community operated in relative autonomy within a broadly taxed agrarian economy (there is no evidence of massive hydraulic works at Teotihuacan). The peasantry
directly controlled production; the state exacted a surplus for redistribution from peasant producers. That, at any rate, was the pattern
in successive subsequent state formations. Second, the argument for
clerical control of agriculture underestimates peasant farming expertise. Settled agriculture, after all, antedated the creation of theocratic
polities by millennia; peasants had successfully farmed, procreated,
accumulated skills and even delivered up modest surpluses without priestly control (though, no doubt, with shamanic intercession,
which is a different thing). They had very likely watched and wor-
shipped the Pleiades, as many 'primitive' peoples – hunter-gatherers
as well as farmers – have habitually done.[40] None of this required an
elaborate clerisy. Furthermore, save in one possible and exceptional
case, that of the Classic Maya of the Petén, the collapse of priestly
control did not signal agricultural disaster.

This argument for the technical autonomy of the peasant is entirely logical, since it is difficult to see how refined astronomical and
calendrical knowledge would fundamentally assist peasant farming.
The onset of the rains was better detected by peasant experience than
by priestly expertise – by sniffing the wind rather than by observing
the phases of Venus. It is in another sphere, that of trade and tribute,
the sphere of circulation rather than production, that priestly skills
(literally) counted. The movement of goods – chiefly non-perishable
goods – is subject to the dictates of man, not nature, and can therefore obey an imposed pattern. A pattern, furthermore, is essential if
tribute is to be paid promptly and in full, if markets are to be held
regularly, and if – to use modern parlance – merchants and manu-
facturers are to meet delivery dates. This is no less true of ancient,

---

[39] Davies, *Ancient Kingdoms of Mexico*, p. 99. Wolf, *Sons of the Shaking Earth*, p. 81, offers a more
plausible resumé of the (presumed) administrative tasks of Teotihuacan's 'theocrats': allocating
land and water, storing grain and trade goods.

[40] Aveni, *Skywatchers*, pp. 30–1, 43–4, gives numerous examples. The appearance of the Pleiades
roughly coincides with the onset of the rainy season.

regulated, non–profit-maximizing markets. Later tributary systems, like that of Texcoco, which was taken over and further developed by the Spaniards, involved complex inventories and schedules: whereby, for example, 530 items of 5 different goods had to be delivered every 80 days.[41] Merchants and officials therefore needed accurate means of measurement, of both goods and times; distant rendezvous could not be governed by the vagaries of the agricultural cycle. And punctuality of payment and delivery served the interests of the state, for it ensured the material provisioning of subjects and constituted daily proof of imperial vigour and legitimacy. In an unusually complex and integrated polity like Teotihuacan, this was of paramount importance. Modern capitalism may have invented the 'time and work discipline'[42] which governs industrial society, and which supplanted the looser, seasonal imperatives of traditional agrarian society; but ancient agrarian societies also possessed their alternative, non-agrarian timetables (calibrated, it is true, in days rather than hours and minutes), which, regulating the sphere of circulation, co-existed with the primordial seasonal rhythms of agrarian production.

We have noted two 'structural' conditions favouring the dramatic rise of Teotihuacan. They may be loosely summarized as trade (or exchange) and religion. It was in these areas, rather than in any ecological munificence or hydraulic specialism, that Teotihuacan achieved pre-eminence. And 'structural' arguments are, today, much preferred by many historians (especially historians of ancient Mesoamerica); conversely, sequential, narrative explanations are frequently spurned (in Mesoamerican studies, they thrive only for the later Postclassic period, for which Aztec codices and Spanish chronicles offer narrative data).[43] Thus, especially where they must rely on the mute, material evidence of archaeological strata, historians tend to deal in broad structural analyses: epochal evolutions are sought out, sudden quantum leaps are suspect. *Historia non facit saltem.* Yet

---

[41] Offner, *Law and Politics*, pp. 14, 102–9.

[42] E. P. Thompson, 'Time, Work-Discipline and Industrial Capitalism', *Past and Present*, 38 (1967), pp. 59–97.

[43] Jones, *Twin City Tales*, pp. 116–17, and Montmollin, *Archaeology of Political Structure*, pp. 8–13, criticize the 'monistic' structural/materialist emphasis of recent research – an emphasis which has, nevertheless, been offset by the recent decipherment of the Classic Maya stelae, with their records of dynastic rise and fall, victory and defeat; see Michael D. Coe, *Breaking the Maya Code* (New York, 1993).

cultural evolution may involve occasional leaps, just as natural evolution supposedly does, at least according to one school. And the
vertiginous rise of Teotihuacan represents a clear departure from
familiar patterns, before and after: it is something of an historical
freak, for which a freakish explanation, analogous to random mu-
tation in the natural world, may be appropriate. How and why did
Teotihuacan burst beyond the bounds of the familiar Mesoamerican
city-state, achieving an overwhelming local primacy, a marked regional hegemony and a size and longevity unparalleled in native
Middle America?

At the beginning of the Christian era an eruption of the volcano
Xitla largely destroyed the city of Cuicuilco in the southern part
of the Valley of Mexico. At the time, Cuicuilco rivalled the emergent Teotihuacan. Its population was about the same, it possessed
a 'massive' ceremonial centre and it may also have been endowed
with an irrigation and town-planning system comparable to Teotihuacan's. Like Teotihuacan, it greedily gathered population to itself,
depleting the surrounding hinterland and establishing a pronounced
local primacy. It may even have begun to export its cultural influence
abroad – perhaps as far as highland Jalisco.[44] Between these incipient metropolises – paramount chiefdoms fast mutating into fully
developed states – lesser communities within the Valley of Mexico
languished, shrank or, like Texcoco and Ixtapalapa, survived as buffer
chiefdoms in the borderlands where the two rivals collided. With
the sudden (if not the total) destruction of Cuilcuilco, Teotihuacan's
hegemony was assured. Elsewhere and at other times ascendant
cities faced formidable rivals who, even if they were defeated and
subordinated, still posed a potential challenge to their conqueror
(as, for example, Texcoco did to Tenochtitlán in the late Postclassic).
The challenge was not purely military: the very presence of a rival
urban centre, possessed of markets, temples and workshops, offered
an alternative to traders, artisans and rural migrants. As a would-be
primate city extended its sway – over peasants, tributaries and lesser

---

[44] Blanton et al., Ancient Mesoamerica, pp. 123–8; Weigand, 'Evidence for Complex Societies',
p. 70. About two hundred years later, the eruption of the volcano Ilopango brought devastation
and depopulation to the southern Maya region (present-day El Salvador): Sharer, The Ancient
Maya, pp. 132–3; though cf. Norman Hammond, Ancient Maya Civilization (New Brunswick,
1994, first pubd. 1982), p. 125, for a caution.

communities – even secondary rivals could present problems, which would increase as the primate city stretched its territorial borders, its ideological legitimacy and its administrative capacity. Primacy thus tended to be precarious and contested. A pattern of shifting political fortunes, experienced by rival city-states within a fragmented regional political system, was as familiar to Mesoamerica as it was to classical Greece or Renaissance Italy. Conversely, the kind of integrating imperial authority briefly achieved by the Macedonians or vainly advocated by Dante was the exception in Middle America too: it was virtually unknown in the Maya lowlands (certainly during the Classic period); it proved beyond the efforts of Monte Albán in Oaxaca; it was precariously established, under the Aztec aegis, for no more than a century in the late Postclassic.

Teotihuacan thus stands as a major exception. That the city could escape these perennial constraints, construct an unusual durable hegemony within the Valley and exert a powerful influence throughout Mesoamerica may have been due in no small measure to the providential, precisely timed, elimination of Cuicuilco. For just as a vigorous Cuicuilco, lodged in the fertile southern quadrant of the Valley, would have contested Teotihuacan's power, acting as a pole for potential dissidents, so Cuicuilco's sudden removal tipped the balance to the north, leaving its own client communities at the mercy of the northern metropolis. Valley hegemony was there for the taking; and, according to the geopolitics of Mesoamerica, who controlled the Valley (no easy accomplishment) controlled, in some degree, the central highlands. Indeed, it would seem likely that Cuicuilco's dramatic demise further validated Teotihuacan's claims to supernatural privilege, as well as to political hegemony. Rome had to defeat Carthage to achieve Mediterranean hegemony; Teotihuacan's Carthage was destroyed by act of God.

Thus favoured, Teotihuacan was able to build the most extensive and durable of Mesoamerican states, one whose influence – perhaps even control – stretched from present-day Guatemala to Zacatecas.[45] As the ambivalence of this last sentence implies, the nature of the

[45] This sits a little uneasily with Mann's notion, based on a comparison of the loose Aztec empire and the more integrated Assyrian or Han (Chinese) empires, that in Mesoamerica 'less caging resulted in less civilization, less permanent institutionalized states, and less social stratification': *Sources of Social Power*, p. 121.

Teotihuacan 'empire' remains unclear. It is certainly necessary to distinguish first the Teotihuacan heartland, located in the Valley of Mexico and its immediate environs (including the obsidian-rich region of present-day Hidalgo), which was subject to the direct political control of the city. Here, within a radius of about 100 kilometres, agricultural production was geared to the city's needs (beyond this radius, the calorific effort required to shift bulk foodstuffs would have been counterproductive in that more food would have been consumed en route than would have reached its destination; such was the tyranny imposed, even on this most sophisticated of Mesoamerican metropolises, by the lack of animal and long-distance water transport). Within this heartland, food was incessantly funnelled into the great city's maw; peasant commuters trekked out of their city tenements to till the surrounding cornfields; and those villages which had survived in the long shadow of the city (for, as we have noted, Teotihuacan's prodigious growth brought extensive rural depopulation) may have done so by specializing in the production of particular crops (such as maguey) for the benefit of urban consumers. Within the heartland, too, it may be inferred, Teotihuacan's theocratic hegemony was most pronounced: rival cities did not exist. Beyond, cities existed and even throve, so long as they accommodated themselves to the Pax Teotihuacana. Indeed, the latter may best be envisaged as uniting – through religious and trade networks – a congeries of city-states, each possessed of local hinterlands of varying sizes: a system analogous to the Sumerian empire of the third millennium B.C.[46]

The city of Cholula, for example, lying some 100 kilometres to the southwest in the fertile and strategic Valley of Puebla, was a major centre of trade, religion and population, enjoying a record of autonomous growth dating back to the first millennium B.C. By the onset of the Classic era, Cholula had established its local pre-eminence, drawing goods, migrants and perhaps cultural inspiration from the petty theocratic city-states of the Puebla-Tlaxcala zone – which, like their Valley of Mexico counterparts, now succumbed to the supremacy of a primate city.[47] Classic Cholula flourished, engaging

---

[46] Mann, *Sources of Social Power*, pp. 89–93, 98–101.
[47] Angel García Cook, 'The Historical Importance of Tlaxcala in the Cultural Development of the Central Highlands', in Sabloff, *Supplement to the Handbook of Middle American Indians*, pp. 256–62.

in massive public works which attest to a theocratic capacity to mobilize labour comparable to Teotihuacan's. One construction, a vast pyramid, several times rebuilt and augmented, and allegedly dedicated to Tlaloc, stands larger than any Egyptian equivalent and constitutes the biggest structure in the ancient Americas.[48] Here, Teotihuacan's influence is significant but not overwhelming; we may suppose a degree of collaborative subordination, with Cholula dominating the Valley of Puebla and serving as a way station for trade and travel between Teotihuacan and its 'Teotihuacanoid' settlements in Tlaxcala, Oaxaca and the Gulf.[49] Significantly, Classic Cholula fell – though the city itself did not vanish – at around the same time as Teotihuacan.

If Cholula represented an established community which prudently accommodated itself to the rising power of Teotihuacan, there were also Classic-era creations upon which the stamp of the new metropolis was indelibly placed: sophisticated, stratified cities, equipped with temples, ballcourts and the familiar Tlaloc motifs: Xochicalco, in southern Morelos; El Tajín in tropical Veracruz; Cacaxtla in Tlaxcala. Each emulated Teotihuacan by building a local hegemony in their respective regions, dominating the rural hinterland and commanding important trade routes which linked the altiplano to the lowlands. Pupils of Teotihuacan, these cities outlived – and may even have helped to topple – their mentor. In Oaxaca, however, the key city of Monte Albán, oldest of the Classic cities, had the temerity to challenge the rising power of Teotihuacan; in consequence, its relations with the new imperial metropolis were, as we shall see, more conflictual than collaborative.

These cities, all subjects, allies or enemies of Teotihuacan, were situated in central Mexico; they were 'highland' cities in terms of their geopolitical location even if some (such as Xochicalco and El Tajín) nestled in semi-tropical or tropical niches. As their later history confirms, they were logical targets for an imperial state based in the Valley of Mexico and drawn, not least by material incentive, to the warmer lowlands of the south and east. In this respect, later Aztec expansion followed Teotihuacan precedent. But Teotihuacan's influence – even control – penetrated much farther. The salient example is

---

[48] Davies, *Ancient Kingdoms of Mexico*, p. 92; Wolf, *Sons of the Shaking Earth*, pp. 94–5.
[49] García Cook, 'Historical Importance of Tlaxcala', p. 267.

the city of Kaminaljuyú, in the region of Guatemala City. Here again an established community soaked up Teotihuacan influence and – given the evident strength of that influence – may even have constituted a form of colony. Fifth-century Kaminaljuyú seems to have experienced a marked 'cultural renaissance', embracing several features of Teotihuacan culture: stone sculpture, imitative architecture, similar construction techniques, the cult of Tlaloc.[50] The fit, in terms of style and artefacts, is close, if not perfect; thus, if political subordination is to be inferred from aesthetic and architectural parallels, it may be legitimate in this instance to entertain the colonization hypothesis (which does not, of course, imply an uninterrupted territorial empire stretching from Teotihuacan to Kaminaljuyú). The sheer distance – over a thousand kilometres as the crow flies – does not rule out such a hypothesis. The Aztecs colonized Soconusco (albeit less durably and succesfully), and Soconusco lies over 800 kilometres from the Valley of Mexico. By analogy, Kaminaljuyú probably served as a key military and mercantile outpost, controlling the southern extremity of Teotihuacan's trading network and organizing the despatch northward of cacao and other southern products.

The insertion of a powerful Teotihuacan client state within the deep south was facilitated by the nature of Classic Maya society, which (we shall see) was more decentralized and fragmented than that of the central highlands. Here, rival cities allied, fought and trafficked, with none achieving more than a loose local supremacy. Political boundaries were shifting and permeable, allowing ready access to cultural and commercial influences from outside (assuming those influences could traverse the formidable distances and terrain involved). Equally, Maya communities were as vulnerable to the incursion of grander, northern states as the squabbling cities of Lombardy were to Hohenstaufen imperialism. Thus, after a long hiatus following the Olmec collapse, during which highland and lowland regions had remained unusually incommunicado, northern influences now surged into the Maya zone, helping to mould the distinctive character of Classic Maya civilization. The fundamentals of that civilization were indigenous; but its contemporaneity with Teotihuacan seems hardly coincidental.

---

[50] Davies, *Ancient Kingdoms of Mexico*, p. 88; Sharer, *The Ancient Maya*, pp. 93–5, 146–7.

At Tikal, largest of the Classic Maya cities, architectural style again mirrored Teotihuacan, and Tlaloc is to be found emblazoned on shields and stelae. Teotihuacan pottery and obsidian have been recovered at other Maya sites, at Copan, Becan and Acanceh, thus stretching from Honduras through the Petén northwards to Yucatán. In the latter region, architectural imitation is evident at Dzibilchaltun, then (A.D. 600) only a small hamlet near the Gulf coast; and, further along that coast, Teotihuacano artefacts have been discovered in the southern Veracruz-Tabasco zone where the Olmecs once flourished.[51] It is plausibly supposed that these finds are evidence of a busy, reciprocal trading relationship, rather than of direct conquest or colonization (Kaminaljuyú, in other words, is not typical).[52] Teotihuacan exerted a powerful demand, at least as regards highly valued trade goods; Tikal – like other incipiently dominant cities in comparable circumstances – established itself as a fulcrum for Teotihuacano commercial (and probably religious/ideological) influence, much to its own advantage. Indeed, Tikal may have combined this integrative role with a similar, albeit secondary, role – linking the lowland Maya to the peoples of the Guatemalan and Salvadorean highlands.[53] Tikal was familiar with warfare, but it seems unlikely that the great network of exchange, of which both Tikal and Teotihuacan were major, collaborating centres, was fundamentally coercive. Apart from the widely dispersed evidence of Teotihuacano influence – suggestive of a fluid movement of goods and people – there are also signs of a Maya presence at Teotihuacan, even of a small Maya barrio.

Thus, although it would be fanciful and probably wrong to suppose that a stern paternalist Pax Teotihuacana prevailed over the

[51] Hammond, *Ancient Maya Civilization*, pp. 133–5; Davies, *Ancient Kingdoms of Mexico*, p. 87; E. Wyllys Andrews, 'Dzibilchaltun', in Sabloff, *Supplement to the Handbook of Middle American Indians*, pp. 325–6.

[52] Webster, 'War and the Evolution of Maya Civilization', in Adams, *Origins of Maya Civilization*, pp. 361–2.

[53] Gordon W. Willey, 'The Rise of Maya Civilization: A Summary View', in Adams, *Origins of Maya Civilization*, pp. 415–16, 420. Schele and Freidel, *Forest of Kings*, pp. 144–64, graphically describe the defeat of Uaxactun at the hands of Tikal in A.D. 378, arguing that Tikal's ruler, Great Jaguar Paw, borrowed both military technology (the spear-thrower) and grand strategy – the idea of a war of conquest, leading to the imposition of a puppet ruler – from his Teotihuacano mentors. Given that Teotihuacan–Maya intercourse had existed for over two centuries, why did the learning take so long? Or did the fourth-century Maya begin to emulate a newly militaristic Teotihuacan?

quarrelsome polities of the Classic Maya, it is entirely plausible
that brisk, long-distance trade – a familar feature of the southern
lowlands, now invigorated by new external influences, acting from
pivotal centres like 'colonial' Kaminaljuyú and 'collaborationist'
Tikal – accompanied and encouraged the cultural florescence and
state-building characteristic of the period. Even martial rulers, keen
on war and expansion, would have been reluctant to disrupt trading networks on which their supply of prestige goods – thus, in
a sense, their very prestige – depended. As in Olmec times, trade
correlated with stratification and state-building, not in some neat,
one-way, causal relationship, but rather by virtue of mutual, functional, reinforcement.[54] The Pax Teotihuacana – to the extent that
it existed, outside the imperial heartland – thus resembled the Pax
Britannica of the nineteenth century: it was patchy and prudential,
serving commercial and ideological interests, relying on select territorial footholds and broader, collaborationist networks, while avoiding grand military campaigns and territorial annexations.

This argument is reinforced if we shift the focus to northern
Mesoamerica. During the heyday of Teotihuacan, the Mesoamerican
frontier advanced northward: not in inexorable, linear fashion, but
like a hollow frontier, capturing new zones, ignoring others, creating
islands – ultimately, an entire archipelago – of Mesoamerican civilization within the vast and hostile expanses of the north. The pattern
is confused but strongly suggests an underlying 'commercial' rationale. To the northeast, Teotihuacan collaborated with clients like El
Tajín, which may have radiated Teotihuacano influence through the
Huasteca (the evidence is not conclusive) and which certainly channelled a stream of ceramic goods down the 'corridor' connecting it
to the highland metropolis.[55] Yet further north, the Classic era witnessed an unusual – and impermanent – development of civilization,
exemplified by ceremonial centres, ballcourts, pyramids and pottery,
in the nomad country of Tamaulipas. Here, the gradual evolution
of farming peoples was stimulated by influences from the south: a
genuine example, perhaps, of 'diffusion', whereby exogenous ideas

---

[54] Webb, 'The Peten Maya Decline', pp. 375, 385.
[55] Pailes and Whitecotton, 'The Greater Southwest', pp. 114–15; García Cook, 'The Historical
Importance of Tlaxcala', p. 223.

and practices (but not entire homologous systems) received a wel-
come reception, without any necessary military conquest. The result
was a marked 'cultural climax' in this hitherto primitive region: for a
time, these northeastern peoples 'were full-fledged though provincial
participants in Mesoamerican culture'.[56] Like the Olmecs, though
on a greater scale, Teotihuacan helped to tease out a latent capacity for stratification, specialization and authority-building: in short,
for civilization. But whereas such trends proved permanent in central Mesoamerica, in the northeast they were ephemeral. Nucleated
sites were civilized islands within a sea of nomadism; present-day
Coahuila, for example, remained the domain of hunters and gatherers. Significantly, these northeastern Classic sites were defensively
located. And their florescence was relatively brief. As the power
of Teotihuacan waned and eventually collapsed, the northeast relapsed into barbarism: the Chichimec ocean rose and swamped the
islands of civilization. Such a process, we should note, was as much
restorative as destructive, and it formed part of a common pattern
of cultural relapse, apparent in much of Mesoamerica – and even
in colonial Mexico. Relapse very likely responded not just to the
collapse of metropolises but also to local pressures and grievances;
for civilization brought its discontents as well as its benefits, and we
should not – romantically, ethnocentrically or teleologically – lament
either its fall or its replacement by a revived, 'tribal' egalitarianism.[57]

Similar growth and relapse (or 'deculturation') occurred in the
Durango-Zacatecas region of north-central Mexico. Here, roughly
A.D. 300–500, occurred a 'sudden burst of prosperity', linked to
the mining and export (not the processing) of jadeite and perhaps turquoise. The settlements of Alta Vista and La Quemada,
though thinly populated, display all the accoutrements of Mesoamerican civilization: pyramids, ballcourts, terraces, stuccoed walls and
a range of artefacts. But Classic civilization penetrated the Gran

---

[56] Diehl, 'Prehispanic Relationships', p. 269.
[57] Diehl, 'Prehispanic Relationships', pp. 267–8, 269, 273. The 'atomized and undifferentiated'
society of the modern Lacandon Maya of Chiapas similarly represents a departure (a decline?)
from a previous condition of greater organization, integration and belligerence (therefore, of
'civilization'?), a departure brought about by the pressures of Spanish colonialism. 'Savagery',
in short, could be an adaptive strategy ('and a largely successful one'), not simply a primeval
condition: Farriss, *Maya Society*, pp. 141–2.

Chichimec with some difficulty. Even a modest build-up of population demanded intensive efforts if cities were to survive on the arid
northern plateau. Furthermore, the 'civilized' settlers and interlopers
impinged upon – and possibly exploited – an existing indigenous population. Such cities, though long-lived, were vulnerable. Alta Vista
was abandoned around A.D. 900, possibly because of the depletion
of its mineral resources. La Quemada, strongly fortified, outlasted
Teotihuacan by centuries, forging new trading relationships with ascendant polities in Central Mexico, and linking them to the peoples
of the American southwest, notably the Hohokam culture of Arizona.
Among the Hohokam many features of Classic civilization (cotton
textiles, ceramics, ballcourts) took root during the Classic era – significantly, among a people committed to a form of hydraulic agriculture. But, around A.D. 1200, La Quemada met a violent end, earning
its name: the 'burned' city.[58]

Although these northern outposts outlived Teotihuacan, it seems
clear that their initial development was bound up with the
Teotihuacano hegemony and, very probably, with the city's voracious demand for raw materials, especially the semi-precious stones
known as *chalchihuites*. Possibly Alta Vista and La Quemada came
into being as colonial bases, exerting a harsh, militarist rule over
'uncivilized' local peoples, whose labour and land were needed to
maintain the flow of goods to the south.[59] At any rate, the Classic period saw the furthest extension north of the Mesoamerican frontier:
a frontier which, like its Spanish successor, advanced into arid and
forbidding expanses lured by mineral wealth, capable of establishing
durable outposts, and radiating a broader 'civilizing' influence as far
as the American southwest, but unable – and probably unwilling –
to create a solid territorial empire or to subjugate a sparse, scattered
and 'savage' population.[60]

---

[58] Richard A. Diehl, *Tula: The Toltec Capital of Ancient Mexico* (London, 1983), pp. 152–5; Charles
D. Trumbold, 'A Summary of the Archaeology in the La Quemada Region', in Foster and
Weigand, *The Archaeology of West and Northwest Mesoamerica*, pp. 260–1.

[59] Trumbold, 'A Summary', pp. 258–63, discusses alternative interpretations of La Quemada,
noting that, compared to central Mexico, archaeological research in the north remains in its
infancy.

[60] Pailes and Whitecotton, 'The Greater Southwest', pp. 114–16, and Hall, *Social Change in the
Southwest*, pp. 43–8, try to locate this process within the broad sweep of North American
'world-system' history.

Within the broad commercial and cultural orbit of Teotihuacan, therefore, new communities were born and old communities flourished; civilization – in the form of states, soldiers, priests, trade and oppression – made inroads upon barbarism. The Classic era in general was also one of population growth, commercial integration and, perhaps, theocratic rule – in which respects it paralleled equivalent 'Classic' phases in other regions of 'primary urban generation', notably Mesopotamia.[61] Important though the role of Teotihuacan was, it would be wrong to see these developments as the product of simple diffusion, proof of the thaumaturgic power of Teotihuacan. In at least one neglected region – highland Jalisco – the processes of nucleation, stratification and apparent state-formation, centred on the community of Teuchitlán, occurred in the absence of any clear Teotihuacano influence.[62] Such processes, it seems, were immanent, made possible by gradual population growth and agricultural development but realized through exchange, redistribution and religion, hence the theocratic caste of government and society. Even in Jalisco, however, the influence and example of Teotihuacan eventually carried weight: Teotihuacan did not engender urbanization and state-formation, but it clearly accelerated and coloured these indigenous processes. By the same token, its fall sent shock waves throughout Mesoamerica. Before considering the sombre termination of this era, however, it is essential to review the two major regional manifestations of Classic culture whose place within Teotihuacan's 'empire' has been mentioned and whose contribution to the evolution of Mesoamerica was profound: the southern civilizations of Zapotec Oaxaca and the Maya lowlands.

II. Zapotec and Maya

General histories of Mesoamerica, fascinated by the successive imperial cultures of the Olmec, Teotihuacan, Toltecs and Aztecs, often relegate Oaxaca to a minor place. Zapotec civilization, it is true, did not set its stamp on Mesoamerica as a whole: its imperialist efforts

[61] Friedrich Katz, *The Ancient American Civilizations* (London, 1989, first pubd. 1972), pp. 17–18, citing Robert Adams; Wheatley, *Pivot of the Four Quarters*, pp. 9, 225–6; Mann, *Sources of Social Power*, pp. 89–93, 130–1.

[62] Weigand, 'Evidence for Complex Societies', pp. 70–90.

were modest and local; its cultural influence did not match that of the civilizations of the Valley of Mexico. But precisely because of its remarkable longevity – and its avoidance of external expansion – Zapotec civilization offers an instructive example of a maize-based, highland culture whose evolution can be traced, in continuous fashion, from its distant agrarian origins (c. 1500 B.C.) down to historical times. It can therefore be particularly suggestive of the forces shaping highland Mesoamerican society.

The transition to sedentary agriculture can, with confidence, be set at a relatively early date. The Valley of Oaxaca, the cradle of Zapotec civilization, was reasonably suited for maize cultivation: frosts were rare (the Valley lies some 700 metres lower than the Valley of Mexico); cultivable land was abundant; shortages of water – which presented the chief obstacle to settlement – could be countered by appropriate innovative responses, as we shall see. Farming villages, conforming to a rough norm (perhaps a hectare in area, with a population of fifty or sixty, grouped in ten or twelve households), were well established by the middle of the second millennium B.C., that is, in advance of the Valley of Mexico, though not of the Olmec heartland. But the transition to agriculture did not produce – still less was it induced by – marked social stratification. Rather, an egalitarian hunting-and-gathering people gradually became an egalitarian farming people.

By the beginning of the first millennium B.C., however, in highland Oaxaca as in highland Jalisco, the first ceremonial centres began to extrude from the pack of simple farming communities.[63] Chief among these was San José Mogote, in the northern (Etla) wing of the Valley of Oaxaca. Here, population started to cohere; an open, ceremonial, perhaps dancing, area acquired an altar-like construction; and signs of trade – imported shells, jade and ceramics – and of local artisanry began to accumulate. Olmec influence can be discerned: again, there is no likelihood of Olmec colonization; rather, as at Tlatilco, Olmec motifs were assimilated by an emergent indigenous tradition, and Olmec artefacts, ideas and, perhaps, migrants were drawn, as if by magnet, to incipiently stratified communities. To put it less impersonally: nascent elites, especially the redistributive

---

[63] Weigand, 'Evidence for Complex Societies', p. 63; Blanton *et al.*, *Ancient Mesoamerica*, pp. 50–8.

chiefs who stood at their apex, coveted Olmec goods and the imprimatur of Olmec civilization, including religion. Thereafter, we may suppose a dialectical process, whereby Olmec influence further reinforced stratification and authority-building.[64] Certainly San José Mogote now developed clear signs of stratification, as hierarchy replaced the 'flat' social structure of previous centuries. By around 800 B.C. San José was a fully-fledged ceremonial centre, endowed with stone buildings, courts and patios. Its population – though no greater than fifteen hundred – dwarfed those of the surrounding villages, some of which, emulating the pre-eminent local centre, now acquired their own lesser public buildings and, it may be presumed, their own lesser elites.

Again, population growth made stratification and nucleation ('urbanization' would be premature) possible. But simple demographic or ecological arguments alone cannot explain the rise of San José. True, the community enjoyed good land and a high water table; but there was abundant agricultural land for the taking elsewhere in the Valley of Oaxaca, hence the collective decision to concentrate was not taken in response to inexorable population pressure (as, we have argued, the initial collective decision to farm probably was).[65] Again, sacred and 'commercial' factors were at work. The new vogue for ceremonial buildings and the conversion of open dancing areas, reminiscent of the Plains Indians, to formal religious precincts suggest the introduction of more elaborate ritual, conducted by a specialist priesthood, possibly involving sacrifice. After the manner of the Olmec, perhaps, the village shaman gave way to the esoteric Brahmin, chosen from a particular (ruling) lineage, carefully trained and closeted in special sacred quarters. Once such a ceremonial centre had achieved a certain demographic and spiritual critical mass (shrines, pilgrimages, successful divine mediation all helped), growth became self-sustaining and also more 'secular' in appearance. Recreation, matchmaking and exchange each played a part (shells, ceramics and mirrors abound at San José), and no doubt the priests and chiefs took care to encourage these activities, conferring on them

[64] Blanton et al., Ancient Mesoamerica, pp. 58–63; Joseph W. Whitecotton, The Zapotecs: Princes, Priests, and Peasants (Norman, Okla., 1984), pp. 32–3; Drennan, 'Religion and Social Evolution', p. 362; cf. Marcus, 'Zapotec Chiefdoms', pp. 193–4.

[65] Blanton et al., Ancient Mesoamerica, p. 53; Whitecotton, The Zapotecs, p. 31.

a sacred legitimacy over and above their mundane utility. Religious sanction underwrote the thriving markets which would become a staple of life in Oaxaca for millennia.

As centres of this kind proliferated (San José eventually lay within a broad network of secondary and tertiary centres), the demographic imperatives changed. Priests wanted workers, converts and acolytes; farming households saw more point in raising their numbers and levels of production, perhaps to satisfy elite demands, certainly because the increased circulation of 'trade' goods offered a new, if limited, opportunity to 'bank' agricultural surpluses. It is also possible that increased settlement and trade, developing in the absence, as yet, of a dominant city, afforded greater incentives for warfare (trade goods represented attractive portable loot), thus encouraging the formation of stronger, more centralized, political authority. Warfare, however, cannot be considered the prime mover in this process (as sometimes is imagined): evidence of warfare is not noticeably apparent in most cases of nucleation and stratification; nor, as we have seen, do these cases correlate with demographic pressure and competition for resources, as the warfare hypothesis would suggest.[66] These incipient towns were not conspicuously 'caged' or constrained; they did not need to behave like prolific mice in an overpopulated maze. Rather, organized warfare and inter-community conflict became more feasible as population cohered and authority emerged; they also became more likely in certain circumstances (e.g., as the emergent elites of roughly comparable rival communities vied for regional supremacy within shifting networks of exchange). Warfare was more a consequence than a cause of stratification and authority-building.[67]

Within the Valley of Oaxaca, the chief beneficiary of these new developments was not San José Mogote but Monte Albán. By around 500 B.C. the first community that we know as Monte Albán was

---

[66] Cf. Service, *Origins of the State*, pp. 43–4, 277–8; Carneiro, 'A Theory of the Origin of the State'.

[67] This is not to deny the prevalence of warfare among many stateless, hunter-and-gatherer, peoples (see Harris, *Cannibals and Kings*, pp. 47–8); however, as Harris observes, p. 48, if 'warfare is a very ancient practice, . . . its characteristics differed in the successive epochs of prehistory and history'. Small, fluid, mobile bands had less to fight over; hence, 'warfare after the development of agriculture probably became more frequent and more deadly' (p. 50) – especially since emergent elites stood to benefit from it. A good example – and *si non è vero, è molto ben trovato* – is Great Jaguar Paw's crushing defeat of Uaxactun in 378 (see n. 53 above).

established on a defensible hilltop in the central part of the Valley. The choice of this site was determined less by ecological factors (even drinking water was lacking) than by strategic considerations, and it perhaps suggests growing military and political conflict in the Valley. The suggestion is further borne out by the defensive rampart constructed along the north and west of the site and by the grisly reliefs – the *danzantes* (so-called dancers who look more like sacrificial prisoners) – which were carved at Monte Albán around the same time. The evidence of warfare therefore seems clear, although it would be rash to generalize this as a standard feature of late Preclassical Mesoamerica, indicative of the supposed primacy of warfare as an agent of state-formation.[68] Monte Albán may be something of a special case; indeed, scholars have suggested that it was founded precisely as a fortified centre by a league of Valley communities who sought to curtail the war of all against all by creating this new hilltop Leviathan. The *danzantes*, with their explicit scenes of death and mutilation, were designed to inspire fear and submission: an early example of the state terrorism which was to flourish in the belligerent Postclassic era.

If this is so, Leviathan prospered. Its rate of population growth (as high as an astonishing 6 per cent a year) was equalled only by Teotihuacan. By 200 B.C. Monte Albán boasted a population of some seventeen thousand, who lived at the centre of a wider tributary zone, the population of which had also expanded. (While Teotihuacan sucked its rural hinterland dry, congregating people within the vast city itself, Monte Albán lived, like a more conventional parasitic pre-industrial city, in symbiosis with the surrounding peasantry.) The neighbouring hillsides, meanwhile, were (at some cost) irrigated and planted, even though better land to the south remained empty; the decision was strategic, and the state, it may be presumed, regulated both the necessary hydraulic operations and the city's supply of foodstuffs and trade goods. Grandiose public works were now constructed: ramparts, pyramids and a so-called observatory, all elaborately decorated with glyphs and figures from a complex pantheon. The observatory (the designation is far from fanciful) was carefully aligned with the constellation of the Southern Cross, the Pleiades

---

[68] Blanton *et al.*, *Ancient Mesoamerica*, pp. 69–70, 76; Webb, 'The Peten Maya Decline', p. 384.

(once again), and the star Capella, whose pre-dawn appearance signalling the bi-annual passage of the sun across the zenith was precisely caught by a 'zenith sight tube' sunk into the building. 'These
cosmic occurrences were so important to the Zapotec priests', Aveni
remarks, 'that they wished to endow their earthly realm with symbols of a permanent heavenly presence'.[69] At Monte Albán, as at
Teotihuacan, we find a markedly stratified society, a sophisticated
and strongly religious elite culture, and as great a capacity for minute
mapping of the heavens as for massive mobilization of human labour
on earth.

   Towards the beginning of the first millennium A.D., however, Monte
Albán entered upon a period of ecological crisis: a conjuncture reminiscent of the Olmec 'collapse', premonitory of that of the Classic Maya, and thus illustrative of the perils of dramatic population
growth and concentration. Monte Albán's 'collapse', however, was a
collapse *manqué*. The crisis was signalled by two ostensibly contradictory but, in fact, complementary trends: locally, the decline and
abandonment of hillside agriculture, accompanied by a significant
fall in the population of the city and its environs; and regionally, a
marked expansion of Monte Albán's military power not only within
the Valley of Oaxaca but also – for the first time – beyond. Monte
Albán's influence now appears as far afield as Cuicatlán, which probably served as a northern military outpost commanding the pass
leading to the Tehuacan Valley. Other towns appear to have been subjugated, and Monte Albán's stone reliefs now record distant armed
conquests associated with the acquisition of territory rather than
prisoners. The exhaustion of the city's rural hinterland (hardly the
most bountiful) seems to have pushed Monte Albán into a phase of
successful aggressive expansion, an option encouraged by the city's
initial military *raison d'être* and subsequent military experience. A
Hobbesian foundation, perhaps, led to a Hobbesian quest for power.
This was an option which lowland communities, Olmec and Maya,
were less likely to follow, for it required a degree of spatial circumscription (or 'caging') and of regional hegemony which those communities usually lacked. The Classic Maya cities feuded incessantly,
but none established the kind of durable regional supremacy which

---

[69] Aveni, *Skywatchers*, pp. 249–57.

characterized highland metropolises like Monte Albán or Teotihuacan – or even, perhaps, the northern bastion of La Quemada – and
which in turn made extra-regional imperialism feasible.[70] The imperial option was typically a feature of highland geopolitics, and it was
one which Mesoamerica's last dominant people, the Aztecs, pushed
to extreme conclusions. In this regard, the Zapotec state of the Classic era, centred on Monte Albán, prefigured aspects of Postclassic
militarism and, to an extent, departed from the loosely theocratic
model associated with Classic polities.[71] Empires of conquest – as
opposed to empires of trade or religion – were symptoms of and supposed remedies for accumulating ecological pressure in the highland
heartland of the empire.

This argument – to be developed in greater detail in the Aztec
context – is borne out by Monte Albán's swift decline (but not total
collapse), which occurred when its territorial ambitions and, perhaps, its theocratic legitimacy faced the mighty challenge of Teotihuacan, which, though younger, soon outstripped the Zapotec city in
size and power. Teotihuacan had a bigger, richer valley to exploit; it
enjoyed privileged access to raw materials, above all, obsidian; and it
benefited from the providential eclipse of Cuicuilco. Between A.D. 300
and 500 Monte Albán's frontier conquests, such as Cuicatlán, were
abandoned; in the Valley of Oaxaca itself new centres like Jalieza
(whose population of 12,000 approached Monte Albán's 17,000) rose
to contest regional pre-eminence, perhaps counting on the sympathy
of Teotihuacan; and Monte Albán withdrew into its own heartland,
where population and agriculture began a gradual revival. Indeed,
now that the Zapotec city had, perforce, reined in its imperial pre-
tensions and accommodated itself to the Pax Teotihuacana (northern
ceramics now appear at Monte Albán, and Oaxaqueño artisans went
to work in the Valley of Mexico), it entered upon a period of renewed
demographic growth and architectural expansion. Monte Albán emulated, in more modest fashion, the efflorescence of Teotihuacan.

---

[70] Blanton *et al.*, *Ancient Mesoamerica*, pp. 83–8. Compare the smaller, shifting polities of the
Maya lowlands, numbering as many as sixty during the first millennium: Schele and Freidel,
Forest of Kings, pp. 59–60, 215.

[71] Whitecott, *The Zapotecs*, p. 78–9, which reminds us that 'the priest-warrior dichotomy is a
matter of relative position': Classic 'theocratic' polities had their kings and martial elites; Postclassic 'militarist' states had their clerisies. The differences derive from broad cultural and
political inclinations, in which respect Monte Albán appears to anticipate later developments.

Again, therefore, Teotihuacan, during its heyday, acted as a model and regulator of Classic highland civilization. To perform these functions it counted on a powerful 'demonstration effect', perhaps backed by occasional coercion, and, it seems likely, on dynastic marriages, which blended Mesoamerican highland elites both genetically and culturally.

Monte Albán's population peaked at around twenty-five thousand. Major public works and residential buildings were constructed. The Zapotec pantheon, in which the indigenous rain and fertility god Cocijo predominated, accommodated newcomers from Teotihuacan – Tlaloc and Quetzalcóatl – with typical Mesoamerican ecumenism.[72] Monte Albán's rivals in the Valley, some suffering the chastening consequences of their own excessive growth, now resumed their old familiar role as demographic and political dependencies of the local metropolis, which – now ten times larger than its nearest rival – recovered its regional supremacy. And with supremacy came an apparent cessation of military campaigning. Supreme in Oaxaca but secondary in Mesoamerica, Monte Albán flourished while Teotihuacan endured. But the latter's fall, signalling the end of the Classic era, sent shock waves throughout Mesoamerica: in Oaxaca, although it did not bring outright or immediate collapse, Teotihuacan's fall initiated a time of troubles, marked by political fragmentation and cultural retrenchment.

In the southeastern lowlands too (we should say, above all) the Classic collapse was a traumatic episode, one that has greatly exercised archaeological minds. But the problem of the Classic Maya civilization is not just why it collapsed, but also why it existed at all. For the Maya – like, perhaps, the Khmer of southeast Asia or the Yoruba of West Africa – transgress many of the anthropological rules supposedly governing the rise of complex societies and states.[73] The Maya region may be roughly divided into three ecological zones: the southern highlands (embracing modern Chiapas and central Guatemala), which, especially following the the eruption of the volcano Ilopango in c. A.D. 250, were of secondary importance,

---

[72] Blanton *et al.*, *Ancient Mesoamerica*, pp. 88–98; Whitecotton, *The Zapotecs*, pp. 49–54.
[73] Farriss, *Maya Society*, pp. 117–19; Wheatley, *Pivot of the Four Quarters*, p. 275; Harris, *Cannibals and Kings*, p. 130.

and the two lowland zones, north and south, which were the principal seats of Maya civilization. Although the more arid north contained major Classic sites, like Dzibilchaltun, and although it was to achieve regional pre-eminence during the Postclassic period, the real locus of Maya culture during the great Classic efflorescence was to be found in the broad belt of tropical territory stretching from the mouth of the Usumacinta River across to the Gulf of Honduras (i.e., present-day Campeche, Quintana Roo, Belize and northern Guatemala). Here the Maya, rather like the Olmecs, inhabited a relatively lush, watered, forested zone, where slash-and-burn agriculture, practised by peasant households, readily yielded the means of subsistence. Plants were varied and abundant (some 200 edible species were available, including staples like maize, beans, squash and manioc, as well as arboreal fruits such as *chicosapote, ramón* and *balche*), and these could be supplemented by hunting, fishing and foraging. Compared to the chill highlands, with their precarious dependence on rainfed maize crops and perennial vulnerability to frosts and drought, this was Eden.[74] It was also a broad Eden: the central Maya lowlands spanned some 100,000 square kilometres, compared to the 7,000 of the Valley of Mexico.

Also relevant to considerations of societal cohesion and state formation is the relative ecological homogeneity of the Maya lowlands. True, there were pockets of diversity, where differential resource endowment encouraged something of the functional interdependence between communities and localities which characterized highland Mexico and Peru. In the Maya lowlands, these pockets tended to be coastal: the salt marshes of northern Yucatán, the riverine niches of the Belize littoral.[75] But in Mesoamerica differential resource endowment depended heavily on altitude, hence the flat Maya lowlands tended towards greater ecological homogeneity. By the same token,

---

[74] Harris, *Cannibals and Kings*, pp. 133–4, stresses the region's constrained water supply, which, he says, favoured nucleation and political control (thus 'removing the problem of the initial growth of Maya ceremonial centres from the realm of heaven to the realm of earth and water'). True for northern Yucatán, this argument is less persuasive for the Petén to the south; and the fact that centres were built near water supplies is poor proof that water supplies dictated settlement. R. T. Matheny, 'Ancient Lowland and Highland Maya Water and Soil Conservation', in Kent V. Flannery, ed., *Maya Subsistence: Studies in Memory of Dennis E. Puleston* (New York, 1982), pp. 158–60, questions the presumed correlation between settlement and water supplies.

[75] Hammond, *Ancient Maya Civilization*, pp. 176–7; William L. Rathje, 'Classic Maya Development and Denouement: A Research Design', in Culbert, *Classic Maya Collapse*, pp. 416–17.

these lowlands lacked major natural barriers, and, since the region displayed a broad linguistic and cultural unity, we may assume that movement, migration and miscegenation were relatively easy. The picture, therefore, is one of broad amplitude and sameness: of a common Maya culture, relatively open and regionally undifferentiated, composed of numerous homologous units, free from the tight circumscription imposed by the mountains of the central highlands. As Michael Mann tersely concedes, 'the Maya were not particularly caged'.[76]

Logically, stratified societies would have been hard put to evolve in these circumstances. People could move – or flee – with ease; communities could fissure, avoiding excessive concentrations of population; subsistence was comfortable and local economic specialization optional rather than enforced. Managerial elites were not required to oversee intensive systems of irrigation or to protect vital trade routes. Nor was a warrior elite required to battle for economic survival: the Preclassic Maya population was comfortably below the region's carrying capacity. In short, the imposition of social control and political authority upon a successful subsistence farming people could not have responded to stark material necessity; furthermore, any such imposition would have been difficult, even impossible, if the people had chosen to resist.

To the extent that stratification and state-building came to the Maya lowlands later than to the altiplano, the ecological rules are to some degree vindicated. Farming was practised – although still supplemented by hunting and gathering – in the middle of the third millennium B.C., by which time the first ceramics were appearing. Long-distance trade, linking the Maya to other regions and introducing 'foreign' goods like basalt *metates* (corn-grinders) and jade, dates to 2000–1500 B.C., and by 1000 B.C. intensive sedentary agriculture formed the economic basis of communities in riverine niches.[77] But social stratification was still not apparent. The excavation of sites like Altar de Sacrificios (c. 1000 B.C.) reveals an egalitarian society, lacking ritualistic public works or burial distinctions; this

[76] Mann, *Sources of Social Power*, p. 119.
[77] Webb, 'The Peten Maya Decline', p. 386; Ball, 'The Rise of the Northern Maya Chiefdoms', p. 107.

pattern, suggestive of a 'flat' segmentary society, also prevailed in the northern plains and central Yucatán, as population gradually spread northwards into these sparsely inhabited zones.[78] Here as elsewhere considerable advance in material culture – evidenced in farming and trade – long antedated the formation of elites, let alone states. This was especially true of the Maya lowlands. One consequence was a marked absence – which, from a geographical and ecological perspective, might appear puzzling – of Olmec influence: an influence which, it has been argued, tended to focus on incipiently stratified communities, whose emergent chiefs were poised to appropriate 'civilized' Olmec goods and ideas. Despite their relative proximity and common lowland environment, the 'flat' egalitarian communities of the Maya were less receptive to Olmec material culture, with its connotations of elite status, than were the incipiently stratified communities of the highlands.[79]

Not until the middle of the first millennium B.C. did Maya villages begin to display modest ceremonial precincts; and not until later – when stratified polities were well established in the Valleys of Mexico and Oaxaca – did Maya chiefdoms (not, as yet, states) begin to emerge, probably around 400–300 B.C.[80] Perhaps significantly, the first and fastest development occurred not in the fecund forests of the Petén, but in the arid northern plains of Yucatán (where Komchen constituted a major centre at the beginning of the Christian era) and in the southern highlands, at Izapa and Kaminaljuyú, where dense populations, rich funerary offerings, ceremonial buildings and the first distinctive Maya stelae (carved commemorative obelisks)

---

[78] Ball, 'The Rise of the Northern Maya Chiefdoms', p. 107, and Willey, 'Rise of Maya Civilization'.

[79] Blanton *et al.*, *Ancient Mesoamerica*, pp. 180–3. Mann, *Sources of Social Power*, p. 119, sees a 'strong diffusion' from the Olmec who thus 'transmitted power capacities to other groups', such as the Maya. This seems greatly exaggerated and symptomatic of the 'diffusionst' approach which, once popular is now in full retreat in Europe as in Mesoamerica: Sharer, *The Ancient Maya*, pp. 72–5.

[80] Ball, 'The Rise of the Northern Maya Chiefdoms', p. 111; Webster, 'War and the Evolution of Maya Civilization', p. 349. Schele and Freidel, *Forest of Kings*, ch. 3, imaginatively recreate the story of incipient state-building – 'the advent of kingship' – at Cerros, on the eastern Yucatán coast, in the first century B.C. They do not, however, relate the process to prior internal dynamics: no chiefs figure; the would-be kings arrive out of the blue, paddling forty-foot dugout canoes; and the people of Cerros, led by their 'patriarchs', 'decide to adopt the institution of kingship' in an oddly sudden, cerebral, almost jacobin fashion. Significantly, perhaps, the experiment fails: after – because of? – a brief orgy of building, 'the Maya of Cerros gave up their brief embrace of kingship . . . they went down to their homes and continued to live around the ruins of their greatness as fisherfolk and farmers once more' (p. 127).

now began to appear.[81] As yet, however, these Maya chiefdoms were relatively small entities compared to the highland metropolises of Teotihuacan and Monte Albán. Thus far the supposed ecological determinants of civilization seem to hold: the harsher, more constrained and variegated, environment of the altiplano, by 'caging' the population, favoured the earlier growth of hierarchical states, possessed of political boundaries (however fluctuating) and of military and managerial capacities.

But, we have seen, such ecological determinants set general limits rather than precise patterns; and the genesis of social hierarchies and states responded to factors other than the ecological. This was particularly true of the lowland Maya. During the Classic era (c. A.D. 250–900) Maya society transcended its supposed ecological determinants and cohered in organized polities, characterized by a marked division of labour, stretched hierarchies, and a complex, sophisticated culture, aesthetically and intellectually brilliant. And (to complete the ecological conundrum) these developments were most pronounced in the forested lowlands of the central Maya region – not in the southern highlands or upon the arid northern plateau. Here, as in the Olmec zone and the highland Valleys of Mexico and Oaxaca, the population began to concentrate around religious centres. By the time of the Classic era, Maya society boasted a network of primary ceremonial centres (Tikal, Seibal, Uaxactun, Yaxchilan, Palenque, Copan and others), spatially scattered (each centre, it has been calculated, presided over a 250-square-kilometre hinterland), and linked, sometimes physically by roads and raised causeways, to subordinate secondary and tertiary centres. The latter served tiny forest hamlets – a dozen of which might share a single ceremonial centre – as well as peasant villages, where populations of 100 to 150 still, perhaps, revered local ancestral deities; meanwhile, ten to fifteen of these lesser ceremonial centres in turn depended on one major centre, which, it is now recognized, could in some instances become a genuine residential city, such as Tikal.[82] The pattern therefore represents a mixture of dispersed and compact settlement, the

[81] Ball, 'The Rise of the Northern Maya Chiefdoms', pp. 124–8; Andrews, 'Dzibilchaltun', p. 339.

[82] Sanders, 'The Cultural Ecology of the Lowland Maya', pp. 327–8; Sharer, *The Ancient Maya*, pp. 467–76.

latter – if archaeological analogies are permitted – probably an evolution of the first.[83] It may be presumed that this gridlike hierarchy
of centres served to integrate the population, to counter the fissile
tendencies of a subsistence-farming people, and to generate, instead,
the elusive 'social bond' which held the Maya together.

Again, cause and function must be distinguished. By what means
and for what reasons (military, demographic, religious, 'commercial') did the Classic Maya ceremonial centres achieve this integrative role? Although population rose both before and during the Classic era, there is scant evidence of sustained demographic pressure,
or of pervasive population growth throughout the region, which
might have compelled nucleation; rather, some regions (like the central Maya zone) boomed, some (like Belize) maintained the steady
growth rates of Preclassic times, and some (the Usumacinta and
Pasión Valleys) declined.[84] War, as we shall note, was a staple feature of Classic Maya society, but organized warfare – as opposed to
sporadic raiding – appears to have followed social nucleation rather
than to have preceded it. Given the obviously religious character
of the Maya centres, the uneven demographic and the random ecological pattern of their distribution, especially at the upper quasi-
urban level, and the global comparisons they inspire, it is reasonable again to suppose an original religious *raison d'être*, which was
in turn linked to patterns of trade and exchange. Special cults and pilgrimages (well known in later Yucatán) thus favoured the growth of
certain sites, lending them a sacred aura and bolstering the position
of priestly elites, who now developed their professional knowledge –
astronomical, calendrical, mathematical – to an unusual degree.

Trade, which we will consider separately, was closely bound up
with this religious specialization. Major centres like Tikal produced a
whole range of manufactured goods – pottery, stelae, stone carvings –
which carried religious connotations; hence, it has been argued, they
could develop a kind of 'Barbie-doll cult complex, based on their own
local cult items'.[85] Linked to this, perhaps, was an early variant of

---

[83] Wheatley, *Pivot of the Four Quarters*, pp. 306–7.

[84] Rathje, 'The Tikal Connection', p. 375.

[85] Rathje, 'The Tikal Connection', p. 380. On the question of Maya trade, see Hammond, *Ancient Maya Civilization*, ch. 8, and Sharer, *The Ancient Maya*, ch. 9.

the pervasive cargo system of later Middle America, whereby aspirant cultists were drawn from the countryside to the city/ceremonial centre. Here, ritualistic observation, which may have been costly in time and goods, offered the aspirants upward mobility and social status, supplied the priesthood with acolytes and recruits and lent the Maya social system a form of integration which linked centre and hinterland, rulers and ruled, thus countering both the fissiparous tendencies of lowland society and the social tensions attendant upon increased stratification. Certainly, patterns of settlement at major centres like Dzibilchaltun strongly suggest a rotational system of religious recruitment, a clear forerunner of the colonial cargo system, which linked lineage, residence, ritual participation and social advancement.[86]

Thus centres that were originally ceremonial and non-residential in function eventually acquired critical mass, attracting a permanent nucleus of population (which, in cases like Tikal, could be considerable) as well as a regular flow of migrants: pilgrims, tributaries, traders, artisans, curious visitors. At Tikal, an ancient community whose roots trace back well into the first millennium B.C., a definite urban community was established by 100 B.C., and a city of some forty thousand by the fifth century A.D. In the process, 'immense sums of energy and resources were expended for religious structure and accoutrements: temples, terraces, pyramids, ballcourts, elaborate stone carvings, masks, and altars'.[87] This religious infrastructure – one might say, with wilful inversion – required a major socioeconomic superstructure. The Great Plaza and its associated monuments at Tikal stood in the midst of an intensely cultivated and built-up area of some 120 square kilometres.[88] It seems clear, therefore, that the old argument as to whether the Classic Maya possessed 'real' cities (dense urban communities) or merely ceremonial centres, scattered amid a dispersed peasantry, has been resolved in favour of the first supposition. Tikal may have been exceptionally large, but, as archaeologists have fanned out from the monumental centres of

[86] Andrews, 'Dzibilchaltun', pp. 327–8.

[87] T. P. Culbert, 'The Maya Downfall at Tikal', in Culbert, *Classic Maya Collapse*, p. 64.

[88] Christopher Jones, William Coe and William Haviland, 'Tikal: An Outline of Its Field Study (1956–70) and a Project Bibliography', in Sabloff, *Supplement to the Handbook of Middle Ameircan Indians*, p. 306; Sharer, *The Ancient Maya*, pp. 152–3.

known sites, in a costly but necessary search for signs of more mundane habitation, evidence of concentrated urban settlement has accumulated. Seibal may have had a population of ten thousand and
Dzibilchaltun one of twenty-five thousand.[89] Some of these cities,
doubtless, depended upon the exaction of tribute from lesser communities within their orbit, so that a fiscal hierarchy of subordination
and superordination paralleled the religious hierarchy which, I have
suggested, formed the basis of Maya social integration. For, it bears
repeating, the 'supersites', the true cities, do not appear to follow
any clear ecological rationale (indeed, cities, by concentrating both
agrarian producers and urban consumers, were economically inefficient): 'the centers were in fact a poor fit for the environment ... This
nucleation was caused not by environmental advantage but rather
by the operation of belief systems and social prestige in conjunction
with kin ties'.[90]

If, compared to Teotihuacan, Maya urbanization was modest,
there was little that was modest about Maya cultural achievement.
Towering temples, taller and more elegant than the squat pyramids
of the altiplano, rose out of the lowland forest; around them were
ranged palaces, ballcourts, commemorative stelae and the outlying
adobe houses of the peasantry. The Maya class structure, like the
Maya temple, was elongated: at the apex stood an elite, in some cases
a known dynastic elite, which embraced secular and theocratic rulers
(the distinction may be hard to draw); below, a subordinate class or
classes of workers and peasants who contributed their goods and
labour, probably according to a tributary system. With this stratifica-
tions, we may hypothesize, went a process of material redistribution,
controlled by the state, which was very likely regressive over time (the
rich got richer, the poor got poorer, the social pyramid got taller and
steeper). The fundamental class divide, which was probably bridge-
able only in rare instances of social mobility, was accompanied by
an advanced division of labour, involving distinct professions and a
hierarchy of status: specialist priests, trained in arcane astronomical
and mathematical knowledge; potters, stonemasons and sculptors;

---

[89] Andrews, 'Dzibilchaltun', p. 329; Sharer, *The Ancient Maya*, p. 471.
[90] Webb, 'The Peten Maya Decline', p. 388; Montmollin, *Archaeology of Political Structure*, pp. 89–
94, develops the argument for Postclassic northern Yucatán, stressing political and religious
power over ecological rationality.

even skilled dentists who beautified the teeth of the well-to-do with jade inlays.[91]

If the model resembled Teotihuacan, where a strong admixture of theocracy and redistribution was also present, this may have been a response in part to direct emulation (diffusion) as well as to local evolutionary logic. Kaminaljuyú, we have noted, represented a Teotihuacano outpost in the Maya highlands, whence its influence – especially its commercial influence – radiated northward: Teotihua-can goods, notably obsidian, and Teotihuacan styles of architecture and aristocratic dress are evident at Tikal, Becan and Dzibilchaltun. The process of diffusion was no doubt complex; northern Yucatán sites were directly linked to the central highlands by sea, hence it need not be supposed that all Teotihuacano influence was channelled circuitously through Kaminaljuyú; and, it must be stressed, diffu-sion required apt – that is, suitably developed and receptive – pupils. Nevertheless, it is plausible to assume that Maya state-formation, be-ginning in the southern highlands, was at least in part 'secondary', that is, a response to the demonstration effect of other, pre-existent, 'primary' states, in this case the distant but mighty metropolis of Teotihuacan.[92]

Cultural efflorescence required abundant labour. Temple IV at Tikal, standing 65 metres high, comprised nearly 200,000 cubic metres of building material. True, the Maya population was growing fast: from between two and five million in 100 B.C. to some ten million at the apogee of the Classic period, c. A.D. 700.[93] Theocratic power and legitimacy may have converted these millions into toiling millions (in fact, given the size of the population, and allowing for a grad-ual rate of construction, an equitable distribution of labour tribute need not have been hugely onerous). But how were the toiling mil-lions fed? In aggregate terms, the maintenance of even so large and growing a population may not have required systematic agricultural intensification; in other words, the carrying capacity of slash-and-burn farming, previously underestimated, may have been adequate. But aggregate calculations of carrying capacity overlook annual

[91] Hammond, *Ancient Maya Civilization*, pp. 186–97.
[92] Harris, *Cannibals and Kings*, pp. 131–2, states the case with characteristic confidence.
[93] Blanton *et al.*, *Ancient Mesoamerica*, pp. 188–9, 205–7.

fluctuations in output as well as permanent concentrations of population which, given the tight limitations of Mesoamerican transport, had to be fed principally from local sources. It is now clear that intense farming was also practised – logically enough around centres, like Tikal, where population was densest. Here and elsewhere, recent research has revealed irrigation ditches and canals, terraces, and quasi-*chinampas* (raised fields amid swamplands), which formed part of an intricate combination of arable farming, horticulture and silviculture (some have stressed the nutritional bounty of the breadnut tree), as well as fishing – a combination which lent itself to cross-fertilization and imparted a certain ecological harmony. The Maya lowlands, in short, were not far behind the central highlands in terms of agricultural innovation and productivity – if they were behind at all.[94] Clearly this raises the possibility of a partially 'hydraulic' explanation of Maya state-building: the elite, perhaps the numerate and literate priestly elite, managed these new, complex and delicately linked systems of production. The argument is particularly plausible for centres (like the Puuc Maya city of Uxmal in northern Yucatán) where local aridity made water storage and control essential for the community's survival.[95] Thus mathematical and calendrical skills, and the development of the New World's most advanced system of writing, would have had direct and practical application.

To the extent that these suppositions may be valid (necessarily they remain conjectural) it must be stressed that the formation of definite political authorities – be they 'super-chiefdoms' or embryonic states – *preceded* these managerial accomplishments, which the super-chiefdom/state made not only possible but even necessary. Wittfogel's thesis, that hydraulic public works require a powerful central state, perhaps encapsulates a valid functional relationship but inverts it. The state encouraged nucleation, population growth and, the extraction from peasant producers of a sizeable surplus, which went

[94] Hammond, *Ancient Maya Civilization*, pp. 154–63; Flannery, *Maya Subsistence*.

[95] Matheny, 'Ancient Lowland and Highland Maya Water and Soil Conservation', pp. 163–4; see also Jones, *Twin City Tales*, p. 345, and Fernando Robles Castellanos and Anthony P. Andrews, 'A Review and Synthesis of Recent Postclassic Archaeology in Northern Yucatan', in Jeremy A. Sabloff and E. Wyllys Andrews, *Late Lowland Maya Civilization: Classic to Postclassic* (Albuquerque, 1986), pp. 58–9, 70, on the Puuc system of *chultunes* (underground cisterns), over a hundred of which honeycombed the site of Uxmal, and which were matched by a complex network of roads (*sacbeob*), the 'skeletons of large political domains'.

to support not only the ruling elite but also artisans, builders and warriors; these processes, in turn, required a more intense and productive agriculture. The sequence, from start to finish, could be read thus, with the proviso that this sequence is an ideal type and that constant interaction between factors must be supposed: natural population increase → farming and modest nucleation → ceremonial centres and redistributive chiefdoms → religious specialization, elite formation, tribute exaction and state-formation → accelerated population growth and concentration (i.e., political, not ecological, caging) → intensive, managed, hydraulic agriculture. The latter therefore, figured less as cause than as outcome of stratification and state-building. In turn, however, it further reinforced the managerial role and political power of pre-existing elites. But it also enhanced the fragility of the social structure, by linking economic production to political organization in a novel fashion. Agriculture was removed from the exclusive domain of the self-governing, self-reproducing peasant household which became a unit within an economic as well as a political part-society. Peasant labour, like peasant produce, was now expropriated and marshalled by elites; peasant political subordination, in other words, was complemented by economic subordination, especially in hierarchical managed communities like Uxmal. A serious disruption of elite rule, as a result, would upset economic organization and carry consequences for society as a whole.

In the Maya lowlands, as elsewhere in Mesoamerica, the concentration of power and population was also served by the development of trade. Maya trade did not achieve the levels attained at Teotihuacan. The lowlands lacked the ecological complementarities which fostered trade on the altiplano: in terms of resource endowment, Maya communities were much of a muchness. Few goods of common consumption could not be produced within the peasant household, obsidian and salt being the best examples.[96] Salt was a major export of northern Yucatecan communities like Komchen and Dzibilchaltun, which traded it for forest products such as wax and honey; control of the salt trade was a coveted political goal.[97]

[96] Hammond, *Ancient Maya Civilization*, pp. 230–5; Farriss, *Maya Society*, pp. 120–5.
[97] Andrews, 'Dzibilchaltun', pp. 324, 331, 339; J. W. Ball, 'A Hypothetical Outline of Coastal Maya Prehistory: 300 B.C.–A.D. 1200', in Hammond, *Social Process*, pp. 181–2.

Apart from this clear north-south, littoral-interior, trading relationship, however, the relative ecological uniformity of the lowlands
tended to restrict trade in basic 'mass-consumption' commodities.
Long-distance trade was another matter: its history stretched back
at least through the second millennium B.C., when canoes ferried
basalt *metates* from the Maya mountains down to Cuello (Belize) and
when jade beads were transported over 250 miles from the Motagua
Valley in Guatemala. Jade, basalt and perhaps cacao were therefore
established as trade goods, whose importation and distribution were
governed by the emergent Maya elite, within a 'suprahousehold pro-
curement system'.[98] In return, the lowlands probably exported tropical products: dyes, spices, perfumes, herbal medicines, fibres, pelts
and plumage.[99] Imports to the Maya zone, being of high weight and
value, were either for elite consumption or for limited elite distribution through the ceremonial network; and they probably constituted
only a small fraction of the goods locally produced and traded. Even
the basalt *metates* which, it has been supposed, were household ne-
cessities, in fact probably were not, since inferior equivalents, made
of native Yucatecan limestone, would have served: 'a basalt *metate*
would be the pre-Hispanic equivalent of a Mercedes-Benz'.[100]

Trade therefore depended less on outright ecological necessity
than on increased stratification and the progressive appropriation
of goods by a rich and powerful elite (a process evident, for example, in the mortuary distribution of jade items during the Classic
period).[101] Trade also depended, as we have noted, on the evolution
of the ceremonial centre network and its corresponding pattern of
urbanization. For patterns of trade, like patterns of settlement, appear to defy any strict ecological logic and to respond, instead, to the
man-made exigencies of that network. Tikal, for example, became
the great entrepôt of the southern lowlands, amassing vast quantities of obsidian and outstripping other regions which, paradoxically,

[98] Hammond, *Ancient Maya Civilization*, pp. 115–16, 225, 229, 231–9; Rathje, 'Classic Maya
Development', p. 411.

[99] B. Voorhies, 'An Ecological Model of the Early Maya of the Central Lowlands', in Flannery,
Maya Subsistence, pp. 70–84.

[100] Farriss, *Maya Society*, p. 124. 'Or', Farriss adds, confounding at least this reader, 'perhaps
more aptly a Cuisinart'.

[101] Hammond, *Ancient Maya Civilization*, pp. 123, 188–9; Sharer, *The Ancient Maya*, pp. 163–4.

lay closer to the sources of supply (Kaminaljuyú, Teotihuacan's commercial 'colony', appears to have been instrumental in determining this pattern). Politico-religious power counted for more than simple geographical location or resource endowment; indeed, it may be that material deprivation fostered trade and thus accelerated stratification and incipient state-building precisely in 'poorer' areas.[102]

Tikal is a clear but exceptional case. Lesser centres, too, fed on the trade routes. Thus, as in the highlands, trade and religion cohered, with ceremonial centres forming links in the network of trade, and with trade goods, such as jade, being invested with symbolic as well as secular value (hence Rathje's 'Barbie-doll cult').[103] It may be supposed that theocratic control and regulation extended to this, the sphere of circulation, as well as to the sphere of (specialized agricultural) production. Certainly, the Classic Maya do not appear to have possessed a distinct class of specialist traders like the Aztec *pochteca*; nor, with the partial exception of Tikal, did the Maya centres contain markets comparable to those of Teotihuacan or Tlatelolco.[104] It is tempting, though perhaps over-bold, to see the limited, largely 'luxury' trade of the Maya as akin to the 'temple trade' of ancient Sumer, that is, a trade in which 'the temple . . . was not only a "house of worship" but a sanctuary, a palace, and a storage place and redistributive center'.[105]

The functional affinity of trade and state-building cannot be discussed without reference to warfare, which some have elevated to the primary factor governing the genesis of states, whether in Mesoamerica or Mesopotamia.[106] Hunters and gatherers, and even small farming communities, did not benefit directly from warfare: their portable surplus, for one thing, was too small; and, even if recurrent skirmishing served both to defend borders and – by encouraging a martial masculine ethic – to encourage female infanticide, thus curtailing population growth, this pressure precisely limited population and ensured that warfare was sustained at a low-equilibrium level.[107]

---

[102] Rathje, 'The Tikal Connection', p. 378–9; Phillips and Rathje, 'Exchange Values', pp. 103–4.

[103] Rathje, 'The Tikal Connection', p. 380; Voorhies, 'An Ecological Model', pp. 86–7.

[104] Hammond, *Ancient Maya Civilization*, pp. 238–9; Sanders, 'Cultural Ecology', pp. 349–53.

[105] Service, *Origins of the State*, p. 207; though note the caveats of Curtin, *Cross-cultural Trade*, pp. 61–7.

[106] Webster, 'War and the Evolution of Maya Civilization'; Hammond, *Ancient Maya Civilization*, p. 132; Carneiro, 'A Theory of the Origin of the State'.

[107] Harris, *Cannibals and Kings*, ch. 4.

A quite different form of warfare – imperialist warfare, one might call it – developed with the rise of states, elites and cities. Large stratified societies played for higher stakes and had an interest in expanding their subject population. Tributaries and trade routes could be won and held by the sword; better still, cities could establish (and defend) trade monopolies, such as that which Quirigua exercised over the Motagua Valley trade or Becan over the salt trade.[108] The desultory skirmishing of tribal bands gave way to the more systematic slaughter of incipient states. Furthermore, in the populous, polycentric world of the Classic Maya, no single polity could impose its will, as Teotihuacan could in the Valley of Mexico or Monte Albán in the Valley of Oaxaca (both, of course, smaller, topographically circumscribed zones). Individual cities tried; and, in the eighth century, Tikal indeed achieved a measure of success. But regional hegemony proved elusive. The Hobbesian state of nature – from which Monte Albán rescued the Valley of Oaxaca, at a price – remained the norm in the Maya lowlands.

War was therefore a constant: 'the earlier, idyllic view of the Classic Maya as the peace-loving flower children of pre-Columbian Mesoamerica has by now been largely discredited'.[109] The late Preclassic (c. 300 B.C.–c. A.D. 200) reveals clear examples of defensive ditches and ramparts (at Becan, for example, where they were kept in good repair in later years too) and evidence of the sudden eclipse of centres, suggesting the adverse fortunes of war.[110] The original concentration of population at Tikal may have involved considerations of defence (which is not to say that warfare *per se* necessitated concentration).[111] During the Classic era, rumours of war abound. The famous friezes at Bonampak show helmeted warriors engaged in frenzied battle; at Palenque captives are to be seen, bound and submissive; a stela at Uaxactun (A.D. 377) reveals the introduction

---

108 Hammond, *Ancient Maya Civilization*, p. 206; Ball, 'A Hypothetical Outline', p. 182. Schele and Freidel, *Forest of Kings*, p. 174, attribute the sudden ending of Tikal's monumental architecture in A.D. 562 to the defeat of the city's ruler at the hands of the rival power of Caracol: 'Double Bird had no doubt been captured and killed, his dynasty ended, and his remaining ahauob (lords) cut off from the vast trade routes which provided their wealth'.

109 Fariss, *Maya Society*, p. 140; Schele and Freidel, *Forest of Kings*, pp. 130–1, 145–6, see a quantum jump in Maya militarism, derived from Teotihuacan and the central highlands, in the later fourth century A.D.

110 Blanton *et al.*, *Ancient Mesoamerica*, p. 188; Webster, 'War and the Evolution of Maya Civilization', p. 337; Schele and Freidel, *Forest of Kings*, p. 174 (see n. 108).

111 Sanders, 'Cultural Ecology', pp. 358–9.

into the Maya armoury of the *atlatl*, the highland spear-thrower. The Maya stelae, in fact, which comprise the most detailed historical sources for the Classic period, are principally records of the accessions, marriages, battles, triumphs and defeats of Maya city-states and their ruling dynasties, some of which, thanks to the mathematical precision of the Maya long count, can be accurately dated. At Palenque and Tikal, for example, entire dynastic sequences can be reconstructed.[112]

The sheer frequency of these carved records, celebrating the deeds of rulers and dynasts, suggests not only a restlessly belligerent elite but also an elite aware of its own precariousness vis-à-vis both rival rulers and, perhaps, dissident subjects; hence an elite constantly concerned to laud its own prowess and bolster its prestige. In fact, a flurry of stelae-erection often appears to have immediately preceded collapse. In the same context, we may note the clear evidence of human sacrifice, especially of prisoners. Although this practice did not reach the epic proportions of Aztec hecatombs, Maya sacrifice probably obeyed similar motives and was 'critical to status reinforcement and political power'.[113] Individuals, families and dynasties displayed their prowess, their divine favour, by sacrificing the prisoners they had taken on the field of battle.

The high politics of the Classic Maya, we may infer, revolved around small, aggressive states and their shifting alliances, cemented by dynastic marriages and tempered in recurrent warfare: a Mesoamerican version of Machiavelli's Italy. Here, too, rulers were resplendent, patronizing art and architecture in the interests of power and prestige; but they were also vulnerable – to war, rebellion and *coup d'état*.[114] Bids for regional hegemony – Tikal playing the part of Florence – were foiled, and, by the late Classic period, as Tikal weakened, political fragmentation appears to have increased.

---

[112] Hammond, *Ancient Maya Civilization*, ch. 7; Schele and Freidel, *Forest of Kings*, chs. 4–8.

[113] Arthur A. Demarest, 'Overview: Mesoamerican Human Sacrifice in Evolutionary Perspective', in Elizabeth P. Benson and Elizabeth H. Boone, eds., *Ritual Human Sacrifice in Mesoamerica* (Washington, 1984), p. 228. As elsewhere in Mesoamerica, sacrifice consorted with a range of penitential and self-mortifying practices, such as bloodletting from tongue, ears and genitals: Schele and Freidel, *Forest of Kings*, pp. 68–71, 87–8, 201–2, 207, 233–5.

[114] Hammond, *Ancient Maya Civilization*, p. 191, compares the life of a 'top-flight Maya craftsman' to that of Benvenuto Cellini. On wars and coups, c. A.D. 400–700: Schele and Freidel, *Forest of Kings*, pp. 127–8, 153, 174, 177–9, 189–90, 205, 211–12: 'a tangle of elite . . . vendettas [which] rivals any in recorded history' (p. 212).

Like the squabbling Italians, therefore, the Maya city–states were vulnerable to better-organized military invaders from the north.

The Maya city-states may also have been vulnerable to protest from within. Classic Maya culture evolved within a theocratic matrix: professional priests had developed a corpus of religious, astronomical, mathematical and historical knowledge which combined practical administrative utility with divination and myth-making. This, like any ideology, served to explain and interpret man's place within the cosmos and, like most ideologies, it also served to legitimize the social order, of which the priestly elite was an integral and privileged part. This did not make the Maya states strict theocracies, however. Over time, secular rulers – who no doubt combined secular and divine legitimacy – acquired greater power and prestige, which they bolstered with sumptuary laws, monumental extravagance and dynastic flag-waving. War tended to encourage this process. Meanwhile, ritual retreated into closeted precincts.[115] Priestly arcana, which had originally derived from a common Maya cosmology, may have become increasingly detached from the concerns and perceptions of ordinary people, especially the mass of peasants upon whose labour the whole impressive edifice rested. We must countenance the possibility (however heretical to some Mayanists, who may be more Mayan than the Maya) that the elaborate rituals, offerings, divinations and calibrations were 'so much mumbo-jumbo to a baffled and indifferent peasantry'.[116] Not that the peasantry lost religion; rather, they lost contact with an increasingly remote, abstract and elitist religion. The ties which had previously bound peasants to ceremonial centres – vestigial local or ancestral cults, early variants of the cargo system – now atrophied. Access to burial in ceremonial

---

[115] On dynastic flag-waving: Schele and Freidel, *Forest of Kings*, pp. 165–6ff. On ritual retreat: Webster, 'War and the Evolution of Maya Civilization', pp. 355–6; Sanders, 'Cultural Ecology', p. 346.

[116] Farriss, *Maya Society*, p. 145. This raises the interesting but difficult question of popular perceptions of elite ideology. Coe, *Breaking the Maya Code*, p. 269, raises the intriguing – and plausible – possibility that Maya script – e.g., as carved on the ubiquitous stelae – was *not* the monopoly of a tiny literate elite but could be read and understood by plebeian Maya too. Even if true, this – *cognitive* – fact does not necessarily imply an enduring *affective* commitment to political – e.g., dynastic – values on the part of those semi-literate plebeians. The dissemination of literacy in Europe is usually held to have been subversive of the old order, not supportive. Of course, printed books and carved stone stelae are very different means of written communication.

centres, for example, became increasingly restricted.[117] As material burdens grew, ideological integration faltered. The scene was set for the collapse of the Classic Maya civilization.

III. The Classic Collapse

The Maya collapse was the most dramatic element in the collective trauma which ended the Classic era throughout Mesoamerica and which ushered in a new phase, a time of troubles marked by political fragmentation, militarization, migration and, in some cases, cultural retreat. Out of this trauma arose new hegemonic civilizations: the Toltecs and Aztecs in the central highlands and the Itzá and Mayapán confederations in Yucatán. Certain broad common features attach to these new cultures, differentiating them from their Classic predecessors and thus justifying the loose Classic/Postclassic terminology. Common causal factors may also have helped bring about the transition: in particular, the bankruptcy of theocratic rule and the rise of secular warlords (albeit these were often manifestations of deeper malaises). Given the relative rapidity of the transition, the dramatic cliché 'collapse' – rather than the more prosaic 'decline' – may in this instance be justified. Unfortunately, Mesoamerican archaeology is more adept at the reconstruction of general *trends* (settlement, urbanization, trade) than of the salient *events* (wars, conquests, revolutions) which punctuate and which may halt, distort or accelerate them. Indeed, the best source for the *histoire événémentielle* of this period – the Classic Maya stelae – were victims of the upheaval; hence, they cannot shed much light on its character. As a result, explanations of the Classic collapse often involve logical inferences drawn from general archaeological data and informed by historical analogy, theoretical models or historians' hunches. The problem with this form of inferential explanation (unavoidable in the circumstances and often conducted with impressive intellectual ingenuity) is that the data appear to allow several distinct but logically coherent reconstructions of what happened: to a degree, you pay your money and take your choice.

---

[117] Sanders, 'Cultural Ecology', pp. 346–7.

First, the nature of the collapse should be clarified. It was far from homogenous. Major communities collapsed, in terms of their areas of settlement, populations and political pre-eminence: Teotihuacan, Monte Albán, Cholula, the cities of the Petén Maya. With this went an evident collapse of the Classic elite and the Great Tradition it had nurtured. General demographic collapse, however, was rare. Usually, population was redistributed rather than annihilated. In the Valleys of Mexico and Oaxaca new communities sprang up: as Teotihuacan shrank to a small fraction (perhaps 3 per cent) of its former size, a pronounced ruralization took place, restoring the old pattern of scattered settlements which had preceded the rise of the great metropolis; in the Valley of Oaxaca, too, a diminished Monte Albán now faced several burgeoning rivals; and Cholula, in the Valley of Puebla, also became a shadow of its former Classic self. Within the Maya zone, the Belize Valley and the northern Yucatán lowlands retained large populations: the former displaying a dispersed, rural and egalitarian character (village settlements embodying the 'Little Tradition' of autonomous peasant culture, now disembarrassed of its 'Great' cultural carapace), the latter retaining an urban, hierarchical and 'civilized' form, most evident in the Puuc Maya cities, such as Uxmal. The Puuc Maya cities were not alone as 'civilized' survivors – and beneficiaries – of the Classic collapse. For, during the time of troubles (more grotesquely, the 'Protopostclassic') which followed the fall of Teotihuacan (c. A.D. 750–900), other centres also flourished: El Tajín, in the verdant Veracruz lowlands; Xochicalco, a fortified hilltop city in Morelos; La Quemada, in the far north; and, later, the new imperial metropolis of Tula, Hidalgo. In contrast, in the Petén zone of the central Maya lowlands, the hearth of the Classic Maya civilization, collapse was complete, all-encompassing and permanent. Centres, cultures and peoples vanished and did not return. Clearly, this extreme experience, obliterating elites and masses, lords and peasants, 'Great' and 'Little' Traditions, requires special explanation.

The fall of Teotihuacan, the dominant centre of the Classic era, must serve as the point of departure: it came early and had widespread repercussions (which is not to say that collapses elsewhere followed, with domino-like determinism, from the initial collapse of Teotihuacan). The dating of this, like many Precolumbian

events, is contentious. There is clear evidence of violence at Teotihuacan: the ceremonial centre of the city was gutted, its buildings and
monuments deliberately vandalized. Some versions put this event at
c. A.D. 650, after which, they suggest, the city lived on, a mutilated but
still viable metropolis (most of the buildings, including the residential blocks, remained intact, and there is no evidence of widespread
massacre).[118] Others, perhaps more plausibly, see the violence and
the terminal collapse of the city (*qua* city) as coeval and occurring
around A.D. 750. According to this point of view, the destruction of
the ceremonial complex brought the destruction of the social bond
which held the urban community together. Population may not have
decamped instantly, but the ideological cohesion – and, perhaps, the
repressive means – which had integrated the mighty metropolis were
gone and certainly by the ninth century Teotihuacan had been reduced to a cluster of villages, its once teeming population cut – by
migration rather than massacre – to a few thousand.

Given the uncertainty of the evidence, explanations of this collapse must remain tentative. It seems clear that, like the late Classic
Maya cities, Teotihuacan lived in a climate of growing militarization
and, perhaps, secularization. Defensive walls become more apparent, and martial scenes – involving specialized warrior castes, such
as the jaguar knights – are more frequently depicted; archaeological finds, too, provide 'accumulating evidence of militarism', and
perhaps of human sacrifice as well.[119] Here, as at Tikal, collapse
was immediately preceded by a spate of building, concentrated
around the Citadel, which may have represented a last attempt
by a desperate elite to buttress its crumbling legitimacy. We may
infer that Teotihuacan's rulers faced serious challenges, some of
which were military and external. Certainly, the threat from the
north was growing: population was shifting south through the Gran
Chichimec, perhaps driven by the dessication of the American southwest; and in consequence the settled communities of the north, outposts of Teotihuacan's 'commercial' empire, had to reckon with military threats, as well as with ruptures in the network of exchange.
Some of these northern 'colonies' survived (e.g., La Quemada); some

[118] Davies, *The Toltecs*, pp. 83–4; Davies, *Ancient Kingdoms of Mexico*, p. 107.
[119] Pasztory, *Murals of Tepantitla*, p. 255; Sanders and Price, *Mesoamerica*, p. 167.

responded with a northward movement of population and influence; but others sent contingents south, perhaps to prey upon Teotihuacan itself.[120]

Old World analogies should be handled with care, but it may be that Teotihuacan, like Rome, suffered from 'barbarian' invasions, stimulated by climatic change and demographic pressures acting far afield. Certainly, the end of the Classic era in Mesoamerica, like the era of the late Roman Empire, was characterized by the retreat of the 'civilized' frontier and the irruption of newcomers from outside. These newcomers, however, were not necessarily shaggy savages; they may well have been 'civilized warrior-traders', displaced from the north by military or commercial misfortunes, such as those who came south during the eighth and ninth centuries and settled the city of Tula. Like Rome, therefore, Teotihuacan perhaps faced its greatest threat from 'barbarians' which it had itself helped nurture, train and 'civilize'.

However, the fall of the city – plausibly assumed to have occurred c. A.D. 750 – was not marked by extensive fighting or bloodshed, and the desecration wrought at the ceremonial centre appears to have been discriminating rather than wanton. This strongly suggests that internal actors and grievances were crucially involved. People knew what they were doing and set about it deliberately: 'to destroy Teotihuacan politically was itself a monumental undertaking, in some ways matching the energy that went into its building'.[121] This also suggests that the Teotihuacan state had already crumbled and was unable to mount effective resistance. To the extent that the events of the mid-eighth century represented a political revolution – and it is plausible that they did – Harrington's comment on the English revolution and civil war may be appropriate: 'the dissolution of this government caused the [civil] war, not the war the dissolution of this government'.[122] Whoever perpetrated the final act of destruction – outsiders, insiders or some unholy alliance of the two – the act itself revealed that the Teotihuacan state had reached the end of its long institutional life.

[120] Pailes and Whitecotton, 'The Greater Southwest', p. 116; Trumbold, 'A Summary', pp. 248ff.

[121] René Millon, 'Teotihuacan: City, State and Civilization', in Sabloff, *Supplement to the Handbook of Middle American Indians*, p. 238.

[122] Christopher Hill, *Reformation to Industrial Revolution* (Harmondsworth, 1969), p. 119.

The reasons for the city's debilitation may be hypothesized. Like other Mesoamerican metropolises, Teotihuacan eventually paid the price for its success. A burgeoning population had to be fed and housed; intensive farming and deforestation (wood supplied not only building material but also fuel for the city during chilly winters as well as for the mass production of building lime) led to soil erosion and declining agricultural productivity. Problems of subsistence were aggravated when a phase of benign, enhanced rainfall ended during the seventh century.[123] Although the population may not have exceeded the Valley's carrying capacity, demographic pressures would have meant heavier work-loads – or tribute payments – and possibly occasional dearths, which the severe constraints on transport would have compounded. It is clear that trade, too, suffered reverses. Northern mining outposts succumbed or were exhausted; commercial relations with the Maya zone were abruptly terminated in the later sixth century. Rising cities, like Xochicalco, in Morelos, may have interrupted Teotihuacan's old corridors of access to the south; even at Cholula, once a key ally or dependency, Teotihuacano influence fades around A.D. 700.[124]

To the extent that Teotihuacan's network of influence depended on non-coercive – that is, religious and 'commercial' – factors, these progressive disarticulations were crucial; and they reflected upon the power and legitimacy of the city's rulers. The final spate of buildings – notably the enhancement of the Citadel – may thus have represented a last-ditch attempt to assert the hegemony of the elite over a large, poor and querulous population. A violent dénouement, of internal origin, is therefore plausible: as commoners rose against rulers, as rulers fought among themselves or as the guardians of the ancient shrines themselves committed a deliberate act of ritual desecration before abandoning the city (as legend suggests that they did).[125] No less than outright revolt, such a theocratic abdication – possibly following Olmec precedent – would offer convincing proof

---

[123] Pasztory, *Murals of Tepantitla*, p. 19; Mark Nathan Cohen, *Health and the Rise of Civilization* (New Haven, 1989), pp. 126, 221, following Storey, notes unusually high and rising malnutrition and infant mortality at Teotihuacan: infant mortality averaged 31%, rising to 39% during the final phase of the metropolis.

[124] Millon, 'Teotihuacan', p. 235; Davies, *Ancient Kingdoms of Mexico*, p. 111.

[125] Davies, *The Toltecs*, pp. 92–3.

of the city's internal crisis, of the failure of hieratic authority, and of the dissolution of the social bond which – assuming coercion alone did not suffice – had held the community together through the centuries since its ancient sacralised foundation. Perhaps (recall again Rome) disaffected groups called on the 'barbarians' at the gates to aid them; or, perhaps, by stifling trade and encouraging militarism, the 'barbarians' simply contributed to the city's accumulating inner crisis.

Whatever the causes, the decline and fall of Teotihuacan sent reverberations throughout Middle America. Some centres – whose rise may have contributed to that decline – now, logically, entered upon a period of florescence, as Xochicalco did. Some erstwhile allies/outposts/dependencies survived, despite the metropolitan collapse: notably El Tajín and Xochicalco which, along with the upstart Tula (of which more anon), comprised the 'successor states' of the central highlands, competitors for hegemony in the wake of Teotihuacan's fall. Other participants in the Pax Teotihuacana, however, fell on hard times, their decline paralleling that of the great city itself. Monte Albán, we have noted, suffered a haemorrhage of power and population analogous to Teotihuacan's; by A.D. 900 most of the city was in ruins, and the Valley of Oaxaca, rent by the feuds of more than two dozen petty city-states, was vulnerable to outside invaders – first Mixtec, later Aztec. At Cholula, recent research suggests that the Great Pyramid and much of the city were abandoned during the eighth century; there follows a marked break in the ceramic sequence, indicating a shift of population and the arrival of new settlers – invaders? – who, in contrast to their civilized predecessors, made do with 'very coarse' artefacts.[126] Cholula's subsequent revival during the Postclassic era thus followed a process of immigration and cultural regression – or, we might say, a cultural *reculer pour mieux sauter* – a pattern which would be repeated elsewhere in the highlands during this turbulent age.

As this sequence suggests, the loss of the religio–mercantile integration and cultural sophistication which had defined the Teotihuacan era was matched by the rise of new, vigorous, belligerent

[126] Davies, *The Toltecs*, pp. 113–16.

polities. Balkanization, political competition, migration and invasion characterize this period which, in Wolf's phrase, saw 'the coming of the warriors'.[127] This political and cultural shift was neatly –
if belatedly and maybe apocryphally – symbolized by the progressive decline of the Zapotec theocracy of Mitla (Oaxaca), an 'island
in time' which preserved some of the old sacred ways through the
centuries of Postclassic militarism, until, around A.D. 1400, the last
hierarch surrendered to the spirit of the age and set up his son as
secular warlord of Zaachila.[128]

Nowhere was this shift clearer or more momentous than in the
southeastern lowlands of the Maya. Here, however, as might be expected, the sequence is less closely tied to the fortunes of Teotihuacan. The latter's influence – evident in pottery, architecture and stelae
inscriptions – appears to attenuate in the later sixth century, at least
a century before the presumed fall of the city. The curtailment of
Teotihuacan's influence coincides with – which is not to say that it
directly caused – a phase of political instability and cultural stagna-
tion, especially at Tikal.[129] But this proved a (hundred-year) hiatus,
not a terminal collapse. Indeed, a collapse would have been unlikely,
given the limited, selective nature of Teotihuacano influence in the
Maya region. The seventh century therefore witnessed the peak of
Classical Maya monumental achievement, at Tikal and elsewhere.

However, we should be careful of equating monumental exuber-
ance with sociopolitical vigour: large-scale building may indicate a
capacity for administrative organization and hence political power,
but it may also reflect the fears of an elite desperately concerned to
enhance its prestige and legitimacy. Such a hypothesis seems plausible for the eighth century when, as we have noted, signs of war, dynastic ambition and frenetic building all accumulate. And, towards
the end of the century, perhaps soon after Teotihuacan's own deba-
cle, the cities of the Classical Maya experienced their own mysterious
collective trauma. The last stelae at Bonampak dates to A.D. 771, at
Yaxchilan to 790, at Piedras Negras to 810. These, the states of the

---

127 Wolf, *Sons of the Shaking Earth*, ch. 6.
128 Whitecotton, *The Zapotecs*, pp. 129–30.
129 Tikal's sixth-century eclipse was linked to the rise of a local rival, Caracol, and to a more
    generalized 'regional crisis' (evidenced, for example, in a shift in ceramic styles): Schele and
    Friedel, *Forest of Kings*, pp. 164, 167–73, 212.

Usumacinta zone, were thus engulfed in crisis by the beginning of the ninth century. Tikal, in the heart of the central lowlands, followed soon after. Benque Viejo, the principal site of the Belize Valley, went into sudden decline around A.D. 830.[130] The impression, therefore, is of a common crisis, concentrated in the late eighth and early ninth centuries, impinging first on the western Maya regions. But specific experiences varied. Some centres witnessed upheaval – even associated with invasion – followed by renewed florescence: Seibal, for example, or the Puuc Maya cities of northern Yucatán, like Uxmal, which prospered throughout the 'time of troubles', albeit by virtue of breaking with the Classic Maya tradition and accepting new ways and rulers.[131]

It is clear that invasion played a major part in the ending of the old order. It was probably not coincidental that the Usumacinta cities, which guarded the southwestern gateway into the Maya region, were the first to fall. But 'invasion' begs many questions. It did not necessarily mean the sudden irruption of non-Maya 'foreigners', carriers of colonial rule; nor was it necessarily a simple military exercise. We should note that the endemic instability of the late Classic Maya involved recurrent war, subjugation and even migration within the Maya zone. Seibal, for example, suffered successive invasions: first, in the late eighth century, by a 'Mexicanized' Maya group (i.e., by Maya who had picked up some of the military techniques of highland states); then, by genuine outsiders, probably from the Tabasco region, during the ninth century. The first invasion directly contributed to local upheaval, the second fed upon it in parasitic fashion. The first reflected belligerent, indigenous power politics – compare, for example, the Peloponnesian War – the second, whereby external (though not wholly unknown) forces, militarily more effective even if culturally more backward, fell upon prostrate city-states, resembled the Macedonian onslaught. The analogy may be pushed further: invasion prompted a re-ordering and revival of Maya culture, at least

---

[130] Gordon Willey, 'Certain Aspects of the Late Classic to Postclassic Periods in the Belize Valley', and Richard Adams, 'Maya Collapse: Transformation and Termination in the Ceramic Sequence at Altar de Sacrificios', in Culbert, *Classic Maya Collapse*, pp. 105, 151; see also the useful map in Schele and Freidel, *Forest of Kings*, p. 381.

[131] Gordon Willey, 'The Postclassic of the Maya Lowlands: A Preliminary Overview', in Sabloff and Andrews, *Late Lowland Maya Civilization*, pp. 25, 27–9.

in the northern Maya zone, where the Puuc-Toltec cities flourished during the Postclassic: first at Uxmal, later at Chichén Itzá.

In the northern lowlands, therefore, the Postclassic was a period not of collapse and cultural disintegration – as it was farther south – but of conquest, fusion and revival: a Hellenistic sequence, we might say. The prevalent motifs – at Seibal, Uxmal and other Puuc sites – suggest that these invaders shared a common non-Maya, northern origin, evident in their features, clothes and weapons.[132] They also display a ceramic and architectural affinity with highland sites like Cholula and Xochicalco; while Chichén Itzá – to be considered later – is steeped in 'Toltec' culture. All display marked 'militarist' tendencies, consonant with the changing ethos of highland Mesoamerica. It is misleading, therefore, to talk of a Maya 'collapse' in this northern zone which, indeed, experienced a notable 'cultural upsurge' during the Postclassic.[133] The Maya may have suffered invasion and defeat, but the invaders grafted their government and culture on to Maya stock, which retained much of its cultural and all of its linguistic attributes. Just as China's northern invaders were recurrently Sinified, so Yucatán's were Mayanized; the same would occur with the even more alien Spaniards. The result, in the Postclassic, was a fusion of cultures and a sustained Mexicanized-Maya florescence.

Outright invasion formed part of a broader inter-state conflict, transmitted from the central highlands. The Classic Maya had, of course, fought and feuded with alacrity. But with the Mesoamerican 'time of troubles' (signalled, rather than initiated, by the fall of Teotihuacan and marked by a continental shift of population from northwest to southeast) the emergent, militarist groups of central Mexico embarked on a kind of *Drang nach Osten*, a thrust – military, migratory and mercantile – towards the Gulf and the eastern lowlands. Here, as ecological reasoning might lead one to expect, they encountered weaker, less integrated states, lacking strong hierarchical organizations (states which, indeed, may have been little

---

[132] Jeremy A. Sabloff, 'Continuity and Disruption during Terminal Late Classic Times at Seibal: Ceramic and Other Evidence', in Culbert, *Classic Maya Collapse*, p. 126. The supposed 'Mexicanization' of the northern Maya is a matter of considerable unresolved debate: see Jones, *Twin City Tales*, pp. 75ff.

[133] E. Wyllys Andrews, 'The Development of Maya Civilization after Abandonment of the Southern Cities', in Culbert, *Classic Maya Collapse*, pp. 243–5.

more than super-chiefdoms); these states, according to a somewhat extreme formulation, represented a 'developmental dead end'
and had either to adapt to the new, centralized, militarist mode or
else face likely extinction.[134] The highlanders' superiority, according
to this thesis, was not simply military but also organizational and
commercial: they controlled valuable trade goods which they could
deny lowland polities like Tikal. The latter were therefore pitched
into an unequal confrontation – political, commercial, military –
which they could not win. Softened up by commercial competition
and sanctions, their historic trade routes interdicted, they eventually succumbed to raiders, invaders or internal dissidents, or some
combination of the three.

    This association of war and trade – both of which flourished in
the Postclassic as never before – is suggestive. Both were activities
which the Maya states/chiefdoms were ill-suited to prosecute in competition with highland polities. It is striking that the processes of
expansion and conquest were one-way, running from northwest to
southeast. There were no countervailing Maya forays into Mexico
(unless we accept the doubtful hypothesis of a Maya foundation of
Tula).[135] In the associated realms of trade and warfare, it seems clear,
the highland states enjoyed distinct advantages, reasons for which
have been suggested. The consequences of this superiority, however,
should not be exaggerated. No doubt it helped undermine Tikal, the
great Maya entrepôt, and it made possible the overthrow of dynasties
in other Maya states. But, alone, it cannot explain the entire Classic
Maya collapse, especially where that collapse was demographic as
well as political and military. Mesoamerican invaders did not prac-
tise genocide; and the curtailment of trade, although it upset elite
patterns of consumption and control, could not have produced massive depopulation.

    Clearly, there was more to the Classic Maya collapse than simply
the pressure of better organized hierarchical states, bent on expansion. If this alone occurred, we must ask: why did the teeming Maya
not resist, as they later resisted the militarily superior Spaniards,
doggedly and to a degree successfully? Puleston has suggested that,

---

[134] Webb, 'The Peten Maya Decline', p. 403.
[135] Davies, *The Toltecs*, p. 204.

as a result of their cyclical view of history, embodied in the Long
Count, the Petén Maya may have been psychologically prepared for
recurrent social traumas, whose onset came every 256 years; this
in turn bred a fatalistic and self-fulfilling expectation of collapse
(which proved temporary in the sixth century, terminal in the ninth).
But this, apart from being an explanation designed 'to set a good
materialist's teeth on edge', cannot accommodate the regional patterns of collapse.[136] Why, above all, did invasion lead to the revival
of civilization in the northern lowlands (the Puuc-Toltec cities), yet
its annihilation in the south, the seat of the Classic Maya culture?
For here, typically at Tikal, military defeat was very likely a secondary factor, the consequence of preceding, internal crisis: 'Tikal
succumbs too easily and rapidly for the trigger to have been external, and foreign incursions in parts of the Maya lowlands seem ... to
be the result rather than the cause of the Maya collapse'.[137] Like its
metropolitan mentor, Teotihuacan, it seems, Tikal fell victim to internal pressures prior to external. And the notion of internal crisis
offers, too, a means to explain a crucial feature of the Classic collapse
in the Maya region: that it was a collapse not only of high culture
and high politics but also of grassroots population and settlement,
which neither military invasion nor collective fatalism could have accomplished. Several additional factors have therefore been scouted:
natural disasters (earthquakes, hurricanes, epidemics); ecological
problems (population pressure, soil erosion, dessication, falling
agricultural productivity); sociopolitical tensions (the weakening of
hierarchical – maybe theocratic – authority; outright peasant revolt).
And, of course, permutations of these factors are feasible.

   Given the catastrophic and complete nature of the collapse of
Maya civilization, in the Petén region and elsewhere,[138] an ecological starting point is appropriate. It seems unlikely that an erosion
of hierarchical authority – even if it was accompanied by war or

---

[136] New *katun* (Long Count) cycles began in A.D. 534 and 790, roughly coinciding with the eclipse
of Tikal and the Classic Maya collapse. The self-fulfilling prophecy theory was propounded
by the late Dennis Puleston: see Sharer, *The Ancient Maya*, p. 346; Willey's comment appears
in 'Dennis Edward Puleston (1940–78): Maya Archaeologist', in Flannery, *Maya Subsistence*,
pp. 11–12.

[137] Culbert, 'The Maya Downfall at Tikal', p. 92.

[138] Willey, 'The Postclassic of the Maya Lowlands', pp. 21–3, 26; Montmollin, *Archaeology of
Political Structure*, pp. 212, 216, 226, on the collapse in the Rosario Valley (Chiapas).

revolution or both – would have led to massive depopulation. In the Belize Valley, for instance, the hierarchs went – or were ousted – but the population remained, still engaged in traditional slash-and-burn farming. Such a pattern – decapitation rather than total dismemberment – might be expected if social conflict alone were to blame, if, that is, peasants rose up against the increasing – and perhaps the increasingly 'irrational' – burdens laid upon them by a priestly caste whose progressive withdrawal into remote, exalted recesses, physical and metaphorical, eroded their legitimacy and provoked rebellion. Such a process – for which there is some evidence[139] – would produce reversion to a more egalitarian, 'flat' social hierarchy, characterized by loose chiefdoms and lineage systems, in place of the previous theocratic city-states. Sociopolitical decapitation, however, should not have led to drastic depopulation. For, although the Maya elite possessed certain managerial functions, such that their overthrow could have detrimentally affected agricultural production (especially intensive irrigated or integrated production), these functions were scarcely so great as to be fundamental to collective social survival. On the contrary, the Maya have throughout history shown great tenacity in what Farriss calls their 'struggle for collective survival,' even in default of developed states and hierarchies; the very ecological base, which, we have noted, militated against state formation, precisely made stateless social survival feasible. Still less would the interruption of trade have threatened the basic existence of the Maya peasantry, as it may have done their ruling elites. Explanations for an infrastructural crisis should therefore be sought in the infrastructure itself, certainly as regards the central lowlands as a whole. A highly urbanized 'super-site' like Tikal may have been exceptional in its degree of elite-managed economic integration, hence in its vulnerability to elite collapse; but, then, Tikal *was* in many respects exceptional. Elsewhere, the causes of collapse must be located within the economic and demographic bases of Maya society.

Ecological evidence suggests that, with the rapid population growth and settlement of the Classic era, at least parts of the Petén must have approached their carrying capacity. The very anomalous character of the Petén Maya civilization – that is, its creation of a

---

[139] Wolf, *Sons of the Shaking Earth*, pp. 104, 106; Sharer, *The Ancient Maya*, p. 345.

high culture and dense population in a humid, forested zone, dependent on swidden agriculture – now became perilously apparent. Soil erosion would have been inevitable, though insidious: it would not have taken the highland form of dramatic flash floods, which people could readily perceive and, to an extent, counter with canals and terracing; rather, it would have gradually leached the forest soils, lessening their ability to support a swelling population.[140] The resulting demographic pressure would have encouraged a switch from land-intensive to labour-intensive cultivation, thus a shift down the continuum which leads from extensive forest exploitation through bush and grass fallowing to intensive permanent cultivation. Such a shift required greater inputs of labour relative to production; it encouraged peasant households to have more, potentially productive, children; and it arguably added to peasant burdens and discontents. For, under 'Neolithic' circumstances, when metal tools (and, in this case, draught animals) were lacking, such a basic, even if incremental, change in production methods involved significant added drudgery – as fields now had to be cleared and kept clear without relying on the old, easier slash-and-burn techniques. And intensive cultivation compounded the problems of soil erosion. However, intensive cultivation did not necessarily offer an escape from subsistence crisis. During the late Classic, it seems, the central Maya zone experienced a progressive climatic dessication which had the effect of drying out the shallow lakes – today's swampy *bajos* – upon which the Petén Maya depended for water and for intensive *chinampa*-style cultivation.[141]

Thus, both land and labour suffered diminishing returns. The Petén population grew (its growth may have been stimulated by these trends, in a manner analogous to the population and poverty equation of the modern world), but it grew at the cost of harder work, lower returns and probable privation. Burial remains show that the late Classic Maya – especially the peasantry – were smaller

---

[140] Sanders, 'Cultural Ecology', pp. 332–41. Needless to say, this explodes the notion of the Classic Maya as living at one with nature in a benign, homeostatic relationship; if they were not 'flower children', no more were they Green activists *avant la lettre*.

[141] Peter D. Harrison, 'The Rise of the *Bajos* and the Fall of the Maya', in Hammond, *Social Process*, pp. 470–508.

(they suffered, according to the jargon, 'stature repression'),[142] and they were probably poorer and sicker. Skeletal evidence also makes clear that deprivation and malnutrition were, as might be expected, unequally shared, with rural populations suffering more than those resident at major ceremonial centres. It is entirely plausible that simmering discontent built up, leading to outright revolt or – perhaps more likely – to sizeable out-migration (the African resort of resistance by flight, which is more efficacious and less risky than frontal assaults on the citadels of oppressive power). And, given their relative openness and homogeneity, the Maya lowlands were eminently suitable for such out-migration, following the ancient practices of community fissure, decampment and resettlement – practices which ideologically bankrupt elites were powerless to contain. Migration, however, is hard to prove empirically. Some argue for a major shift of population to the southwestern highlands, though the evidence is scant; it has also been suggested that the vigorous Puuc cities of northern Yucatán developed by acquiring – whether by force or natural attraction – migrants from the declining Petén.

Even if the migration hypothesis is valid, as it may well be, it cannot fully explain the scale of the depopulation. One would expect migration to fall off as a new equilibrium was established appreciably below the region's carrying capacity; instead, the Petén appears to have become a virtual wilderness, with once flourishing centres like Tikal reduced to ghost-towns, frequented only by a handful of squatters, looters or nostalgic cultists. Additional hypotheses which might account for this phenomenon are necessarily inferential. Of the various 'natural' explanations, hurricanes and earthquakes are unconvincing (neither would eliminate whole populations). Disease – certainly of humans, possibly of crops – is much more plausible. It is well known that pre-industrial societies can fall victim to a Malthusian syndrome: demographic growth leading to malnutrition, vulnerability to disease and consequently major epidemics.[143] In the

---

[142] Sanders, 'Cultural Ecology', p. 345. By modern, 'Western' standards, the Classic Maya were short to begin with: Ah-Cacaw, ruler of Tikal, was – at 167 cm (5 ft. 6 in.) – 'a veritable giant' among his people: Schele and Freidel, *Forest of Kings*, p. 195. The same authors, p. 380, note a differential of 10 cm between elite and subjects.

[143] Emmanuel Le Roy Ladurie, *The Peasants of Languedoc* (Urbana, 1974). Note also the interesting thesis of Mary Kilbourne Matossian, *Poisons of the Past: Molds, Epidemics and History*

case of the Petén Maya, the dense population and resulting malnutrition can be evidenced; signs of disease are also apparent, though they cannot be measured over time. A careful analysis concludes that 'important health problems existed' and that 'a chronic precarious health status' could have contributed to the Maya collapse.[144]

The nature of the hypothetical epidemic cannot be known: malaria, we have noted, was absent (though not, perhaps, yellow fever); and there is clear evidence of yaws, a global infection related to syphilis and among the oldest-known of human diseases.[145] Certainly, forms of infestation would have flourished, and would have been easily transmitted, in the hot, humid conditions of the Petén; and it seems rash to suppose that, prior to the arrival of the Spaniards (who, to be sure, brought a host of fresh diseases), the Maya lived in a state of splendid, disease-free isolation. A particularly plausible hypothesis links disease and dessication: as the lakes of the Petén turned into swampy morasses, flies and mosquitoes, once the prey of fish, flourished with impunity, acting as the vector of contagious disease. The censers which proliferated in the Postclassic period, sending their pungent fumes into the tropical air, may have served not only to honour the gods but also to repel insects.[146] Thus, if a virulent infection (such as yellow fever) struck a dense, possibly underfed, poorly resistant population, its effects could have been catastrophic – to the extent that, as in parallel cases, the population would fall beyond a point of no return. In such circumstances, the victims could include not only the human population but also the bacteria or viruses themselves, which would pay for their excessive virulence and their failure to establish a stable, endemic relationship with their human hosts by suffering extinction. The impact of such a rogue infection would therefore be sudden but also chronologically and regionally confined (it would meet the objections of

---

(New Haven, 1989), that ergotism – food poisoning derived from fungal infections of grain – may have been (co-)responsible for major epidemics and even 'mass psychoses' in history. Maize blight has been mentioned as a possible cause of the Maya collapse: Kent V. Flannery, 'Preface', in Flannery, *Maya Subsistence*, p. xxi, citing Brewbaker.

144 F. P. Saul, 'Disease in the Maya Area: The Precolumbian Evidence', in Culbert, *Classic Maya Collapse*, p. 323.

145 William McNeill, *Plagues and People* (Oxford, 1977), p. 177. Cohen, *Health and Civilization*, p. 37, raises the possibility that 'early primitive human groups may have suffered from some diseases that no longer occur in human populations'.

146 Harrison, 'The Rise of the *Bajos*', p. 489.

those who point out that the presumed disease did not devastate northern Yucatán – where, of course, ecological conditions differ significantly).[147] And such rogue infections – one-off bacterial or viral onslaughts – are not unknown in history.[148]

Neither archaeological nor, of course, written sources can confirm or disprove this hypothesis. Disease is not easily detected and measured by archaeological methods, and even increased mortality – a mortality which necessarily escapes the confines of ceremonial burial – may be elusive. The hypothesis therefore remains largely inferential. Interestingly, the earliest of the three major recorded epidemics which affected Mesoamerica has been dated at c. A.D. 780, just at the threshhold of the Classic Maya collapse.[149] This epidemic struck the central highlands. But, given the frequent historical association between war, migration and epidemics (the Mongol invasions offer the classic example), it is tempting to speculate that the time of troubles which followed the fall of Teotihuacan encouraged the spread of new infections and that the Petén Maya, hitherto relatively isolated, densely concentrated in a hot, humid environment and suffering declining material conditions, were uniquely vulnerable. Given that the hypertrophy of the Classic Maya state, with its greedy consumption of limited resources, also represented an outstanding form of what McNeill has imaginatively termed 'macroparasitism',[150] it is further tempting to conclude that the Petén Maya fell victims to a double parasitic attack: that of 'macroparasitic' overlords and of microparasitic organisms. By their combined virulence, they killed off the bodies on which they depended; thus, host and parasite, lord, peasant and protozoa, all perished together.

---

[147] Andrews, 'The Development of Maya Civilization', pp. 261–2.

[148] McNeill, *Plagues and Peoples*, pp. 52–3. Paul Slack makes the point that 'if a violent epidemic occurs only once, it produces a single shock which may be quickly forgotten': 'Introduction' in Terence Ranger and Paul Slack, *Epidemics and Ideas: Essays on the Historical Perception of Pestilence* (Cambridge, 1992), p. 7.

[149] Sherburne F. Cook, 'The Incidence and Significance of Disease among the Aztecs and Related Tribes', *Hispanic American Historical Review*, 26 (1946), pp. 320–5.

[150] McNeill, *Plagues and People*, pp. 54ff.

THREE. The Postclassic Era

The time of troubles which supervened with the decline and fall of Teotihuacan affected most of Mesoamerica. It was characterized by the fall of old polities; by the movement of population, especially from north to south; and by the introduction of new sociopolitical and aesthetic motifs, suggestive of a more harsh and martial culture: sacrifice and cannibalism; warrior cults, ballcourts and skullracks; perhaps aggressive new religious movements. If a single cause for this complex cultural shift is to be identified, it would be the influence of the immigrant peoples who, having fought and traded in the hostile environment of north ern Mexico, embarked on a progressive move to the south, as Teotihuacan (once their commercial mentor) declined and collapsed. Within these fortified quasi-colonial outposts (Alta Vista and La Quemada would be the prime examples) developed a people who were accustomed to war, trade and a harsh, even Darwinian, social ethic.[1] Their penetration of central Mexico, coming at a time of Balkanization and conflict, helped mould a new culture which displayed less theocratic, more martial, characteristics. As in the Old World, marcher lords proved capable of exercising

---

[1] Wolf, *Sons of the Shaking Earth*, ch. 6. The presumed shift from ('theocratic') Classic to ('militarist') Postclassic is open to objections and qualifications (note Wolf's own misgivings, *Sons of the Shaking Earth*, p. 270); however, even if the *nature* of the shift is debated, the *fact* of a shift remains; as against this view, some have chosen to stress the timeless stasis – or 'structural unity' – of Mesoamerican civilization, from the Olmecs to the Aztecs: see Sanders and Price, *Mesoamerica*, p. 126, citing Michael Coe.

a powerful influence over the more populous sedentary societies with whom they coexisted.

I. The Toltecs

The most celebrated and important of these early interlopers were the Toltecs, whose 'empire' succeeded (after a decent interval) the hegemony of Teotihuacan in central Mexico and, in many respects, prefigured that of the later Aztecs. Within this triple succession of highland empires, however, the Toltec empire is the most obscure. The Toltecs, Renfrew observes, are 'a shadowy people'.[2] Recent research, combining archaeological excavations and patient analysis of written records, has alleviated some of this obscurity and dispelled some hoary myths.[3] But the picture remains far from clear, and the historian who contemplates the Toltec empire is tempted to recall Voltaire's famous dismissal of the Holy Roman Empire – 'that agglomeration which was neither holy, nor Roman, nor an empire'. For the Toltecs, too, were heavily mythologized, above all by those accomplished mythologizers, the Aztecs. In Aztec eyes, the Toltecs were numinous forebears: warriors, empire-builders, subtle craftsmen of magic and material artefacts, the offspring of gods and the fortunate inhabitants of a fabulous city – Tollan (Tula), the 'Place of Reeds'. For historians, the Toltecs provide a connecting link between the two great metropolis-empires of Teotihuacan and Tenochtitlán; and the Toltec empire offers an organizing concept with which to order the fundamentally disorderly period of the early Postclassic. Aztecs and historians alike may well have joined in imaginative conspiracy; as one expert has observed, also paraphrasing Voltaire, 'if no Toltec empire had existed . . . the Aztecs would have perforce invented it'.[4] And at least one heretical scholar (long ago) pronounced the Toltec empire a pure figment.[5]

---

[2] Colin Renfrew, 'General Editor's Foreward', in Diehl, *Tula*, p. 7.

[3] Diehl, *Tula*, ch. 3; Davies, *The Toltecs*; Katz, *Ancient American Civilizations*, pp. 123–4; Jones, *Twin City Tales*, pp. 311–15.

[4] Davies, *The Toltecs*, p. 344.

[5] Davies, *The Toltecs*, p. 29, citing Daniel Brinton (1887).

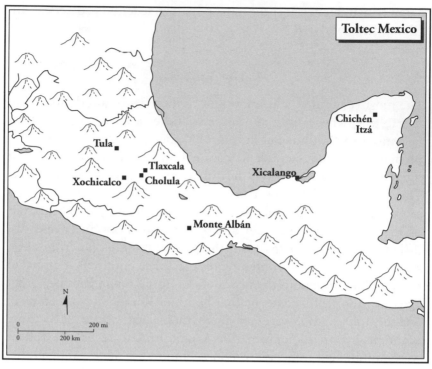

Map 4

Certainly, compared to Teotihuacan and Tenochtitlán, the Toltec metropolis of Tula (now generally accepted as Tula, Hidalgo) was a small city of recent origin. Though the site had known human habitation since before the time of Christ, the city itself dated from the eighth century and, at its peak between A.D. 950 and 1150, its population did not exceed forty thousand.[6] It was therefore about one sixth the size of Teotihuacan and perhaps only a tenth that of Tenochtitlán. Like the former – but unlike the latter – Tula enjoyed a marked local primacy: it was jostled by no neighbouring cities; and, in the absence of any communities above the level of villages, it is likely that the total population of the Tula region (the heartland upon which the Toltecs could draw directly for labour and staple goods) was no more than double that of the city itself. While the Aztecs commanded two million in the Valley of Mexico, the Toltecs controlled

[6]   Diehl, *Tula*, pp. 15, 60, 106.

perhaps eighty thousand in their more constricted ecological niche at the confluence of the Tula and Rosas Rivers.

Though dwarfed by the giant metropolises of Teotihuacan and Tenochtitlán, Tula enjoyed brisk population growth through the ninth century. Substantial immigration boosted numbers, and a system of intensive agriculture, irrigation and terraces helped maintain them.[7] A partially hydraulic explanation of Toltec state-building is therefore plausible – with the recurrent caveats that state-formation preceded irrigation (not vice versa) and that while irrigation may have *facilitated* the formation of a centralized, hierarchical polity, it did not ineluctably require it. Smaller than Teotihuacan, Tula also enjoyed a briefer floruit. Within two hundred years of achieving greatness it entered upon its terminal crisis; Tula's lifespan was therefore no more than a third of Teotihuacan's.

The scope of Tula's imperial sway, too, should not be exaggerated. Davies, relying on ethnohistorical sources (and rightly suspicious of the archaeological technique which 'converts potsherds into people' and aesthetic parallels into relations of political sub- and superordination), suggests that Tula's empire embraced the Valleys of Mexico, Puebla and Morelos, to the south, as well as the plains of Hidalgo to the east: an area of some 12,000 square miles (the size of, say, Belgium), which cannot compare with the later Aztec empire's 140,000 square miles (equalling Finland or Japan).[8] Diehl, however, relying more on archaeological evidence and inference, excludes the Valley of Mexico from his 'minimally defined' Toltec empire but includes the centre-west region of the Bajío, stretching as far as Zinapécuaro (Michoacan) to the west and La Quemada (Zacatecas) to the north. Yet, the same author readily admits, such boundaries are 'completely conjectural'.[9] Zinapécuaro and La Quemada were major centres of Toltec trade, the first supplying obsidian, the second turquoise. It is unclear though whether these were direct dependencies, perhaps garrisoned by Toltec troops, or merely trading partners.[10] Even if they were dependencies, it is inconceivable that

---

[7] Diehl, *Tula*, p. 41.

[8] Davies, *Ancient Kingdoms of Mexico*, pp. 144, 220.

[9] Richard A. Diehl, 'Tula, Hidalgo', in Sabloff, *Supplement to the Handbook of Middle American Indians*, pp. 290–1.

[10] Diehl, *Tula*, p. 111.

they represented outposts of an integral territorial empire. The later, greater, Aztec empire had its own gaping holes (Tlaxcala, Yopitzingo and Tototepec, as well as the Isthmian belt separating conquered Soconusco from the imperial heartland); in earlier times, too, Teotihuacan and its putative colony Kaminaljuyú were never linked by unbroken Teotihuacano domains. Tula, much smaller than either of these metropolises, can hardly have exercised a more perfect supremacy. Very likely, Tula's political and military domination was patchy and variable, mediated, in some cases, through junior allies like Otumba and Culhuacán (both within 60 miles of Tula), offset, in other cases, by powerful rivals such as Cholula, in the Valley of Puebla, Xochicalco, in Morelos, and the emergent Tarascan state centred on Tzintzuntzan to the west.

Furthermore, apart from its modest size and manpower, Tula does not seem to have enjoyed a 'commercial' or ideological hegemony comparable to Teotihuacan's. True, obsidian was again a key item of trade, produced close by at Pachuca (within Tula's immediate orbit), processed at and distributed from Tula itself. Tula also produced ceramics in bulk; but the city's own demand ran to nearly a million items a year. The quality of production was mediocre, and there is little archaeological evidence of widespread exports; indeed, the record suggests 'relative material poverty' (e.g., jade artefacts are wholly missing); and, although some experts, drawing upon Aztec analogies, suggest that Tula possessed a vigorous merchant class, excavations have failed to reveal a major market.[11] Even in its immediate hinterland, Tula failed to establish a mercantile monopoly comparable to Teotihuacan's.[12] Davies is surely right to conclude, therefore, that Tula's mercantile role was 'rather restricted' and that the Toltec city – and putative empire – cannot compare with either Teotihuacan or Tenochtitlán in economic performance.[13] Aztec tales of Toltec material splendour would appear to be, like many other Aztec tales, mythical inflations.

---

[11] Diehl, *Tula*, pp. 67, 113–14; Blanton *et al.*, *Ancient Mesoamerica*, p. 150; Diehl, 'Tula, Hidalgo', pp. 288–9; Davies, *The Toltecs*, p. 278.

[12] That is to say, it failed to develop a 'dendritic' market system comparable to Teotihuacan's: Santley, Kerley and Kneebone, 'Obsidian working', pp. 129–30.

[13] Davies, *The Toltecs*, pp. 281–4.

Rather clearer and less contentious is Tula's stark military – even sanguinary – ethos, evident in the city's ample skullracks, in the predatory beasts and sacrificial motifs which characterize its stone reliefs and in its serried ranks of *atlantes*, the massive, armoured, grim-faced stone warriors of Tula.[14] Thus, as Wolf remarks, the Toltec era signalled the 'coming of the warriors', not because warriors were unknown in the preceding Classic age, but because now endemic warfare and warrior cults seem to predominate as never before in Mesoamerica. Possibly, militarism flourished in combination with a new aggressive religious cult (or cults). Certainly, images of the god Quetzalcóatl (the feathered serpent) and his intimate enemy Tezcatlipoca (the smoking mirror) now proliferate, displacing – or, sometimes, absorbing – the once pervasive Tlaloc. Just as the militarization of Mesoamerica derived in part from the irruption of northern peoples, inured to a harsh, warlike existence in the arid plains and mountains of the north, so, too, the new cults displayed a distinctly northern flavour and represented the triumph of belligerent sky gods over the more placid terrestrial deities of central Mexico. In the eleventh century, for example, the cult of Quetzalcóatl flourished in the far north, at Casas Grandes (Chihuahua) and among the Anasazi of (present-day) New Mexico.[15]

True, notions of religious exclusivism and proselytization were less rooted in Mesoamerican culture than they were, say, in medieval European or Islamic cultures. In Mesoamerica, sundry gods and cults coexisted, fused, split and evolved in a manner more reminiscent of the Roman Empire. However, if Roman cults 'were all considered by the people as equally true; by the philosopher as equally false; and by the magistrate as equally useful',[16] such tolerant heterodoxy was alien to Mesoamerican religion, which combined a complex, shifting pantheon with immensely powerful beliefs and rituals. Mesoamerican religion embodied the intricacy of polytheism and

---

[14] Diehl, *Tula*, pp. 65–7.

[15] Wolf, *Sons of the Shaking Earth*, pp. 102, 111–17; Pailes and Whitecotton, 'The Greater Southwest', pp. 116–17. Tula also appears to have pioneered the military orders that would culminate in the eagle and jaguar knights of the Aztec empire: Diehl, *Tula*, p. 63. Ross Hassig, *War and Society in Ancient Mesoamerica* (Berkeley, 1992), p. 84, traces the lineage to Teotihuacan.

[16] Edward Gibbon, *The Decline and Fall of the Roman Empire* (London, 1966; first pubd. in Everyman, 1910), vol. 1, ch. 2, p. 29.

the militancy of monotheism. The Postclassic era also witnessed an intimate union of religion and politics. Later Aztec expansion depended on a reinforcing religious ideology, linked to sacrifice and to military power; and it is entirely plausible – if difficult to prove – that Toltec expansion similarly harnessed new gods and rituals to militarist *Realpolitik*. Thus, religion and politics still cohered, as they had during the Classic age (and the notion that the Toltec state represented a halfway point in a linear progress from Classic theocracy to late Postclassic secularism seems excessively neat). But the nature of this ancient union changed. The archaeological record suggests that the palace now usurped the temple's previous pre-eminence; military motifs outnumber religious ones; military castes (such as the eagle and jaguar knights) rival priestly elites. By implication, religion now underwrote a military and imperial state, rather than offering the fundamental *raison d'être* of social cohesion as (we have tentatively argued) it did during the Classic era. The indissoluble union of government and religion remained – a central feature of Mesoamerican culture (thus there could be no investiture contest, as in medieval Europe, no Henrician reformation, as in sixteenth-century England). But with the climacteric which ended the Classic era, with the fall of old empires and the rise of new, northern-influenced polities, that union underwent a decisive shift and ushered in a period of endemic military conflict and conquest. As Demarest observes, the Toltec state 'was to become the archetypal Postclassic state', based on a quasi-Darwinian ideology of militarism and sacrifice.[17]

The role of religious ideology, however, was not wholly autonomous or solely determinant. Rather, it reponded to changed sociopolitical circumstances. Crucial to any understanding of Tula's rise and fall is its geopolitical location. It lay some 50 miles north of the central Valley of Mexico, in territory that, compared to the latter, was more arid, less hospitable. Of all Mesoamerica's major centres (Teotihuacan, Tenochtitlán, Monte Albán, the Maya cities of the southeast) Tula was the most peripheral, the one closest to the

---

[17] Demarest, 'Overview: Mesoamerican Human Sacrifice in Evolutionary Perspective', pp. 231–2. Jones, *Twin City Tales*, pp. 328, 332, 360, similarly stresses the novelty and radicalism of Toltec art and architecture which, anticipating Aztec practice, combined 'glitz and gore' and proclaimed a 'radically new conception of sovereignty' premised on *force majeure*, rather than on religious sanction or dynastic legitimacy.

raw Chichimec frontier. This frontier, we have noted, was in full retreat as Teotihuacan declined and fell; Chichimec peoples, possessed
of varying degress of 'civilization', were moving south, the first mover
in this great *Völkerwanderung* being the progressive dessication of
northern Mexico and the American southwest.[18] Over time, Tula was
both creature and victim of this protracted trend. The decisive settlement which propelled Tula to greatness appears to have involved
(at least) two migrant groups. One, a typically martial people of
northern origins (described as the Tolteca-Chichimeca), originated
from distant outposts of settlement established in the Zacatecas-
Durango region during the Pax Teotihuacana. The city of Alta Vista
(Zacatecas), a Teotihuacan trading partner (or colony), which was
finally abandoned around A.D. 900, evinces many Toltecoid characteristics (skullracks, sacrifice, cannibalism, colonnaded halls), all suggestive of a harsh, military society.[19] We do not know whether a
declining Alta Vista sent its migrants south to Tula; and, historians
stress, such migration is best seen as a continual flow – a leaching
of population from north to south – rather than as a distinct event, a
kind of Mesoamerican Great Trek. Nevertheless, the northern provenance of many of Tula's settlers is both clear and significant. The
city also maintained close ties to the Bajío, the centre-west region
of Mexico, jammed between the civilized centre and the barbarous
north. Hitherto marginal to Mesoamerican evolution, the Bajío supplied Tula with obsidian, ceramics and, perhaps, migrants; Diehl also
includes the region within the putative Toltec empire.[20]

The second group of settlers, in contrast, derived from the Gulf
region, specifically the great Mesoamerican crossroads of southern
Veracruz-Tabasco, where they had perhaps arrived first as refugees
from the declining Teotihuacan. These people, the Nonoalca,
less numerous than the Tolteca-Chichimeca, were carriers of the

---

[18] Pedro Armillas, 'The Arid Frontier of Mexican Civilization', *Transactions of the New York
Academy of Sciences*, n.s. 3 (1969), pp. 697–704. Diehl argues that the migrations were incremental rather than dramatic; we should think in terms of the 'composite arrivals of countless
small groups': *Tula*, p. 49. In this, the Mesoamerican *Völkerwanderung* resembled the second
wave of Europe's 'barbarian invasions': those which involved 'a slow, piece-meal [Frankish]
advance in Gaul, an obscure plethora of landings in England, and a gradual series of shifts
southwards into Italy', as compared to the decisive military expeditions of the early fourth
century: Perry Anderson, *Passages from Antiquity to Feudalism* (London, 1978), pp. 112, 121.

[19] Diehl, *Tula*, pp. 152–3.

[20] Diehl, *Tula*, p. 119; Diehl, 'Tula, Hidalgo', pp. 279, 290.

Mesoamerican Great Tradition: as the Toltec *Kulturvolk* they imparted old values to the new migrants from the north, rather as
the Latin and Greek churches 'civilized' the barbarian invaders of
Dark Ages Europe.[21] The Nonoalcas supplied the brains, the Tolteca-
Chichimeca the brawn (literally, it seems, since skeletal evidence
suggests that these northern migrants were physically bigger). This
combination proved particularly effective during the time of troubles of the early Postclassic. The Chichimeca settlers (rough-hewn
warriors, not nomadic savages) were progressively 'civilized' (we will
note later parallels in the Valley of Mexico); trade and artisanry, public works and religious ritual flourished. Meanwhile, there were further infusions of northern stock, which in turn were reciprocated
by the diffusion of Toltec cultural influence to the north and west,
evident in archaeological finds in Zacatecas, on the Pacific coast
at Guasave (Sinaloa), at Casas Grandes (Chihuahua), and among
the Anasazi of the American southwest.[22] This influence should not
be seen as a one-way transmission, from Tula to the north, however. Tula was itself the product of a northern culture, nurtured in
colonial outposts like Alta Vista and La Quemada. Initially stimulated by the growth of Teotihuacan – and the great city's demand
for valuable minerals – these outposts outlived their mentor, acting as commercial and cultural links along the long corridor from
central Mexico to the American southwest. La Quemada, a fortified
'castle-town' in Zacatecas, may have been a Toltec creation, which
served to transmit turquoise from the far north to its imperial master;[23] other settlements probably enjoyed less formal relations with
the southern city. Either way, Tula's hegemony helped knit together
a loose archipelago of communities, stretching through the Bajío
and Zacatecas to Chihuahua and New Mexico. This was no unitary
empire, but a loose diaspora, characterized by a degree of cultural
kinship and by elusive patterns of sub- and superordination.

In many repects, therefore, Tula's strength and (relatively) brief
pre-eminence were military in origin (not commercial or religious),
and they depended on the successful – but risky – incorporation

---

[21] Davies, *The Toltecs*, p. 167.
[22] Diehl, *Tula*, pp. 154–7.
[23] See the discussion in Trumbold, 'A Summary of the Archaeology in the La Quemada Region',
pp. 258–63.

of newly arrived 'barbarians' into Mesoamerican civilization. The Nonoalcas offered high culture and thus a certain political legitimacy, the Tolteca-Chichimecas brought military prowess and useful connections to their northern cousins. Tula's location, on the northern borders of civilized Mesoamerica, exemplified this syncretizing function. Tula thus played a role analogous to that of the Danubian provinces of the late Roman Empire: at once the shield of the empire, the cradle of emperors and the portal through which successive barbarian peoples entered the imperial heartland.

The creation of military prowess and conquest, the Toltec empire was vulnerable to the vicissitudes of military fortune; politically, the Toltecs lived and died by the sword. It is in this light that the famous Toltec 'invasion' of Yucatán should be considered. Sources both written and archaeological reveal the intimate relationship – the 'uncanny parallels' – which linked Tula and the northern Yucatán city of Chichén Itzá.[24] Here, we are no longer talking about a diffuse 'influence'. The two sites display similar architectural styles, similar military and animal motifs (notably, jaguars and feathered serpents), the distinctive recumbent Chac Mool figures (perhaps altars dedicated to Tlaloc), almost identical ballcourts, the same sombre skullracks and *atlantes*. How did this close kinship arise? Did the Toltecs conquer Chichén and create a southern dependency (compare Teotihuacan's 'colony' of Kaminaljuyú)? Or did a resurgent Yucatán inspire Tula's aesthetics and politics, as Kubler has suggested?[25] Or was the relationship a more complex one of mutual influence, possibly attributable to shared origins?

In general, it seems likely that population and influence again followed the traditional Mesoamerican route from northwest to southeast and that Yucatán was recipient rather than donor, conquered rather than conqueror. On the other hand, the two cities flourished contemporaneously, roughly in the two centuries after A.D. 950, and, although the argument that Chichén, being the greater (in cultural

---

[24] Davies, *Ancient Kingdoms of Mexico*, p. 149; Jones, *Twin City Tales*, p. 3.

[25] Davies, *Ancient Kingdoms of Mexico*, pp. 152–3; Kubler is cited by Jones, *Twin City Tales*, p. 65, which forms part of a lively discussion of contrasting interpretations – or, as she puts it, p. 75, 'this seemingly endless swamp of misconceptions, corrections and exasperations'. Clearly, where experts are in such disagreement, the synthetic historian can do little but tread carefully and intuitively.

and architectural terms), must have been the first mover, is fundamentally suspect, it need not follow that the polar opposite is true and that the close parallels derive from direct Toltec conquest. Why, for example, would Tula seek such distant conquests?

Nigel Davies offers a fuller and generally convincing explanation, which involves, first, the notion of shared origins and, second, the (common) thesis of a two-fold process of conquest in northern Yucatán. According to Davies, Tula and Chichén owed their common culture to a shared lineage, which derived from the culturally fecund region of the Gulf coast where the Olmec had once flourished. From here, the Nonoalca migrated to Tula, bringing a sophisticated culture derivative of Teotihuacan. From here, too, migrants moved east into the Maya zone, as the Classic era ended amid war and catastrophe. These eastward migrants, the Putún, or Itzá, brought to Yucatán a new elite and a new elite culture, redolent of the highlands and characterized by a martial spirit, military motifs, the cult of the feathered serpent and an aesthetic markedly different from that of the local Maya. The Putún/Itzá came to control the coastal trade of Yucatán and established their capital at Chichén Itzá, 'at the rim of the well of the Itzá'.[26] Although the Itzá spoke Maya, their 'dress, weapons, religion, architecture and economic acitivities all reflected considerable acculturation to central Mexican norms'.[27] In particular, they probably possessed a superior politico-military organization, which facilitated their conquest of the peninsula, as well as superior weaponry, including the famous *atlatl*, or spear-thrower (this superiority would have been all the more marked if, as Von Daniken assures us, the *atlatl* was in fact an extraterrestrial laser gun).[28]

The original Itzá established themselves at Chichén in the early tenth century. Later in the same century (987 is the preferred but

[26] The Putún/Itzá were responsible for 'old' Chichén, the southern part of the dual site, which displays a syncretic Puuc Maya/Toltec character. Recent research has tended to stress the Maya element and to question J. Eric S. Thompson's bold thesis of a far-flung and enduring Putún Maya coastal and commercial empire: Jones, *Twin City Tales*, pp. 71–4; Davies, *The Toltecs*, p. 187; and Sharer, *The Ancient Maya*, pp. 348–9, and, for a full description of the site, pp. 388–402.

[27] Davies, *The Toltecs*, pp. 213–14.

[28] Davies, *The Toltecs*, p. 223; however, consonant with their reinterpretation of the Classic Maya as secular, ruthless and warlike, Schele and Freidel, *A Forest of Kings*, p. 152, see highland military technology, incluing the *atlatl*, entering the Maya region centuries earlier.

highly speculative date) a second wave of conquerors arrived, led –
so the Books of the Chilam Balam record – by Kukulkán, the Maya
name for Quetzalcóatl. These were assuredly Toltecs: 'everything
about them suggests direct ties with the Tula Toltecs'.[29] A Toltec elite
was thus grafted on to existing Maya stock, and the martial state
which they established became the centre of a regional empire which
dominated northern Yucatán for some two hundred years (c. A.D.
1000–1200) before it, in turn, was overthrown and replaced by the
Mayapán confederacy in the early thirteenth century. The defeated
Itzá fled inland, establishing an independent realm at Tayasal, in
northern Guatemala, where they resisted first Maya, then Spanish
attacks until the end of the seventeenth century.[30]

The Itzá people left a solid memento of their achievements at
Chichén, from which it may be inferred that their regime wrought a
political transformation in Yucatán. The cloistered precincts of the
Classic Maya theocracy gave way to spacious plazas and ballcourts,
designed to accommodate, impress and (bearing in mind the military motifs and sacrificial practices) intimidate a mass audience.
The changed architectural style bespoke a change in the social bond
holding Maya state and society together, at least in the northern part
of the peninsula.

Though Chichén displays sufficiently close kinship to Tula for the
historical account of Toltec conquest to be broadly accepted, clearly
the two did not constitute twin poles of an empire, still less of a
unitary empire. The Toltec 'Mayan march' derived from old historic
liaisons (e.g., the common Nonoalca background of both Toltecs and
Putún) and formed part of that grand, secular movement of population from northwest to southeast, from highland to lowland. It did
not create an enduring link, however, of the kind which joined Teotihuacan and Kaminaljuyú. The Fine Orange pottery of the southern
Gulf coast, which the Putún Maya produced and traded, is not to
be found at Tula; Toltec trade seems to have been skewed to the

---

[29] This second wave of migrants was responsible for 'new' Chichén Itzá – the northern half of the
dual site – which bears the clear stamp of Toltec militarism: Jones, *Twin City Tales*, pp. 362–3,
and Diehl, *Tula*, pp. 145–9, which notes the problems which the Books of the Chilam Balam
present as sources ('they make the Book of Revelations sound like a straightforward newspaper
account').

[30] Diehl, *Tula*, pp. 150–1; Sharer, *The Ancient Maya*, pp. 408, 423, 747–5.

north – to the Huasteca, the Bajío and the far north – rather than to the south; in this respect, the Toltec and Aztec commercial networks appear to have differed significantly.[31] Toltec conquest may have created new kingdoms, but these did not cohere in an integrated empire, nor even in an integrated trading system. Like the contemporary Norman diaspora in Europe (the kindred realms of Normandy, England, Sicily and Syria), the Toltec achievement embraced widely different regions, united only by common origins and certain shared political and cultural traits; there was no central direction, no political, commercial or ideological integration (of the kind which both Teotihuacan and Tenochtitlán achieved, to a degree); rather, over time, there was a centrifugal dissipation of martial energy, followed by progressive local assimilation and differentiation. By the thirteenth century the Itzá were essentially Maya, just as the Plantagenets were essentially English.

Tula's empire was therefore limited and circumscribed. Within the imperial metropolis itself, too, divisions were apparent: between the Nonoalca and Tolteca-Chichimeca groups, and between rival dynastic factions which perhaps derived from this prior ethnic dichotomy and perhaps expressed themselves in terms of counterposed religious cults. Certainly legend has it that the fall of Tula was signalled by a battle between Quetzalcóatl and Tezcatlipoca, gods emblematic of the Nonoalca and the Tolteca-Chichimeca, respectively. One consequence was further out-migration which, early in the twelfth century, led to Toltec colonization of the Puebla-Tlaxcala region, notably of the (then modest) city of Cholula. Such southern moves were also stimulated by pressure from the north, aggravated by continued dessication. Tula's northern trade routes decayed; La Quemada fell to local insurgents, possibly Huichol rebels tired of Toltec oppression.[32] More migrants trekked south to Tula, following the paths trodden by their ancestors. Given Tula's hybrid (Nonoalca-Chichimeca) origins, it would be wrong to see these northern migrants as barbarians battering the gates of a beleaguered civilized city. Generations of Chichimeca – of varying degrees of 'civilization' – had taken the road

[31] Diehl, *Tula*, pp. 114–16.
[32] Diehl, *Tula*, pp. 155, 162–3.

south, towards the cities and valleys, the loot and lusher pastures, of Mesoamerica, much as the hordes of an inhospitable Scandinavia had taken the road to Miklagard. For generations, these migrants had been accommodated within Tula's politico-military system; or they had passed on, associating themselves with Toltec and Toltecoid cities to the south, notably in the Valley of Mexico.

By the late twelfth century, however, the combination of internal and external pressures proved too much for Tula's limited powers of political management. Drought, overpopulation, plague and famine afflicted the city (whose available natural resources were strictly limited).[33] A dynastic battle, waged between Huemac and Topiltzin, aggravated the situation. Legends tell, as legends are wont to do, of sorcery, intemperance and moral decline. Toltec hubris invited retribution. Around 1175 an already weakened metropolis fell to external attackers – Huastec or Chichimec or some combination of the two. Tula experienced a 'catastrophic end', marked by fire and pillage (which, in turn, afford a ready alibi for archaeologists whose finds do not measure up to ethnohistorical accounts of Toltec material splendour). Unlike Teotihuacan, however, Tula survived, a chastened provincial town rather than a mighty imperial metropolis. Its population leached away, especially through migration to the Valley of Mexico, where the old Toltec ally of Culhuacán now assumed the mantle of Toltec civilization and culture. Possibly the Toltec diaspora reached further – to Puebla, Oaxaca and Campeche.[34] Thus, pockets of Toltec settlement, characterized by their self-conscious and self-regarding Toltec culture, survived down to the age of Aztec supremacy, affording a basis, both political and ideological, for Aztec claims to Toltec lineage. Toltec princes and princesses were eagerly sought out; the Toltec achievement was sedulously inflated and mythologized. And the legend of the defeated Topiltzin/Quetzalcóatl, who would return from the east after a cyclical interval, also lived on, affording the rationale for Moctezuma's awed reception of Cortés in 1519.

[33] Diehl, *Tula*, pp. 98, 158–64.
[34] Diehl, *Tula*, pp. 15–60; Davies, *The Toltecs*, pp. 408–9; Kent V. Flannery, 'Oaxaca and the Toltecs: A Postscript', in Kent V. Flannery and Joyce Marcus, *The Cloud People: Divergent Evolution of the Zapotec and Mixtec Civilizations* (New York, 1983), pp. 214–15.

II. The Coming of the Aztecs

Following the fall of Teotihuacan, the Valley of Mexico had experienced demographic and political dispersal. The old imperial
metropolis shrank and several lesser centres of population grew.
None, however, achieved regional supremacy; between c. 700 and
950 six clusters existed, vying for power, their constant feuding evidenced in their choice of defensible hilltop sites.[35] External powers
overshadowed Valley politics: first the Teotihuacano successor states
of Xochicalco and Cholula, then the rising metropolis of Tula, which,
we have seen, imposed a kind of loose Pax Tolteca, and a degree
of renewed political integration, until its own demise in the twelfth
century. A key ally of Tula was the city of Culhuacán which, surviving
Tula's fall, lived on like a Mexican Ravenna, an island of old imperial civilization washed by waves of barbarian invasion.[36] For by the
late twelfth and early thirteenth centuries Chichimec migrants were
establishing petty new realms in the Valley. Xolotl and his fur-clad nomads came to rest at Tenayuca on the western shore of Lake Texcoco
(we are told); Aculhua and the Tepanecs, possibly originating from
Toluca and Michoacan to the west, settled at Azcapotzalco; and many
other groups, of diverse language and culture, settled, fought and jostled in the fertile lacustrine Valley. Neither the size nor the precise
origins of these populations can be confidently given.[37]

Initial attempts at empire-building – by Xolotl – proved more
rhetorical than real, and it was not until the later fourteenth century
that clear alignments of power became evident within the Valley. By
then, the old Toltec client city of Culhuacán was in decline, while
Texcoco, an offshoot of Xolotl's Tenayuca people, had developed
into a powerful commercial centre, a magnet for migrants from as
far afield as Oaxaca and the lynchpin of a broad confederation of

---

[35] Blanton *et al.*, *Ancient Mesoamerica*, p. 146.

[36] Burr Cartwright Brundage, *A Rain of Darts: The Mexica Aztecs* (Austin, 1972), p. 12, calls
Culhuacán a 'rump Toltec state'. See also Nigel Davies, *The Toltec Heritage* (Norman, Okla.,
1980), pp. 28–9.

[37] Davies, *Toltec Heritage*, p. 43, gives the wild numerical estimates of chroniclers; Robert
S. Santley, 'Recent Works on Aztec History', *Latin American Research Review*, 19/1 (1984),
p. 266, deflates both the scale and the distance of the migration, with which Offner, *Law and
Politics*, pp. 19–24, concurs, noting the obscurity of Xolotl's origins and ethnicity. See also
Charles Gibson, *The Aztecs under Spanish Rule: A History of the Indians of the Valley of Mexico,
1519–1810* (Stanford, 1964), pp. 9–20, on the migrant 'tribes' of the Postclassic.

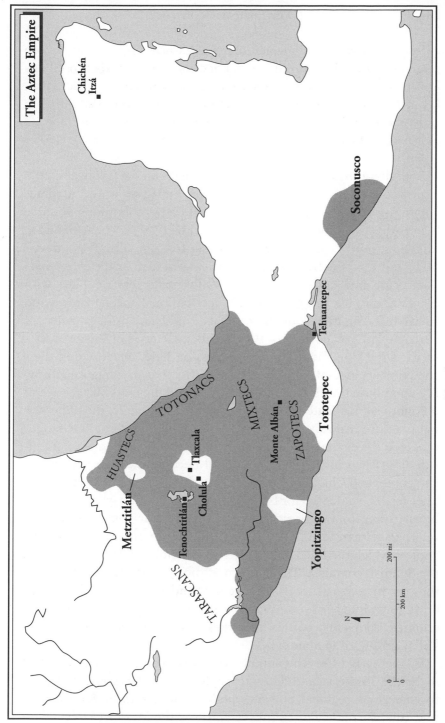

The Aztec Empire

Chichén Itzá

Soconusco

Tehuantepec

TOTONACS

HUASTECS

MIXTECS

Metztitlán

Monte Albán

TARASCANS

Tenochtitlán

Tlaxcala

Cholula

ZAPOTECS

Tototepec

Yopitzingo

N

0   200 mi

0   200 km

Map 5

cities – the first of several such alliances. Under Quinantzin, whose reign ended c. 1377, Texcoco extended its conquests, landholdings and tributaries in the eastern Valley. Azcapotzalco, its chief rival, lay across the lake to the west, where it claimed a regional lordship inherited from Xolotl and successfully pursued a policy of imperial expansion which culminated in the long reign of Tezozómoc (1371– 1426).

Both these rivals depended for their growth on the favourable ecological conditions of the Valley, where land and water were abundant, communications swift and easy and climatic conditions equable (each adjective should be prefaced by: 'relatively'). The Chichimec migrants, initially nomadic, became settled agriculturalists, developing more productive means of cultivation, such as the *chinampas* (lacustrine mud gardens) which the Valley made possible. Thus, with a greater surplus being generated, occupational specialization and social differentiation could proceed at a rapid pace. And the rulers of Texcoco and Azcapotzalco – the chief beneficiaries of this process – spurred the transition along by enclosing land, encouraging their sometimes reluctant subjects to farm rather than to forage and drawing upon both the agricultural expertise and the cultural prestige of the more sophisticated Toltecoid centres. Meanwhile, the old external pressure from the north may have abated, as climatic changes rendered the distant dry lands more habitable. So sedentary agriculture flourished in the Valley; Nahuatl became the *lingua franca* of its people; and Chichimec princes eagerly married into Toltec royal lineages. The potential for both dramatic population growth and political expansion was present. As we consider how this potential was realized, we can for the first time draw upon written sources – the codices which recorded Valley myth and history, and which survived the Spanish conquest. Their interpretation is contentious; however, they permit a departure from structural and archaeological analysis, and a foray into *l'histoire événementielle*, the history of dynasties and empires, coups and battles. And these the turbulent history of the Valley produced in abundance.

By the early fifteenth century, Azcapotzalco and Texcoco looked to be the likeliest candidates to exploit the Valley's potential and to emerge as regional powers, modest successors to Teotihuacan and Tula. By mid-century, however, it was the Mexica (Aztecs) who proved the chief beneficiaries of ecological plenty and Darwinian politics and whose heterogeneous empire, built at breakneck speed, now far outstripped both their contemporary rivals and, eventually, their historic predecessors.[38] Ethnohistorical sources permit a fairly detailed account of the military exploits of the Mexica; however, it is no less important, although rather more difficult, to *explain*, rather than simply to *narrate*, their rise to supremacy. The Mexica arrived in the Valley in the mid-thirteenth century, a minor band of multi-ethnic migrants who had trekked from some point of departure – the legendary island of Aztlan – somewhere in the northwest (possibly Nayarit).[39] Like other southbound migrants, the Mexica had been influenced by mainstream Mesoamerican civilization, and they were not simply fur-clad savages; perhaps, like the original founders of Tula, they represented an amalgam of 'pure' Chichimec and more 'civilized' elements. Van Zantwijk posits a 'Mexican' rank-and-file subordinated to a consciously Toltecoid 'Aztec' elite; accordingly, the term 'Aztec' – which we will use hereafter – denoted a cultural, political and ideological identity rather than a strictly ethnic one.[40] Certainly the Aztecs' long odyssey involved splits, separations and fresh recruitments, as such *Völkerwanderungen* usually did. Along their circuitous route, which may have taken them via Coatepec and even Tula itself to their ultimate destination in the Valley of Mexico, they periodically paused to farm; they appear to have possessed some calendrical knowledge as well as a complex pantheon; they may even have served, briefly, as mercenaries of the failing Toltec power. The rudiments of Mesoamerican civilization, including military power politics and human sacrifice, were therefore familiar to them; they were no innocents abroad. Indeed, they were driven

---

[38] Nomenclature presents a problem: although 'Aztec' is the most common usage, and I shall stick to popular convention by using it, the term 'has no very precise meaning' (Gibson, *Aztecs under Spanish Rule*, p. 1); it is best reserved as a generic label for the Postclassic inhabitants of the Valley of Mexico who formed the basis of the 'Aztec' empire – a multi-ethnic political and cultural entity. Most, though not all, of these inhabitants spoke Nahuatl and are also known as Nahuas. Among them were the Mexica, the founders of the city of Tenochtitlán, and eventually the dominant group in the Aztec empire. On the derivation of the names (Aztecs: people of Aztlan, 'Place of Cranes'; Mexica: etymology disputed), see Davies, *Ancient Kingdoms of Mexico*, p. 167.

[39] Brundage, *Rain of Darts*, pp. 20–6.

[40] Rudolph Van Zantwijk, *The Aztec Arrangement: The Social History of Pre-Spanish Mexico* (Norman, Okla., 1985), p. 14.

on by a powerful belief in their own collective and divine destiny, which was conferred on them by their classically Toltec patron deity, Huitzilopochtli, through the medium of four priest-rulers. Such beliefs were common among migrant tribes in both Mesoamerica and the Middle East: on their arrival in the Valley of Mexico, the hordes of Xolotl immodestly staked claims to 'the entire earth'.[41]

What distinguished the Mexica/Aztecs was their ability to weather misfortune and thus to prove to themselves – and to others – that divine blessing was indeed real and efficacious. 'This people', a Culhua observer later reckoned, 'is specially favoured by the god'.[42] But divine favour was not immediately apparent. Newly arrived in the Valley, the Mexica stood low in the scale of local prestige, serving as mere 'menials and vassals'.[43] Accordingly, they were integrated into regional power politics as dependent clients of established cities like Tenayuca. In the late thirteenth or early fourteenth century, with their numbers increasing and their quasi-theocratic 'tribal' organization mutating into monarchy, the Aztecs (as we will now term them) established themselves at Chapultepec, the well-watered bluff which today overlooks downtown Mexico City from the west. The Machiavellian politics of the Valley did not, however, allow them a secure enjoyment of this desirable niche close to the western shore of Lake Texcoco. Nor did the Aztecs themselves encourage peaceful coexistence. Already, they had gained a reputation for belligerence; they were 'great villains', 'bad people of evil ways', according to Culhua sources.[44] Twice they were attacked, and in 1319 (or perhaps 1349) they were dislodged from Chapultepec by the burgeoning local power of Azcapotzalco.

Valley politics worked on the principle of *vae victis* (woe to the vanquished). The Aztecs were scattered in the swampy fastnesses which surrounded the nearby lake; some fled to neighbouring cities and very likely to slavery; the majority of the stricken tribe reached

[41] Nigel Davies, *The Aztecs: A History* (London, 1977), pp. 10, 14–15, 17; Offner, *Law and Politics*, p. 22.

[42] Davies, *The Aztecs*, p. 32. The Culhuaque (people of Culhua) are another semantically shadowy group; in this case, the 'Culhua observer' was a member of the city of Culhuacán, an early overlord-cum-mentor of the Mexica: Gibson, *Aztecs under Spanish Rule*, pp. 10–11.

[43] Davies, *The Aztecs*, p. 27.

[44] Davies, *The Aztecs*, pp. 31, 32.

Culhuacán where they threw themselves on the mercy of the Toltec successor state (was this a deliberate choice?) and suffered the further humiliation of seeing their ruler sacrificed. Culhuacán, a prestigious power in decline, faced an awkward dilemma, recalling that of the Sabines after the Battle of the Caudine Forks. Like the Sabines, who briefly held the upstart Romans in their power, the Culhua chose neither to crush nor to comfort their temporary victims. After some debate, they despatched the Aztecs to the rocky, snake-infested wasteland of Tizaapán (where the National University of Mexico now stands). Here, Aztec resourcefulness proved itself, stimulated, if later records can be trusted, by the tireless exhortations of the divine Huitzilopochtli. Reverting to old ways, the Aztecs took to hunting; the very snakes which were supposed to be their scourge became their sustenance; and, in a manner almost too anthropologically good to be true, they also reverted to their earlier, collective, priestly leadership. Their initial battle for subsistence won (to Culhua astonishment), the Aztecs began to carve out cultivable fields among the laval rocks, to construct temples and houses and to trade skins for woven cloth.

This period of recuperation during the first half of the fourteenth century was important in several respects. The Toynbeean challenge of Tizaapán provoked an appropriately positive response. Huitzilopochtli's exhortations proved effective, reinforcing the Aztecs' sense of manifest destiny (it was now, too, that the Culhua spy grudgingly conceded the fact of Aztec divine favour). And the liaison with Culhuacán, though initially dependent and humiliating, gave the upstart Aztecs an entrée into Toltecoid high culture and politics. Soon, they were again serving as ferocious and successful mercenaries in Culhuacán's wars against Xochimilco, to the south, and they began to trade and intermarry with the Culhua, thus enhancing their status and acquiring – no doubt deliberately – their hybrid title, 'Culhua-Mexica' (it was of the 'Culhua' which Cortés's first Gulf interlocutors spoke when they referred to the Aztecs). Like the ancient Toltecs, therefore, the Aztecs grafted ancient culture on to barbarian stock.

Culhua concern at this transformation – of down-and-out vassals into doughty warriors – was compounded by a famous incident which, according to legend, ended the Culhua-Aztec liaison. Urged by Huitzilopochtli, the Aztecs sought a Culhua princess to grace their community. Acceding to this – a familiar enough – request, the Culhua ruler Achitometl offered his own beautiful daughter. She was promptly executed and flayed, and her skin, according to custom, was used to drape an Aztec priest. The Aztecs then brazenly invited Achitometl to a feast where, like Titus Andronicus, he was presented with the remains of his offspring, not baked in pies but adorning a prancing priest. 'Immediately', we are told, 'fighting broke out', whereupon Huitzilopochtli (a god of war for whom discretion was sometimes the better part of valour) advised his acolytes: 'I know well; go from here calmly and cautiously'.[45] Divine counsel conspired with pressing circumstances, and the Aztecs resumed their travels.

Again, they made for the sanctuary of the lagoon. Here, on a rushy islet, probably in the year 1325 (or 1345), they beheld a portent which Huitzilopochtli had foretold: an eagle, perched on a cactus, devouring a snake.[46] Here, therefore, they founded their new settlement, at the 'place of the cactus', or Tenochtitlán. The spot, as well as its portentous selection, was suffused with symbolism: it harked back to the old Aztec homeland of Aztlan (said to be another insular fastness), and its reeds recalled the great Tollan ('place of reeds'), by implication place of multitudes. The eagle stood for the sun and the Aztecs' divine mentor, Huitzilopochtli; the cactus, whose pulpy red fruit resembled the human heart, symbolized the act of sacrifice which was to play so central a part in Aztec ritual. And the luckless snake represented, perhaps, the old 'earth-serpent' of Olmec provenance, now consumed by the eagle, symbol of more bloody aerial deities.[47]

But symbols do not fill bellies. The spot so chosen also offered distinct practical advantages. It was ecologically congenial, offering drinking and irrigation water, as well as shellfish and waterfowl; over time, in response to mounting population pressure, the Aztecs could

---

[45] Davies, *The Aztecs*, p. 33. Brundage, *Rain of Darts*, p. 31, gives a different version. Susan D. Gillespie, *The Aztec Kings* (Tucson, 1989), pp. 58–61, equates the princess with the goddess Toci and sees this unusual union as symbolizing the marriage of the 'barbarian, hunter, Chichimec, north[ern], male' Aztecs with the 'civilized, farming, . . . south[ern], female' Culhua-Toltecs.

[46] Different dates are given: Davies, *The Aztecs*, p. 36, prefers 1345; Brundage, *Rain of Darts*, pp. xii, 34, suggests 1369; 1325 is the 'traditional date': Davies, *Ancient Kingdoms of Mexico*, p. 171.

[47] Davies, *Ancient Kingdoms of Mexico*, p. 173; Luckert, *Olmec Religion*, pp. 136–7. For related legends and interpretations, which are abundant, see also Burr Cartwright Brundage, *The Fifth Sun: Aztec Gods, Aztec World* (Austin, 1983), pp. 144–5; David Carrasco, *Religions of Mesoamerica* (San Francisco, 1990), pp. 73–4.

emulate their Valley predecessors by constructing *chinampas* – mud gardens of great productivity. Nevertheless, their lack of cornfields led the Aztecs to cast envious eyes towards the fertile lakeshore controlled by the Tepaneca. The lake also facilitated transport (canoes were perhaps forty times more efficient than land-based porterage)[48] and offered a degree of security which was enhanced by the Aztecs' occupation of a buffer zone, located between the rival powers of Azcapotzalco and Texcoco.

Initially, times were hard: 'the small city was ... little more than a sprawling hamlet of reed huts, net racks, and canoe anchorages'.[49] But, ensconced in their ecological and geopolitical niche, the Aztecs laboured and prospered. So, too, did the kindred community of Tlatelolco, another island settlement, established by Aztec folk following their earlier eviction from Chapultepec. Eventually the two communities would be linked by causeways to form the great lacustrine metropolis of Tenochtitlán-Tlatelolco, the 'Venice of the Western world'.[50]

As settlement led to population growth and renewed integration into Valley power politics, the pressure to assume a monarchical form of government revived. Tlatelolco therefore sought a Tepanec prince, while Tenochtitlán gave refuge to – and then elected as its ruler – a scion of the deposed Culhua ruling house, Acamapichtli, who boasted both Mexica and Culhua-Toltec blood.[51] Acamapichtli and his son Huitzilihuitl swiftly consolidated their religio-legal power. Though elected by a council of tribal elders, they claimed divine status and took pains to enhance it. Huitzilihuitl, for example, 'began to make laws and regulations for the state, especially as far as the cult of the gods was concerned, which was something over which all the lords and kings showed a special zeal, since they considered themselves to be their living representatives, and thought that whatever honour was done to the gods was also done to

[48] Ross Hassig, *Trade, Tribute and Transportation*, pp. 60–6. On Aztec land hunger, see Brundage, *Rain of Darts*, pp. 36, 51; on the scale and productivity of the *chinampas*, see Sanders, 'The Agricultural History of the Basin of Mexico', pp. 133–5.

[49] Brundage, *Rain of Darts*, p. 46.

[50] Brundage, *Rain of Darts*, pp. 27, 29, 58; the phrase was coined by William Prescott, *History of the Conquest of Mexico* (London, 1929; first pubd. 1886), p. 9.

[51] Gillespie, *Aztec Kings*, pp. 26–8ff., gives abundant details of the foundation and progress of the dynasty.

themselves'.[52] Tenochtitlán's early rulers also encouraged the formation of a new noble elite, closely tied to the state and emancipated
from the nobles' earlier association with particular *calpulli*, or corporate clienteles. The traditional bonds between nobility and people, mediated through seven such corporate groups, each possessed
of its own gods and rituals, were attenuated, and something more
resembling an 'imperial nobility', wedded to the state, came into
being.[53]

The outcome was a regime which displayed the familiar 'secular'
features of the Postclassic era: militarist and expansionist, it possessed a mighty ruling house, architecturally honoured by lavish new
palaces and served by a powerful aristocracy and warrior elite; yet
the regime also rested on theocratic principles, at least to the extent
that religion and ritual were essential props of 'secular' power. The
Aztec prince (the *tlatoani*) mediated between men and the gods, and
he carried the responsibility for sustaining the fragile balance of human existence (hence, we shall see, the obsessive preoccupation with
sacrifice). Religion suffused politics; that is to say, the conventional,
'modern' distinction between the two, between the sacred and the
secular, did not apply.

But this was not a static situation. Over time, *tlatoani* power, rooted
in religious sanction, eclipsed the residual authority of *calpulli* and
elders. In the process, the early 'man-gods' of the Mexica – glorified
shamans, folk wizards, populist messiahs – gave way to rulers who,
though they possessed a powerful religious legitimacy, were essentially secular and imperial rulers, served by extensive priestly and
warrior elites. By the fifteenth century the Aztec *tlatoani* enjoyed
an absolutist divine right which the Bourbons would have envied
and the Sublime Porte would have understood.[54] The difference between this extreme Postclassic polity and the 'theocratic' regimes of
the Classic era was less any new, legitimating, 'secular' ethos, than
it was the novel employment of religious sanctions and symbols in
the service of great dynasties, who espoused grandiose military and

---

[52] Davies, *The Aztecs*, p. 48.
[53] Van Zantwijk, *Aztec Arrangement*, pp. 18–19, 82–3; Brundage, *Rain of Darts*, pp. 48–50.
[54] Serge Gruzinski, *Man-Gods in the Mexican Highlands, Sixteenth to Eighteenth Century*
(Stanford, 1989), p. 26.

imperial aims, vastly transcending the interests of kin, village and local community. And it was because these conflicting interests, dynastic and local, elite and popular, diverged to an unprecedented degree that coercion – and terror – also came to play an unprecedented role in Aztec politics.

Consideration of the internal dynamics of the developed Aztec state must wait for a moment. Initially, the Aztec state was small and threatened by powerful neighbours. Like Prussia, vulnerably placed on the north German plain, the Aztecs responded by developing a vigorous and Machiavellian foreign policy, underwritten by force. They accepted, as it were, *der Primat der Aussenpolitik*: the primacy of foreign policy. To survive, let alone to prosper, Tenochtitlán had to bob and weave in the pugilistic ring of Valley politics. Above all, it had to come to terms with the prevailing Tepanec power, masterfully directed by the wily Tezozómoc. Under his rule, Azcapotzalco seemed bent on creating a regional empire along Toltec lines. Enemies, like Culhuacán to the south and Xaltocan to the north, were ruthlessly crushed and incorporated into an expanding tribute system which, although it faced continued defiance from independent principalities like Chalco and Texcoco, came to embrace most of the Valley and stretched west to Toluca, south into Morelos, and even – following the traditional lure of the rich lowlands – southeast towards Puebla and the Gulf.[55]

Military and Machiavellian, Tepanec expansion followed Toltec precedent; but, even more clearly and significantly, it foreshadowed later Aztec practice. For the Aztecs – the soldiers of Tenochtitlán and the redoubtable canoe flotilla of Tlatelolco – now served as valuable subordinates of Tezozómoc. That they were subordinates is not in doubt: as tributaries they were squeezed (ruthlessly and capriciously, if the stories are true); and as mercenaries they were constantly deployed – against Culhuacán, their old master and mentor, whose destruction they contrived; against lakeside Tenayuca; against the Otomí city-state of Xaltocan, which they defeated in 1395; and against Chalco, which was repeatedly battered but never subdued. Thus, Tenochtitlán served as the bludgeon of Tepanec

---

[55] Van Zantwijk, *Aztec Arrangement*, ch. 5; Brundage, *Rain of Darts*, pp. 38ff.

imperialism, especially in the rich southeastern quadrant of the Valley.[56]

Contemporary politico-military organization, however, did not permit monolithic imperial control. Though Tenochtitlán served Tepanec interests, it benefited in the process and, indeed, enjoyed a limited autonomy. It feuded endlessly with Chalco, even in defiance of Tepanec policy, and it acquired new lands, like those of the defeated Xaltocan, which vitally augmented its initially limited patrimony.[57] Recognition of Tenochtitlán's rising status came when Azcapotzalco relaxed its tribute demands and allowed its Aztec allies to take fresh water from Chapultepec (mud, offal and salt made the lake waters undrinkable). Apart from war, the Aztecs also pursued the classic strategy of dynastic marriage: Huitzilihuitl married a Tepanec princess, daughter of Tezozómoc himself. Now, it was noted, the Aztecs had begun to wear cotton clothes (the spoils, perhaps, of southern conquests) and to construct stone temples and houses on their populous island. The merchants of Tlatelolco also prospered, plying the lake in their canoes, trading luxury goods with the cities of the mainland. The island cities grew; but their position was far from secure. Floods and famine afflicted Tenochtitlán in the 1380s.[58]

As the fourteenth century drew to a close, therefore, the Aztecs were established as important actors in Valley politics: successful warriors, junior partners of the ascendant Azcapotzalco (whose rulers regarded the Aztecs with mingled appreciation and anxiety) and frontline forces in the impending showdown between Azcapotzalco and Texcoco. For by now 'it was inevitable that either Texcoco or Azcapotzalco would have to dominate the other; neither could suffer the other's independence'.[59] The early fifteenth century witnessed a dramatic denouement in which the Aztecs, playing a typically martial and Machiavellian role, emerged with their external power greatly enhanced and their internal organization subtly revolutionized. In the crucible of the 1420s the future Aztec empire was forged.

---

[56] Davies, *The Aztecs*, p. 45; Brundage, *Rain of Darts*, pp. 88–9.
[57] Davies, *The Aztecs*, p. 51; Offner, *Law and Politics*, p. 39.
[58] Brundage, *Rain of Darts*, pp. 52–3, 60; Van Zantwijk, *Aztec Arrangement*, p. 282.
[59] Offner, *Law and Politics*, p. 39.

III. The Aztec Revolution in Government

This crucial period of conflict and realignment stretched from 1409 to 1428. In 1409 the new ruler of Texcoco, Ixtlilxóchitl, who was linked by marriage to the Aztec ruling house, took a defiant stand against Azcapotzalco; by 1415, full-scale war was under way. Initially successful, Ixtlilxóchitl was tricked, defeated, ousted and killed.[60] Both his defeated city and his fugitive son, Nezahualcóyotl, were now dependent on the favour of the Aztecs, whose power and prestige continued to wax. Indeed, the balance of power within the Tepanec-Aztec alliance was palpably shifting, and, in the domestic struggle which divided Azcapotzalco following the death of Tezozómoc (1426), an anti-Aztec faction, led by the impetuous Maxtla, took control. Maxtla trained his sights on his overmighty Aztec subjects. He cut off their supply of mainland goods, reimposed heavy tribute and, according to one account, engineered the deaths of both the Aztec *tlatoani* Chimalpopoca and his colleague, the king of Tlatelolco. Alternatively – and more plausibly – Chimalpopoca fell victim to an Aztec palace coup (1426), which replaced a supposedly pliant appeaser with a new, belligerent faction, keen to resist Maxtla and the Tepanecs.

Just as the crucial transition from Roman Republic to Roman Empire was mediated by an illustrious triumvirate so, too, was the formation of a militantly imperialist Aztec state the work of three power-politicians, whose talents effectively blended: the new *tlatoani*, Itzcóatl ('obsidian serpent'), an experienced and capable warlord, the bastard son of Acamapichtli; his nephew and heir-apparent, Moctezuma Ilhuicamina; and Moctezuma's younger brother, Tlacaélel, 'an unusual man...of unquestioned brilliance', who, under the title, thereafter institutionalized, of Cihuacoatl ('woman snake'), assumed the role – roughly – of high priest, or grand vizier.[61] Of course, this Aztec triumvirate, like its Roman counterpart, could not act out its historic role without broader support. So, in squaring up to Azcapotzalco, its members appealed to both the martial spirit and the material greed of the Aztec elite who (if the story is

---

[60] Offner, *Law and Politics*, pp. 41–2; Brundage, *Rain of Darts*, pp. 62–5; Davies, *The Aztecs*, p. 56.

[61] Davies, *Toltec Heritage*, p. 19; Davies, *The Aztecs*, p. 63; León-Portilla, *Broken Spears*, p. xxii.

true) struck a strange bargain with the commoners of Tenochtitlán: if the war undertaken by the nobles and warriors was successful, the commoners would thereafter serve and provide for them; if it failed, 'they could take their vengeance and devour them in dirty and broken pots'.[62]

Whether true or not, the bet neatly encapsulated the dynamic options open to the Aztecs at this crucial juncture in their history: victory would confirm and decisively accelerate the processes of social stratification, state-building and military expansion; defeat would abort them, bringing about the subjugation and possible political dissolution of the city. Odd though the Aztec wager seems, it broadly parallels events elsewhere. For in Mesoamerican and Mesopotamia alike, periods of crisis and conflict similarly afforded the crucibles in which new, powerful secular authorities were established, sometimes even on a similar basis of conditionality.[63]

In the Aztec case, the nobles won their bet and escaped the dirty cooking pots. The young prince of Texcoco, Nezahualcóyotl, who had seen his father, Ixtlilxóchitl, ousted, pursued and hacked to death by the Tepanecs, became the architect of a grand anti-Tepanec alliance, which embraced Tenochtitlán, Tlatelolco and Texcoco, as well as extra-Valley powers, such as Tlaxcala and Huejotzingo, who had no cause to love the Tepanecs. Azcapotzalco was attacked, besieged for three months and finally subdued, amid pillage and massacre. In subsequent campaigns (1428–33) erstwhile Tepanec tributaries – Coyoacán, Xochimilco, Ixtapalapa, Culhuacán – were defeated and their temples symbolically razed. His father avenged, Nezahualcóyotl recovered his royal birthright in Texcoco, which he ruled, a poetic Solon, for forty years (1431–72). His Aztec allies acquired valuable agricultural land on the west side of the lake and asserted their supremacy over their insular neighbour, Tlatelolco. Joined by a Tepanec city, Tlacopan, which had prudently defected to the winning side, Tenochtitlán now led the dominant confederation with the Valley, a Triple Alliance of Tenochtitlán, Texcoco and Tlacopan. This novel development ended the endemic inter-city warfare which had consumed generations of Valley people; for the first

---

[62] Davies, *The Aztecs*, pp. 65–6.
[63] Wheatley, *Pivot of the Four Quarters*, pp. 311–12.

time since the hegemony of Teotihuacan, one pre-eminent authority controlled the Valley and thus enjoyed the potential for expansion beyond.[64]

Itzcóatl's political coup, swiftly crowned by military victory, was now complemented by political revolution (a term which is not used lightly, but deliberately). For the ensuing changes were swift, purposive and politically engineered; they were not the overdetermined outcome of long-incubating economic or ecological pressures (the first movers in much Mesoamerican historiography).[65] Such pressures defined the broad limits of action, it is true; but within those limits political options existed and politico-military decisions counted. Even the most fervent Anglo-Saxonist would accept that the events of 1066, which were not overdetermined, had momentous consequences for England; so, too the events of the 1420s set Tenochtitlán, the Valley of Mexico and Mesoamerica as a whole, upon a new course. Precolumbian history, like most history, admitted of sudden genetic mutations, as well as long evolutionary sequences.

As a result of their winning bet and victorious campaign the Aztec nobility was showered with material rewards: chiefly land but also rights to tribute, in the form of both goods and labour owed to them by fellow-Aztec commoners as well as conquered peoples. The bulk of Azcapotzalco's land, for example, was distributed among the Aztecs, and it was the elite – Moctezuma and Tlacaélel, in particular – who benefited; lesser towns also faced the gradual appropriation of their lands by Aztec, nobles, or, like Coyoacán, they were saddled with onerous labour services.[66] The ancient corporate associations of the Aztecs, the *calpulli*, which controlled peasant access to land, received only a modest allocation; thus, in both Tenochtitlán and

---

[64] Strictly speaking, therefore, the 'Aztec empire' was the 'empire of the three city league'. The process of alliance and conquest is described in Brundage, *Rain of Darts*, pp. 75–84, and Davies, *The Aztecs*, pp. 71–84.

[65] Van Zantwijk, *Aztec Arrangement*, pp. 279–80, refers to these events as a 'violent political revolution'.

[66] Offner, *Law and Politics*, p. 93; Brundage, *Rain of Darts*, pp. 83, 86. Gibson, *Aztecs under Spanish Rule*, p. 20, reminds us that the Mexica never enjoyed territorial dominance in the Valley of Mexico; Aztec supremacy was based on alliances, tribute and – later – extra-Valley conquests. For a good resumé, see Pedro Carrasco, 'The Territorial Structure of the Aztec Empire', in H. R. Harvey, ed., *Land and Politics in the Valley of Mexico: A Two-Thousand-Year Perspective* (Albuquerque, 1991), pp. 93–112.

Texcoco (where the rewards of imperialism were similarly skewed in their distribution) the balance was decisively tipped away from the old, more egalitarian, form of property-owning; and, at the same time, power shifted from traditional *calpulli* elites to the ascendant warrior aristocracy. The *calpulli* – which were never the simple egalitarian clans they have sometimes been imagined – now became residential associations, units of fiscal, religious and economic organization, firmly integrated into the new hierarchical state structures. Indeed, the state created new *calpulli* as it saw fit. The *calpulli* may thus be best seen as analogous to parishes: residential units of administration possessed of a certain corporate religious identity.[67] They served to control rather than to represent; and they no longer generated popular religious leaders – charismatic 'man-gods' – as they had in the past.[68]

Again, this erosion of an earlier equality and absorption of corporate associations into a centralized state were not trends confined to Aztec, or even to Mesoamerican, history.[69] The ascendant aristocracy, for example, acquired a growing number of outright serfs (*mayeque*) and slaves: as in Rome, therefore, the rise of empire favoured the growth of a slave-owning patriciate, just as it demoted the old 'tribal' associations (Roman *gentes*, Aztec *calpulli*) along with their respective authorities (the Roman tribunate, the Aztec *calpullec*). But, even more than the aristocracy, the monarchy throve on warfare and empire – hence it is no surprise that prince and nobles revelled in both. Although the Aztec *tlatoani* was elected – and thus subject to some initial elite control – his power and splendour grew in tandem with his empire, and both were sedulously fostered by successive *tlatoque* and their entourages. The political revolution of 1428, possibly masterminded by Tlacaélel, involved an 'ideological reformation' which embraced almost all aspects of Aztec society. The pomp and privilege of monarchical rule were inflated, bolstered by complex sumptuary laws and flaunted at successive, spectacular coronations: Moctezuma I's in 1440 and Ahuitzotl's in 1486. Itzcóatl was

---

[67] Van Zantwijk, *Aztec Arrangement*, pp. 16–17, 83; Brundage, *Rain of Darts*, pp. 48–50; Offner, *Law and Politics*, pp. 169–70; Inga Clendinnen, *Aztecs* (Cambridge, 1991), pp. 20–1, 39–40, 64.
[68] Gruzinski, *Man-Gods*, p. 25.
[69] Wheatley, *Pivot of the Four Quarters*, pp. 311–16.

the first Aztec prince to order his image carved in stone; his successor, Moctezuma I, claimed a miraculous birth and semi-divine status.[70] Although the *tlatoani* still figured as an active war-leader (the circle of electors, a narrow aristocratic coterie which shrank with time, saw this as a key criterion), his position nevertheless became more remote, withdrawn, exotic and imperial. Moctezuma II (1503–20), who carried the practices of Oriental despotism to their Mesoamerican limits, could not be touched or looked upon directly; no one could enter his secluded presence wearing shoes; he lived surrounded by a servile army of slaves and servants, cooks and concubines.[71]

Yet, notwithstanding the sensual luxury of their palaces, Aztec rulers and the Aztec elite more generally adhered to a stern Catonist ethic which stressed duty and deference, restraint, temperance and a rigorous respect for draconian law.[72] Aztec children, especially those of the elite, had this harsh morality drummed into them at school; and Aztec boys acquired a martial ethic, which embodied sentiments of 'super-heated masculinity'.[73] As 'protector of the toiling masses and master of mighty warriors', the *tlatoani* in particular carried an awesome responsibility which, in the case of Moctezuma II, weighed upon the hag-ridden monarch like a dead albatross.[74] In part, the monarch's duties were secular: he led armies in battle, subjecting himself to the meritocratic military ethos which suffused Aztec society. (Tízoc, who preferred building to campaigning, ruled suspiciously briefly and suffered a sudden, possibly contrived,

---

[70] Davies, *The Aztecs*, p. 88; Brundage, *Rain of Darts*, pp. 108, 119.

[71] When, forty years after the conquest, a Spanish friar asked an elderly Indian what Moctezuma had looked like, his interlocutor told him that 'though he [the Indian] had lived in proximity to the ruler, he did not know, since he had never dared to look': Thomas, *Conquest of Mexico*, pp. 44–5. See also Davies, *The Aztecs*, pp. 209, 214–16, where Moctezuma II's absolutist tendencies are seen to generate a 'kind of counter-revolution', with which Clendinnen, *Aztecs*, p. 128, concurs.

[72] Offner, *Law and Politics*, pp. 223, 254–78; Clendinnen, *Aztecs*, pp. 49–51, 130–1; Warwick Bray, *Everyday Life of the Aztecs* (London, 1968), pp. 62–4. It is possible that Aztec order and discipline were, in retrospect, exaggerated: first, by post-Conquest (Indian) informants who pined for the good old days; second, by Spanish friars and officials (e.g., Motolinía and Zorita) who admired such attributes and sought to reassert them amid the flux and chaos of the Conquest.

[73] Brundage, *Fifth Sun*, p. 201; Clendinnen, *Aztecs*, ch. 5.

[74] Davies, *The Aztecs*, p. 153; Offner, *Law and Politics*, p. 146, recounts Nezahualcóyotl's kingly self-justification, prompted – like Henry V's eve-of-battle musings – by querulous plebeians. On Moctezuma II, see Thomas, *Conquest of Mexico*, pp. 46–7, 272.

demise in 1486). Aztec rulers also prided themselves on their self-less enforcement of rigid legal codes which, in the wake of the 1428 revolution, were carefully codified and vigorously applied. Laws – like the fourteenth-century legal code of Texcoco – which had suited a more sparse, fluid and rural society were overhauled and enforced by a sophisticated magistracy in courts which were 'solemn, orderly, and greatly respected and feared by the populace'.[75] As well they might be: at Texcoco, drunks were enslaved for their first offence and strangled for their second; drunken aristocrats, however, for whom the principle of *noblesse oblige* acquired unusual relevance, were strangled for their first offence. Thieves, too, were strangled, 'even if the theft was only of seven maize ears'; adulterers were stran-gled, burned or had their heads crushed with heavy stones. Concu-bines who were too free with their favours were 'given over to the youths of the town to be gang-raped'.[76]

Though promulgated by kings, Aztec law was considered to be of divine inspiration; it cemented the peaceable public order which the legalistic Spaniards admired in Aztec society; and it underpinned the power of the Aztec elite, their property and (through a barrage of sumptuary laws) their privileges. In Texcoco, where the celebrated code of Nezahualcóyotl prevailed, the result was 'a homogeneous frame of social control', which disciplined the swelling population 'through terror or something akin to terror'. This internal terror, of laws rigorously – and rapidly – enforced, thus complemented the yet more overt external terror of imperialist war and mass sacrifice. In the process, the looser egalitarian society of early Aztec times was pummelled and manipulated by an emergent state apparatus, in a manner reminiscent of Rome or Ch'in China.[77]

Yet this state apparatus, for all its coercive and hierarchical as-pects, did not lack legitimacy. Aztec society had its share of social conflict. Corporate groups (such as nobles and merchants) contested

---

[75] Offner, *Law and Politics*, pp. 51, 83, 147–8; note also Brundage, *Rain of Darts*, p. 128.

[76] Though 'the male involved apparently went unpunished': Offner, *Law and Politics*, pp. 254–78, which concludes (p. 282) with the striking statement that the hundred-year survival of the Texcoco legal system 'is convincing proof of its excellence', and that its overthrow as a result of the Conquest 'can only be viewed as a tragic loss for the Aztecs, the Spaniards and modern Mexico'. By the same token, Britain might consider the reintroduction of hanging for sheep-stealing.

[77] Offner, *Law and Politics*, pp. 80, 82–3.

with each other. But examples of overt class conflict – of lords combatting peasants, for example – were rare.[78] Despite mounting inequalities, the regime itself seems to have escaped outright censure or opposition (one must say 'seems' because the nature of the historical evidence hardly allows a confident argument *ex silentio*). No doubt this had a lot to do with expedience: there were rewards, material and psychic, for obedience, just as there were harsh penalties for dissidence. But the political and legal order also enjoyed a powerful divine sanction. Laws were god-given – 'flashes that the great king Moctezuma (Ilhuicamina) had sown in his breast from the divine fire' – and they were usually applied with severe impartiality. Nezahualpilli, lord of Texcoco, cut a swathe through his own family, executing flirtatious sons and daughters, hard-drinking concubines and an adulterous wife, her three lovers and two thousand attendants.[79]

Such arbitrary authority rested upon religious (or, we could say, ideological) bases. Just as religion had helped establish the first stratified states, back in the Mesoamerican Preclassic, now religion underpinned the most powerful and stratified state of the Postclassic. Indeed, the Aztec state may be seen as an example of Weber's 'hereditary charismatic' category. The *tlatoani*, mediator between men and gods, embodied charisma: that 'certain quality of an individual...whereby he is set apart from ordinary men and treated as endowed with supernatural powers or qualities'.[80] Furthermore, this Weberian model is not (as sometimes is alleged) static; it conforms to the perceived dynamics of Aztec development, which we are here surveying. Charisma, Weber observes, is 'a phenomenon typical of...expansive political movements in early stages'; over time,

---

[78] Offner, *Law and Politics*, p. 146; Katz, *Ancient American Civilizations*, pp. 194–6, 210, though working within a broadly Marxist tradition, sees little sign of popular discontent or protest in the Aztec heartland (the outlying empire being a different matter); the argument is developed in Katz, 'Rural Uprisings in Preconquest and Colonial Mexico'. Van Zantwijk, *Aztec Arrangement*, p. 278, refers to a peasant revolt in 1432. Given the Aztecs' aptitude for rewriting history and making myths – and the ease with which posterity overlooks the discontent of the illiterate poor – it may be risky to infer (*ex silentio*) that the people of the Aztec Valley of Mexico lived in happy social solidarity. However, Alfredo López Austin, *The Human Body and Ideology: Concepts of the Ancient Nahuas* (2 vols., Salt Lake City, 1988), presents a sophisticated 'idealist' argument that Aztec animism – specifically, notions about the human body, the individual's life cycle, sin, sorcery and sacrifice – underpinned a broad social legitimacy.

[79] Offner, *Law and Politics*, pp. 159, 237, 242.

[80] Max Weber, *The Theory of Social and Economic Organization* (New York, 1964), p. 358.

however, it necessarily becomes subject to routinization, that is, the mediation of charismatic authority through administrative, including bureaucratic, systems.[81] Indeed, a fundamental problem of the Aztec state arose from the tensions inherent in this process as the divine responsibility of the charismatic leader, requiring war, expansion and sacrifice, clashed with the day-to-day needs of government and economy (the need to police the empire, maintain its borders, collect taxes and, above all, feed the burgeoning Valley population). We shall consider these tensions shortly.

Here, it is the genesis of charismatic authority which demands attention. Charismatic elements may be discerned even during the divinely directed wanderings of the early Aztecs. But it was with the 'ideological reformation' of the 1420s that the religious imprimatur of charismatic authority was indelibly placed upon the nascent Aztec state. The 'supreme achievement' of that reformation lay in 'the elevation of Huitzilopochtli and the formulation of an imperial cult that united the patron deity, Mexica military ambitions, and the sun into a vision of a constant struggle between the forces of the universe'.[82] It is therefore probably wrong to attribute the harsh religion and ritual of the mature Aztec empire to the atavistic legacy of nomadism and the supposed obsession with energy conservation which it imparted.[83] To do so is to assume continuity when there is rupture – and, perhaps, to misconceive the nature of early Aztec nomadism anyway.

The apparent continuity of the cult of Huitzilopochtli is itself misleading. Huiztilopochtli ('Hummingbird of the South' – 'an amiable etymology for so ruffian a deity', Prescott observes)[84] was something of an upstart within the traditional Mesoamerican pantheon. As patron deity of the inconspicuous Aztecs, his fourteenth-century cult in the Valley of Mexico was 'probably quite modest'.[85] But as Aztec power grew (not least thanks to Huitzilopochtli's regular advice and intercession) so the god's persona grew too, plagiarizing the

---

[81] Weber, *Theory of Social and Economic Organization*, p. 370.
[82] Geoffrey W. Conrad and Arthur A. Demarest, *Religion and Empire: The Dynamics of Aztec and Inca Expansionism* (Cambridge, 1984), p. 38; León Portilla, *Broken Spears*, pp. xx–xxi.
[83] Cf. Duverger, *Fleur létale*.
[84] Prescott, *Conquest of Mexico*, p. 28, n. 2.
[85] Conrad and Demarest, *Religion and Empire*, p. 27.

attributes of older deities in the characteristically permissive fashion of Mesoamerican religion. Huitzilopochtli was a ragbag deity, 'hastily thrown together out of the odds and ends of [other] divinities'.[86] Thus, a minor tribal deity (perhaps a deified chief of past generations) became the potent demiurge which obsessed the Aztecs and appalled the Spaniards. And this transformation, while it depended on the validation of Aztec survival and success (recall the story of the Culhua spy), was also consciously fostered, above all by Tlacaélel, the 'high priest and ideas man' of the 1428 triumvirate.[87]

The new cult of Huitzilipochtli thus underwrote Aztec expansion, perhaps as the new Quetzalcóatl cult had underwritten that of the Toltecs.[88] Accordingly, new history books had to be written, in which the Aztecs' Toltec heritage was stressed, the alliance with the Tepanecs was glossed over, and the role of Huitzilopochtli was inflated (as a result, the written sources almost certainly exaggerate the cult's distant origins and historical continuity). And, to maintain the pretence, old texts had to be destroyed (Spanish bishops were not the first bookburners in Mesoamerica). In addition, a centralized universal education was created, through which all children passed – nobles and commoners to their different schools, in which a 'harsh discipline' prevailed and teachers disseminated the official line in ethics, cosmology and religion.[89] These new schools were staffed by priests, and, just as the old corporate leaders ('elders') gave way to centralized imperial officials, so traditional shamans were replaced by hieratic professionals, the carefully trained and materially privileged agents of an Erastian empire. All the ingredients of later Spanish 'ideological control' were therefore prefigured in the Aztec state: a militant official religion, the repression of heterodoxy, intimate Church-State collaboration and powerful legitimizing myths (for Huitzilopochtli read Santiago).

---

[86] Brundage, *Fifth Sun*, pp. 149–50.

[87] Conrad and Demarest, *Religion and Empire*, p. 41.

[88] Davies, *The Toltecs*, pp. 121–2. During the Postclassic the Tlaxcalans, too, developed a new, belligerent 'state cult', centred on the god Camaxtli, while the Tarascans, to the west, established a 'state religion' embodying the 'Curicaueri sun-warrior cult': Conrad and Demarest, *Religion and Empire*, pp. 70, 83; Helen Perlstein Pollard, *Taríacuri's Legacy: The Prehispanic Tarascan State* (Norman, Okla., 1993), pp. 135ff. These parallel trends – whether the product of diffusion or of independent genesis – lend weight to the idea of a loose, common, Postclassic culture.

[89] Bray, *Everyday Life of the Aztecs*, pp. 34, 62–4.

The runaway cult of Huitzilopochtli was synonymous with human sacrifice: a topic vital for any understanding of Aztec society ('sacrifice may ... be said to have been the central fact in Aztec life')[90] but one that is subject to intense debate and considerable misunderstanding. At the outset, the topic should be stripped of sententious moralizing or tit-for-tat comparisons with Spanish atrocities. It is easy to be liberal at the expense of the Middle Ages, as Marx observed. The historian's task is to explain, not to parade moral sensibilities. By way of explanation several preliminary points should be made. First, the fact of Aztec human sacrifice, linked to cannibalism, is undeniable (though attempts have been made to deny it and to blame Spanish myth-mongering).[91] Second, human sacrifice stood – if the metaphor may be allowed – atop a pyramid of sacrificial and ascetic practices, including fasting, self-punishment and self-mutilation (bloodletting with cactus spines, the gashing of ears and thighs) and the sacrifice of both material goods and animals (quails were a favourite). A stern social and religious ethic thus demanded stern self-discipline and mortification. Like U.S. Marine recruits, novice warriors were subjected to harsh initiation, involving fasting, bloodletting, abstinence and abuse.[92] Boys in general experienced a tough educational regimen. Lazy or defiant boys were 'beaten, pricked with maguey spines, then bound hand and foot and laid naked on the wet ground for a day, or else were held over a fire of chile peppers to inhale the bitter smoke'.[93] Thus, in Aztec Mexico as in Victorian Britain, the builders of empire were trained for their adult tasks.

Third, such Aztec practises were neither new nor confined to the Aztecs. Evidence of mortification, such as ritual bloodletting, can be found in Formative-period villages in Oaxaca; two millennia later Bernal Díaz encountered Totonac priests, 'their ears ... cut to pieces as a sacrifice'.[94] The supreme human sacrifice, too, was well known

[90] Brundage, *Fifth Sun*, pp. 196, 208.
[91] Yolotl González Torres, *El sacrificio humano entre los mexicas* (Mexico, 1985), pp. 14–15.
[92] Brundage, *Rain of Darts*, p. 110; Clendinnen, *Aztecs*, pp. 71, 112–14. For a grim analysis of puberty rites and their rationales, see Farb, *Man's Rise to Civilization*, pp. 71–4.
[93] Bray, *Everyday Life of the Aztecs*, p. 59. Girls suffered similar mortification.
[94] Kent V. Flannery, 'Contextual Analysis of Ritual Paraphernalia from Formative Oaxaca', in Flannery, *Early Mesoamerican Village*, p. 344; Bernal Díaz, *The Conquest of New Spain* (Harmondsworth, 1981, first pubd. 1963), p. 124.

in Mesoamerica prior to the Aztecs. Archaeological evidence (knives, bones, murals) attests to the practice of human sacrifice at Teotihuacan, among the Classical Maya and, *a fortiori*, at both Monte Albán and Tula. The Tarascans of western Mexico, contemporary enemies of the Aztecs, also perpetrated human sacrifice.[95] But if, in their practice of human sacrifice, the Aztecs were unoriginal, it cannot be doubted that they carried it to unprecedented lengths – more than any other society the world has known (with the possible exception of the eighteenth-century kingdom of Dahomey).[96] This quantitative shift, furthermore, was sufficiently great to constitute a qualitative change in the social, the religious and, perhaps, the material significance of the practice. Where, for example, the Classical Maya had practised the individual and personalized sacrifice of prisoners, the Aztecs organized collective, depersonalized holocausts, such that historians have noted the 'staggering differences . . . in tone and scale between the late Postclassic solar/warfare/sacrifice complexes and the individualistic, prestige-reinforcing rituals of the Classical period'.[97] Aztec sacrifice was to earlier precedents what industrial was to artisan production.

Forms of sacrifice varied, depending on the god who was to be honoured and succoured. 'Honoured' and 'succoured' – rather than 'propitiated' – because the cosmic rationale appears to have been less that of sacrifice designed to appease an irate god, than sacrifice required to help the god in his perennial struggle to maintain the fragile cycle of existence. Aztec gods, in this respect, were like Catholic saints – personal allies to be invoked and aided. To the extent that the Aztecs posited a Supreme Being (Tloque Nahuaque: 'The Immanent One') he was a colourless and cultless individual, revered chiefly by the intellectual poet-king Nezahualcóyotl.[98] Monotheism had no foothold in the Aztec world-view (we will later note how this facilitated Catholic conversion, as Catholic saints and Aztec gods were

---

[95] González Torres, *El sacrificio humano*, pp. 56–62; Sharer, *The Ancient Maya*, pp. 143, 245–6; Linda Schele, 'Human Sacrifice among the Classic Maya', in Benson and Boone, *Ritual Human Sacrifice in Mesoamerica*, pp. 7–45; Davies, *Ancient Kingdoms of Mexico*, pp. 110–1; Pollard, *Taríacuri's Legacy*, pp. 134, 143.

[96] Davies, *Ancient Kingdoms of Mexico*, p. 229; Gonzalez Torres, *El sacrificio humano*, p. 51.

[97] Conrad and Demarest, *Religion and Empire*, p. 229. Brundage, *Rain of Darts*, pp. 101–2, notes that the Aztecs also outdid the – belligerent, sanguinary, Postclassic – Toltecs.

[98] Brundage, *Fifth Sun*, p. 67.

promiscuously assimilated). Sacrifice therefore served a multitude
of ends: above all, it sustained the sun in its course; but it also aided
Tlaloc in bringing rain, or Xipe Totec ('Our Lord the Flayed One') in
ensuring the rebirth of spring. Aztec gods served as allies, succoured
by sacrifice, who contested the inexorable destructive forces – an
Aztec anticipation of the astrophysicist's entropy, according to one
imaginative analysis[99] – which ceaselessly threatened man and the
universe. War was essential as a generator of sacrifical victims, to
which end special contrived 'flowery wars' were fought, the booty
being neither land nor tribute but prisoners destined for the sacrificial block.[100] In some instances, victims assumed the guise of the
gods themselves: they were feted, honoured and caparisoned before being despatched in the manner appropriate to each particular
cult. For Mixcoatl, god of hunting, victims were shot full of arrows;
for Tonatiuh, the sun god, or for Xipe Totec, captured prisoners,
equipped only with flowery staves, fought unequal battles with fully
armed warriors; children were chosen for Tlaloc (some were dumped
into a 'divine sump hole' in the middle of Lake Texcoco) and an ample supply of propitious tears was assured by first drawing the finger
nails of the infant victims.[101]

But the commonest sacrificial practice, especially associated with
Huitzilipochtli and the sun, was the removal of the victim's heart.
With the victim held down, face-up, distended on a kind of humped
slab, the priest (or king) swiftly slashed the abdomen with an obsidian knife, inserted his hand, and ripped out the still palpitating heart,
which was consigned to the flames. Amid a welter of blood, the body
was then hurled down the temple steps (often bouncing past fresh
victims, who were mounting the slick and bloody stairs). The mutilated corpses, piled on the 'blood mat' at the pyramid's base, later
provided food for a feast or were traded in the market; the skulls
were often preserved on racks in the temple (*tzompantli*).[102]

The scale of this human sacrifice, certainly unprecedented in
Mesoamerica, cannot be quantified. The gory temples and loaded
skullracks horrified the Spaniards: their estimates of 50 victims

---

[99] Duverger, *Fleur létale*.
[100] Brundage, *Rain of Darts*, pp. 96–101. The Tarascans, like the Tlaxcalans, also took part in such
contrived carnage: Pollard, *Taríacuri's Legacy*, p. 106.
[101] Davies, *The Aztecs*, p. 171; Brundage, *Rain of Darts*, p. 132; Clendinnen, *Aztecs*, pp. 94–110.
[102] Brundage, *Rain of Darts*, pp. 103–4; González Torres, *El sacrificio humano*, pp. 153ff.

per temple per year (Cholula had 430 temples); or of 136,000 skulls which they counted on the *tzompantli* of Tenochtitlán's Great Temple, cannot inspire great confidence, yet they may not be wildly wrong.[103] Bernal Díaz carefully counted over 100,000 skulls at Xocotlan (Zautla): 'I repeat that there were more than 100,000'.[104] At the inauguration of the Great Temple, in 1487, 80,400 victims were said to have perished in a mighty holocaust lasting four days, which left the sacrificers, including the emperor Ahuítzotl, blood-drenched and exhausted.[105] Even if this figure is deflated tenfold (as Davies suggests, somewhat arbitrarily), it remains a hecatomb. Apart from such grand events – sacrificial Olympics, stage-managed in massive plazas with chauvinistic pomp and circumstance – there were recurrent, lesser sacrifices, made to various deities, by private citizens: by merchants, who won prestige by acquiring and sacrificing slaves; by warriors, who, according to the prevailing military meritocracy, achieved glory and promotion by capturing and sacrificing prisoners, whose parts they were privileged to consume. Thus, while total estimates are impossible, it is clear that fifteenth-century Mexico witnessed a steep increase in human sacrifice, which was in turn linked to Aztec expansionism, to a parallel increase in tribute of all kinds, to the internal dynamics of Aztec society – and, some have said, to ecological pressures and protein deficiency. The provision of sacrificial victims brought not only divine favour but also terrestrial advancement and, perhaps, full bellies.[106]

---

[103] Anthony Pagden, ed., *Hernán Cortés, Letters from Mexico* (New Haven, 1986), pp. 35–6, 75; Thomas, *Conquest of Mexico*, pp. 25–6, which notes that Ortiz de Montellano chooses to deflate Andrés Tapia's 136,000 to a more reassuring 60,000. On the aggregate figures, see González Torres, *El sacrificio humano*, pp. 79–80, citing Sherburne F. Cook, and Conrad and Demarest, *Religion and Empire*, p. 78 (nn. 127, 129).

[104] Díaz, *Conquest of New Spain*, p. 138.

[105] Davies, *The Aztecs*, p. 167. On the significance of the Great Temple, see Eduardo Matos Moctezuma, *The Great Temple of the Aztecs: Treasures of the Aztecs* (London, 1988), and Johanna Broda, David Carrasco and Eduardo Matos Moctezuma, *The Great Temple of Tenochtitlan: Center and Periphery in the Aztec World* (Berkeley, 1987).

[106] 'Cultural materialist' explanations of Aztec human sacrifice, stressing protein deficiency and cannibalism, include Harris, *Cannibals and Kings*, pp. 158–66, and Michael Harner, 'The Ecological Basis for Aztec Sacrifice', *American Ethnologist*, 4/1 (1977), pp. 117–35. A careful critique is offered by Bernard R. Ortiz de Montellano, *Aztec Medicine, Health, and Nutrition* (New Brunswick, 1990), pp. 85–94. It is worth mentioning that the (presumed) link between cannibalism and protein deficiency is not simply outlandish speculation, there being good evidence of the phenomenon in other contexts: 'protein starvation is probably . . . the ultimate reason why cannibalism was widespread in traditional New Guinea highland societies': Diamond, *Guns, Germs, and Steel*, p. 149.

It is one thing to describe, another to explain. The conventional (and, at one level, correct but incomplete) explanation for these practices is derived from Aztec cosmology and religion, specifically from the belief that the cycle of life required constant sacrificial inputs if it was to maintain its momentum.[107] This belief was not confined to Mesoamerica, but it acquired particular vigour there. The positive function of sacrifice, including human sacrifice, was widely accepted; perhaps sometimes even by the victims themselves. In some cases, sacrifice was considered just, even privileged (there are stories of captured warriors who demanded their own sacrifice); certain victims underwent elaborate preparations, which helped ensure that the final act was consummated with an air of pious submission rather than irreverent resistance (drugs, drink, exhaustion and hunger also helped ensure the passivity of many victims).[108] At any rate, some form of compliance must have been induced, otherwise it would be difficult to envisage how the hieratic rulers of a Neolithic society could achieve the clockwork precision of the 1487 hecatomb.

Thus, given the prevalence of (self-imposed) asceticism in Aztec society, it is quite plausible that some victims made the supreme sacrifice compliantly, in the sense of submitting to a harsh but ineluctable destiny. The subjective psychological wellsprings of such submission can hardly be fathomed; but it may be possible to view Aztec sacrifice – in all its manifestations – in terms of Barrington Moore's analysis of asceticism as a means to achieve control over the world, to tap subliminal energies and to overcome threatening destructive forces.[109] Certainly the devotees of the gods acquired cachet and authority by virtue of their spiritual exertions: 'those who fasted during the year were feared and venerated; they had earned the exclusive title "Brothers of Huitzilopochtli"'.[110] We could go further and see 'self-inflicted suffering [as] one possible response to a high level of frustration produced by uncertainty about the natural and social environment and the inability to control it'; a response

---

[107] González Torres, *El sacrificio humano*, pp. 72–82, offers a useful resumé of theories. Clendinnen, *Aztecs*, pp. 89–104, and Carrasco, *Religions of Mesoamerica*, pp. 85–91, are resolutely idealist (as against materialist) in their explanations.

[108] Clendinnen, *Aztecs*, pp. 104–11; González Torres, *El sacrificio humano*, pp. 251–4.

[109] Barrington Moore, Jr., *Injustice: The Social Bases of Obedience and Revolt* (London, 1979), pp. 50–5.

[110] León-Portilla, *Broken Spears*, p. 74. Note also Brundage, *Fifth Sun*, p. 214.

generated by 'a general religious environment' and 'despair about the possibility of happiness on this earth' (recall the maudlin poems of Nezahualcóyotl). Such a syndrome, Moore suggests, may be 'a characteristic though not inevitable reaction to social change and strain in pre-industrial times'.[111] At this intangible, psychological level Aztec society perhaps had something in common with its almost contemporary European counterpart of the fourteenth and fifteenth centuries: a macabre society of bloodied flagellants and ecstatic priests, of baneful portents and gory theatrical executions; a society convinced of the fragility of terrestrial existence and characterized by the paradoxical juxtaposition of sybaritic luxury and spartan asceticism.[112]

In this respect, sacrifice formed part of a powerful shared ethic, uniting rulers and ruled, conquerors and conquered. The subordinate peoples of the Aztec empire, though they bitterly resented Aztec immolations, did not question the basic legitimacy of such practices. Nor can it be doubted that rulers like Moctezuma II took their theocratic role seriously and felt compelled to maintain the rate of sacrifice, especially when emergency overtook the state. Held captive by the Spaniards, Moctezuma 'never ceased his daily sacrifice of human beings', despite Spanish protests; but now, he lamented, 'the gods no longer replied as of old'.[113]

These overt, articulated beliefs gave a certain cohesion to Aztec society, functioning, perhaps, like harsh rituals of tribal initiation. But here we shift from manifest to latent function: from the obvious acceptance of sacrifice to the less obvious rationale which underlay it. We also enter a minefield of speculation. However sincere the practitioners of sacrifice, it is reasonable to assume that social and political pressures underwrote such collective behaviour, that it was not simply the product of a peculiar Aztec psyche. It is also necessary to explain why the Aztecs took a familiar Mesoamerican phenomenon and carried it to such unprecedented extremes. This

---

[111] Moore, *Injustice*, p. 54.

[112] Cf. J. Huizinga, *The Waning of the Middle Ages* (New York, 1954), chs. 1, 2, 11.

[113] Díaz, *Conquest of New Spain*, pp. 264, 276. Previously, Moctezuma had welcomed Cortés and the conquistadors into the communion of human sacrifice, ordering an Aztec representative: 'if he [Cortés] does not like the food which you have given him, and if he is desirous of eating human flesh, and would like to eat you, allow yourself to be eaten. I assure you that I will look after your wife, relations and children': Thomas, *Conquest of Mexico*, p. 189. The Tlaxcalans made similar offers: p. 249.

quantitative and qualitative shift makes it implausible to interpret mass sacrifice in terms of the atavistic legacy of tribal nomadism.[114] Many Mesoamerican peoples inherited such a legacy, but only the Aztecs practised sacrifice on such a scale. Two alternative theories warrant mention: they have the merit of explaining not only the 'why' but also the 'when' of Aztec sacrifice; and (though they are espoused by different authorities) they are not entirely incompatible.

The first theory, couched in the language of cultural materialism, links mass sacrifice to cannibalism and sees it as a response to population pressure and food shortages, epecially shortages of protein, which the Aztec empire certainly suffered from the mid-fifteenth century (famines were recorded in 1452–54, 1492, 1500 and 1505, and we know that the 'worst [famine] year' of 1454 spurred special sacrificial efforts, as priests, led by Tlacaélel, 'discovered that the awful disaster that had befallen their world had been caused because the gods were angry at the niggardliness of human sacrifice as practised by the Aztec cities').[115] It is important not to caricature this theory. It was not a question of diminishing the population through sacrifice: after all, most of the victims were 'foreign' prisoners, many from outside the Valley of Mexico. It would have been more rational for the Aztecs to have left them in provincial subjection, required to produce and convey foodstuffs to the Valley. Furthermore, the evidence of perceived population pressure is ambiguous. Aztec policy, with its exaltation of motherhood and its reliance on military might, hardly displayed overriding Malthusian preoccupations. Nor did rulers like Nezahualpilli, who opposed a modest colonization scheme (which would have shifted eight hundred inhabitants of Texcoco and Tenochtitlán to serve in garrisons in Guerrero) on the grounds that it 'would impose an excessive population drain'.[116]

---

[114] On the scale and novelty of Aztec sacrifice: Demarest, 'Overview: Mesoamerican Human Sacrifice in Evolutionary Perspective', pp. 234–6; cf. Duverger, *Fleur létale*, which stresses distant origins.

[115] Brundage, *Rain of Darts*, pp. 132–3. Ortiz de Montellano, *Aztec Medicine*, pp. 77, 83, notes the incidence of famine but discounts any causal link to sacrifice, arguing that the Aztec response – improved irrigation and enhanced tribute – was both rational and effective. The argument is not wholly convincing.

[116] Davies, *The Aztecs*, p. 175. The thesis that sacrifice represented a form of population control (see Sherburne F. Cook, 'Human sacrifice and warfare as factors in the demography of precolonial Mexico', *Human Biology*, 18 [1946], pp. 81–102) is now discredited: Conrad and Demarest, *Religion and Empire*, pp. 165–6.

The 'nutritional cannibalism' thesis should not be so easily rejected, however (although often it is). If the burgeoning Aztec population lacked – and lusted for – protein, sacrifice offered a ready alternative and, for this reason, could have exercised a strong appeal. Here we enter a complex debate concerning the 'carrying capacity' of the Aztec homeland. There is no doubt that it was heavily populated by the fifteenth century (Tenochtitlán alone comprised a third of a million inhabitants) and that dearths, even famines, were recurrent. A principal reason was the transport bottleneck: canoes facilitated swift transport within the (overpopulated) Valley of Mexico, but to import food from without required the services of human porters (*tlamemes*) whose capacities were limited and whose own energy (i.e., food) consumption made their efforts counterproductive beyond a certain distance.[117]

Some authors, such as Sahlins, stress the varied supply of available protein: the Aztecs lacked cattle, pigs, sheep and goats, but they could hunt deer, catch fish, snare birds and gather grubs. Critics, such as Harris, are scathing: Harris calculates that the average Aztec consumed annually about the equivalent of two herring and three-quarters of a duck; as for the notion that the populous Aztecs got their essential protein by hunting, it 'is worth about as much as the suggestion that New York City could get its meat from deer captured in the Catskills'.[118] Certainly it is significant that the Aztecs, alone among the major, populous, urbanized civilizations of the world, lacked grazing animals; it is therefore plausible that any accessible source of animal protein would have been coveted and that those

---

[117] Ross Hassig, 'Famine and Scarcity in the Valley of Mexico', in Isaac, *Economic Aspects of Prehispanic Highland Mexico*, pp. 318–19; and Ross Hassig, *Trade, Tribute and Transportation*, pp. 28–40. In what has become a fairly technical debate, Ortiz de Montellano, *Aztec Medicine*, pp. 80–4, queries Hassig's calculations and takes a more optimistic view of Aztec productivity and logistics. The 'truth' may lie somewhere between these contrasting views. That the Aztec empire – like many pre-industrial empires – faced food-supply constraints seems clear. (See, e.g., Michael E. Smith and Cynthia Heath-Smith, 'Rural Economy in Late Postclassic Morelos: An Archaeological Study', in Mary G. Hodge and Michael E. Smith, eds., *Economies and Polities in the Aztec Realm* [Albany, 1994], pp. 363–70, which points to mounting poverty even in the lush lowlands of Morelos.) However, the severity of those constraints and their relation to political and religious practices are more contentious questions.

[118] Marvin Harris, *Cultural Materialism: The Struggle for a Science of Culture* (New York, 1979), p. 337. Ortiz de Montellano, by means of some grisly calculations ('we conservatively assume that all victims were 60-kg males, 16 percent protein – similar to the 16.5 percent in lean beef and lamb . . . and 90 percent digestible'), responds that the (average) nutritional benefit gained from Aztec sacrifices was similarly exiguous: *Aztec Medicine*, pp. 90–4.

in charge of its distribution would have enjoyed unusual power. For the theory does not state that cannibalism made possible the mass consumption of tasty life-saving protein: it suggests, rather, that cannibalism was a form of a privilege, controlled by king and priests and conferred on particular beneficiaries (those who provided the prisoners; those who served the *tlatoani* with distinction; those who waited at the foot of the bloody pyramid). 'Commoners (including women) might occasionally partake of human flesh, but by and large its consumption was a privilege reserved for the nobility, the merchants, and the priests'.[119] By means of sacrifice the Aztec rulers kept the sun in its allotted course; but at the same time, they distributed material favours in a context of theatrical horror: an imperial policy, as it were, of meat and circuses.

Here the materialist theory blends with the political. Domestically, the latent function of sacrifice was to legitimize the role of the *tlatoani* and his immediate entourage (a role greatly enhanced with the revolution of the 1420s). Constant sacrifice attested to the political virility and social indispensability of the new ruling class. It linked rulers and ruled in a system of rewards and sanctions which underwrote the revamped, imperialist Aztec state. Warriors won promotion by hauling in prisoners of war for sacrifice (even though this might be militarily counterproductive in terms of battles won and territory subdued); merchants bought prestige by offering up slaves for the slab. In the massive redistribution of goods which the Aztec empire undertook (which, in a sense, *was* the Aztec imperial economy), sacrificial victims were a basic commodity. Rulers ruled by redistributing such commodities, and their (better-off) subordinates gained preferment and honour by playing their part in the great redistributive system. This system was so pervasive and – in terms of certain economic principles – irrational, that the Aztec state has, with justice, been termed a gigantic 'potlatch state', a state predicated on the collection, redistribution and conspicuous consumption of a vast quantity of diverse goods.[120] Sacrifice represented a hypertrophied

---

[119] Brundage, *Rain of Darts*, p. 110; cf. Brundage, *Fifth Sun*, p. 217; Clendinnen, *Aztecs*, pp. 91–5; R. C. Padden, *The Hummingbird and the Hawk: Conquest and Sovereignty in the Valley of Mexico, 1503–1541* (New York, 1970), p. 98.

[120] A good example of the lavish deployment of wealth in order to achieve prestige, potlatch-style, is provided by Aztec merchant feasts: Frances Berdan, *The Aztecs of Central Mexico: An Imperial Society* (New York, 1982), p. 33.

form of potlatch, with humans playing the part elsewhere reserved for pigs.

But if sacrifice afforded a means of gaining prestige and advancement, it also represented an obvious form of intimidation, a reminder of the awesome power of the state and its divine mentor, Huitzilopochtli (this argument is not incompatible with the proposition that some sacrificial victims accepted their lot stoically). The celebratory conclusion of military campaigns and ceremonies like the dedication of the Great Temple were massive spectator events, carried out atop lofty pyramids, with thousands gathered in the precincts of the city below; and these thousands included not only the populace of Tenochtitlán but also dignitaries from other states, who were invited, urged and even required (under military sanction) to attend.[121] Such foreign spectators were feted, showered with gifts and given grandstand seats, but the purpose, clearly, was 'to ensure that their [the Aztecs'] enemies... should be conscious of the greatness of Mexico and should be terrorized and filled with fear'.[122]

Sacrifice – with its attendant ritual, splendour and ostentation – thus served to impress but also to intimidate both the local population and provincial subordinates. It was the supreme manifestation of the 'potlatch state', and it had to be carried out on a gargantuan scale, dwarfing competition. Enemies, of course, spurned such invitations: not because they abhorred sacrifice *per se*, but because they repudiated Aztec claims to supremacy. The Tarascans, recently victorious over an Aztec army, considered the invitation to Ahuítzotl's coronation, which they promptly received, to be 'demented'; the Tlaxcalans, also old foes of the Aztecs, refused to compromise their independence by attending and thereby tacitly accepting the Aztec yoke.[123] Others had no choice: better to attend as spectators than as participants. The regular flow of victims, from province to metropolis, thus exemplified and underpinned imperial relations – however economically irrational it might have been. The people of Cempoala resented the annual tribute of their 'sons and daughters' taken to Tenochtitlán as young Athenians were to Mínoan Crete; but they

---

[121] Davies, *The Aztecs*, p. 142.

[122] Davies, *The Aztecs*, p. 162. The 'terrorist' argument is developed by John M. Ingham, 'Human Sacrice at Tenochtitlan', *Comparative Studies in Society and History*, 26/3 (1984), pp. 379–400.

[123] Davies, *The Aztecs*, p. 163.

did not dare resist until the bold Cortés, playing the part of Theseus, urged them on and directly challenged this hated suzerainty.[124] Just as a form of internal 'terrorism', vested in the law, bolstered the Aztec elite vis-à-vis the Mexica masses, so the sacrificial cult afforded a means of imperial control which both impressed those masses and intimidated tributary peoples throughout central Mexico. It provided a constant reminder of the bet the Aztec elite had won back in the 1420s, when they had staked their enhanced social status on military victory and when the compliant masses had accepted enhanced subordination in return for vicarious participation in the meat and circuses of Aztec imperialism.

The overt ideology of sacrifice was thus linked to powerful political and class considerations. It did not well up from a murky Aztec psyche. Furthermore, these considerations were not necessarily latent and subconscious. Tlacaélel, it seems, appreciated the political efficacy of the Huitzilopochtli cult and its sacrificial obsession. Possibly he invented – and certainly he developed and justified – the 'flowery wars', the contrived conflicts whose primary purpose was the collection of sacrificial victims.[125] This is not to say that his fostering of cult, war and sacrifice was cynically instrumental, that he did not believe in them himself. On the contrary, politicians are particularly adept at convincing themselves (and others, if they are lucky) of self-evident truths which also happen to redound to their political benefit: this would seem to apply as well to absolute monarchs, Manchesterite liberals, racist imperialists and even recent exponents of supply-side economics. As an empire-builder, Tlacaélel was perhaps no more cynical than Cecil Rhodes. And where Rhodes espoused the mission of the Anglo-Saxon people, Tlacaélel built up the cult of Huitzilipochtli, an 'ideological adaptation' which efficiently served the interests of the emergent Aztec elite during the turbulent and hungry mid-fifteenth century.[126]

It is not surprising, therefore, that the cult failed to promote the collective well-being of the Aztec masses; that, apart from the occasional haunch of meat, they got no more than the psychic reward of

---

[124] Díaz, *Conquest of New Spain*, pp. 110–11.

[125] Miguel León-Portilla, *Aztec Thought and Culture* (Norman, Okla., 1963), p. 162, on Tlacaélel's flair for innovation; Brundage, *Fifth Sun*, pp. 205–7, on the flowery wars.

[126] Conrad and Demarest, *Religion and Empire*, p. 53.

adhering to a conquering cult and, perhaps, of indulging in a certain sadistic *Schadenfreude*: there, but for the grace of Huitzilopochtli, go I. Over time, however, even these diffuse rewards – and the elite's more tangible political pay-off – suffered diminishing returns. The cult of militarism, expansion and sacrifice, highly functional to the creation of empire, became a runaway juggernaut which even its makers and initial benefactors could not control. War became the empire's *raison d'être* and sacrifice an integral part not only of external policy but also of internal social dynamics. By the early sixteenth century, we will note, the diminution of returns had become so evident that the last Aztec emperor, Moctezuma II, attempted to modify the system, to brake the juggernaut. By then it was too late: just as Teotihuacan and the classic Maya centres had, arguably, suffered from the gross hypertrophy of an initially functional role (the exercise of theocratic rule and ritual), so the Aztec rulers found themselves locked into a system of open-ended war, expansion and sacrifice which had outrun its earlier, probably contrived, utility. The union of (genuine) cosmological belief with (self-serving) political – and, perhaps, material – interest eventually proved unstoppable.

IV. The Aztec Empire

The events of the 1420s thus brought to power an elite committed to a radical politico-ideological project. But the ecological context within which they implemented this project was crucial (at least by way of imposing broad limits, if not specific directions). Victory over the Tepanecs brought an accession of land and tribute; part of this tribute, rendered in the form of labour by Tepanec dependencies within the Valley, was used to develop Tenochtitlán's communications and productive resources: causeways linking the island to the mainland, the fertile mud gardens (*chinampas*), flood-barriers and – a vital productive resource in the ideological sense – the Great Temple itself. These were big undertakings. The *chinampas* eventually covered 10,000 hectares (some 25,000 acres); the causeways required twenty-five million man-days of labour. Again, state mobilization of labour – for hydraulic works or other collective projects – followed rather than preceded imperial aggrandizement. Indeed, the major development of *chinampa* agriculture did not take place until

Map 6

the mid-fifteenth century, when imperial expansion was already well under way.[127]

By then, such measures were vital since the burgeoning Aztec state faced the threat of overpopulation. During the entire 'Aztec period' (roughly 1200 to 1500) the population of the Valley of Mexico grew a remarkable fivefold, reaching over one million, some two hundred thousand of whom were concentrated in the dual city of Tenochtitlán-Tlatelolco. This greatly exceeded (by perhaps a factor of four) the previous peak in Valley population, achieved during

[127] Van Zantwijk, *Aztec Arrangement*, p. 282. On the *chinampas*, see also Hassig, *Trade, Tribute and Transportation*, pp. 47–53, 275; Sanders, 'Agricultural History of the Basin of Mexico', pp. 133–4; and Jeffrey R. Parsons, 'Political Implications of Prehispanic Chinampa Agriculture in the Valley of Mexico', in Harvey, *Land and Politics*, pp. 17–42.

the Classic era hegemony of Teotihuacan. Although the relationship between state- and empire-building on the one hand and population growth on the other is debatable, it is clearly no coincidence that this surge in population accompanied the reassertion of the Valley's geopolitical prominence within Mesoamerica (during the same period, for example, the population of the Valley of Oaxaca declined).[128]

Success brought its own problems, however. Archaeologists have calculated that even the swollen population of the Aztec era did not exceed the notional 'carrying capacity' of the Valley.[129] But there is a touch of armchair agronomy to these calculations. They may broadly hold in an average or good year. But, like many agrarian civilizations, the Aztecs were vulnerable to occasional climatic vicissitudes – those departures from the mean which brought dearth and famine in their wake. Indeed, the Valley of Mexico was particularly vulnerable to freak frosts and droughts: since these had a severe impact on the depopulated Valley of colonial times, it is very likely that they also afflicted the more numerous Postclassic population, *chinampas* and hydraulic systems notwithstanding. The *chinampas* helped counter the threat of frost and drought, but they tended to increase both the danger of flooding and the progressive salinization of the lake. Furthermore, even with its *chinampas*, Tenochtitlán could supply only a fraction (perhaps 5 per cent) of its total subsistence needs; it had to draw the rest from the surrounding hinterland.[130] The city's provisioning thus remained a chronic problem. There is early evidence of water shortages, later compounded by food shortages which were triggered by exceptional frosts. A sequence of lean years occurred in 1450–4: the lake flooded in 1450 and froze in 1450–1, when snow fell in the Valley; there followed three years of drought and dearth. The people went hungry; families sold their children into slavery; and, unusually, vultures hovered in the thin highland air.[131]

---

[128] Blanton *et al.*, *Ancient Mesoamerica*, pp. 102, 163–6, 223–4.

[129] The arguments are complex and inconclusive: Ortiz de Montellano, *Aztec Medicine*, pp. 72–84, reviews the evidence, noting (p. 82) carrying capacity estimates which range from approximately 900,000 to 1.5 million, at a time (1519) when the Valley's population stood at about one million. See also Blanton *et al.*, *Ancient Mesoamerica*, pp. 164–6.

[130] Hassig, *Trade, Tribute and Transportation*, p. 57.

[131] Brundage, *Rain of Darts*, 130–1; Davies, *The Aztecs*, pp. 92–3. Ortiz de Montellano, *Aztec Medicine*, pp. 77–8, arguing for Aztec abundance, sees the famine of the 1450s as freakish; compare Hassig, 'Famine and Scarcity', pp. 304, 308–9, and Clendinnen, *Aztecs*, pp. 38, 64–6, 73, which describes a 'frugal' economy, familiar with dearth, poverty and begging.

Although Tenochtitlán now controlled most of the Valley – and a good deal more besides – it could not overcome these environmental constraints. The network of state granaries characteristic of the Inca empire, and of other centralized ancient empires, did not exist in the more fragmentary Aztec empire; nor could military expansion conjure this threat, for expansion was not geared to the rational exploitation of food resources. Perhaps, as Davies suggests, 'after their experiences in the famine, the Aztecs must have hankered after . . . well-watered lands to the east', which became the target of Moctezuma I's campaigns.[132] But the transport of bulk foodstuffs from the lowlands to the altiplano was no easy matter (a porter bringing maize from Tuxtepec to Tenochtitlán would have consumed, on his round trip, some 80 per cent of his load); and subsequent lowland conquests do not appear to have alleviated the Valley's vulnerability to shortages in bad years. Nor is this surprising, since the bulk of lowland tribute came in the form of luxury goods which, even if, like cacao beans, they were edible, were destined for elite tables and could play no part in assuaging the hunger of the masses.[133] In contrast, bulky staple goods, such as corn (or firewood), were produced and delivered by tributaries within the Valley. Chalco, once defeated, became Tenochtitlán's breadbasket – a role it retained down to the nineteenth century.[134] Here, canoe transport – which was forty times more efficient than human porters – made a substantial difference. Perhaps ten thousand canoes plied the Valley lakes; some, reaching fifty feet in length, could carry a ton of grain.[135] But communities in

---

[132] Davies, *The Aztecs*, p. 99. On the absence of granaries: Conrad and Demarest, *Religion and Empire*, p. 78 (n. 134); though cf. Hassig, *Trade, Tribute and Transportation*, pp. 97, 107.

[133] Van Zantwijk, *Aztec Arrangement*, p. 283; Offner, *Law and Politics*, pp. 14–15, 104, 106; Hassig, *Trade, Tribute and Transportation*, pp. 32–4, 114; Blanton *et al.*, *Ancient Mesoamerica*, p. 248, concur with Hassig's negative evaluation of Aztec long-distance porterage; Ortiz de Montellano, *Aztec Medicine*, pp. 83–4, is more positive, perhaps excessively so.

[134] Brundage, *Rain of Darts*, p. 125; Gibson, *Aztecs under Spanish Rule*, pp. 308, 324. Hence the people of Chalco complained to Cortés 'that the Mexicans make the men work like slaves, compelling them to carry pine-trunks and stone and firewood and maize overland and in canoes and to perform other tasks, such as planting maize-fields': Díaz, *Conquest of New Spain*, p. 210.

[135] Hassig, *Trade, Tribute and Transportation*, pp. 56–64; although Hassig questionably asserts (p. 64) that 'speed . . . does not seem to increase wth the size of the canoe', it does, roughly according to the ratio $1.55 \times \sqrt{\text{waterline}}$ length; thus, a 16-foot canoe (at the lower end of the Aztec range) would be *potentially* capable of 6.2 miles per hour; a 49-foot canoe (the upper end), 10.8 miles per hour: Bill Riviere, *The Open Canoe* (Boston, 1985), pp. 11–12. Actual speeds were much lower: about 2 miles per hour.

the immediate hinterland were, of course, subject to the same climatic vicissitudes as Tenochtitlán itself.[136] The 'nutritional cannibalism' argument, which we have reviewed, obviously derives strength from this evidence of recurrent dearth, just as critics of the thesis posit a – more dubious – condition of alimentary abundance.

If conquest failed to conjure dearth, the alternative lay in Valley hydraulic agriculture. The construction of dykes and *chinampas* had yielded results during the reign of Moctezuma I (1440–68). But these were clearly not enough. Moctezuma's grandson, Ahuítzotl (1486–1502), decided – logically but precipitately – to divert the water supply of the city of Coyoacán north to Tenochtitlán. Coyoacán's ruler, protesting and prophesying doom, was murdered; labourers 'as numerous as . . . ants in an antheap' dug the new aqueduct; and, following the appropriate ritual, which included the sacrifice of infants to Tlaloc, the water coursed north in such abundance that the lagoon overflowed, flooding ficlds and cities. 'Ahuítzotl was mortified', Davies writes, 'the hero of so many distant triumphs had met his Waterloo [*sic*] on the home front'.[137] The flood of 1499 ensured famine in 1500 (one scholar estimates that famine stalked the land as frequently as every four years).[138] And famine worsened in the early sixteenth century as the Aztec empire reached its territorial maximum under Moctezuma II. To the extent that hunger bred expansion, therefore, it did so less because of rational economic considerations than because of the politico-ideological factors already mentioned; that is, rulers sought to please the gods and appease their own hungry subjects by glorious campaigns of conquest, crowned by spectacular

[136] Chiefly frost and rainfall (drought rather than floods), compounded by insect pests: Hassig, 'Famine and Scarcity', pp. 308–9. Gibson, *Aztecs under Spanish Rule*, pp. 310–17, notes 'harvests of great irregularity' in the Valley of Mexico throughout the colonial period – a theme to which we will return later.

[137] Davies, *The Aztecs*, pp. 192–5; Brundage, *Rain of Darts*, pp. 222–3.

[138] Harner, 'The Ecological Basis'. Harner may well overstate his case; but the evidence of mounting population pressure and sporadic dearths seems strong: see Van Zantwijk, *Aztec Arrangement*, pp. 278, 282; Parsons, 'Settlement and Population History', p. 98; Clendinnen, *Aztecs*, pp. 30, 73, 135; Padden, *Hummingbird and the Hawk*, p. 100. Enrique Florescano, *Precios del maíz y crisis agrícolas en México, 1708–1810* (Mexico, 1986; first pubd. 1969), chs. 2, 3, notes recurrrent poor harvests, dearths and epidemics, following a roughly eleven-year cycle, during the later colonial period, a time when population was substantially smaller. Of course, economic and ecological conditions had also changed considerably following the Conquest; hence, colonial evidence can be no more than suggestive. However, the likelihood is that Spanish innovations (crops and animals) boosted productivity and consumption, which would tend to confirm a pre-Conquest vulnerability to dearth.

holocausts. To the extent that the holocausts implied cannibalism and afforded additional protein, this was a bonus; but the rationale of the 'Aztec arrangement' was political rather than practical; war offered an outlet more than a solution to mounting demographic pressure. Like modern blitzkrieg campaigns, those of the Aztecs responded to short-term political – rather than long-term economic – objectives.

Meanwhile, campaigns came thick and fast, first within, then, increasingly, beyond the Valley. A chronological narrative of these campaigns would be long and tedious. Rather, it is the expanding geographic scope which deserves attention and which suggests some key features of Aztec empire-building. Within the Valley most of Azcapotzalco's old dependencies soon fell under Aztec sway: though they (usually) retained their old ruling dynasties, they were now obliged to supply goods and labour for Tenochtitlán or to its Triple Alliance partners, Texcoco and Tlacopan. The latter two enjoyed a certain primacy in the northeast and northwest sections of the Valley respectively, leaving Tenochtitlán the richer southern section; however, over time Tenochtitlán's power and income swelled until the Triple Alliance assumed a distinctly lopsided aspect.[139] Aztec supremacy did not go entirely uncontested, however. Chalco held out, as it had against the Tepanecs; indeed, given its natural resources (and assuming a neat translation of resources into military strength) Chalco should have emerged the chief beneficiary of the fall of Azcapotzalco. As it was, the Aztecs – would-be conquerors of Chalco in 1376 – returned to the fray in 1444, advancing the usual trivial grievance by way of self-justification. Intermittent fighting went on for some twenty years, punctuated by the great famine of 1451–4. The war yielded a regular crop of sacrificial victims but no definitive result. Typically, the Aztecs resolved to bypass this obstacle and seek easier victims outside the Valley. Chalco survived, a declining, independent enclave, until treason delivered it into Aztec hands in 1465.[140] Eight years later, Tenochtitlán's twin city of Tlatelolco was defeated in a fratricidal struggle which

[139] Offner, *Law and Politics*, pp. 90–1, 233; Conrad and Demarest, *Religion and Empire*, pp. 79–80.
[140] Davies, *The Aztecs*, pp. 89–90, 121–2.

(the usual personalistic *casus belli* notwithstanding) represented a further assertion of Tenochtitlán's power within the Valley.[141] In 1498 the ruler of Coyoacán was slain and the city's water supply expropriated. Even the allied powers of Texcoco and Tlacopan waned to the point where Aztec rulers meddled in these cities' succession struggles; and, conversely, the allies dragged their feet when called upon to sustain the empire's endless wars. By the early sixteenth century the Triple Alliance had become a one-man band.[142]

By then, too, the Aztecs were ranging far beyond the Valley. Indeed, it is probable that this outward urge stemmed from the Aztecs' limited local patrimony: Valley rivals might be defeated, but they could not be sweepingly dispossessed; their rulers and peoples usually remained *in situ*, rendering tribute which, however lavish, could not provide such rich pickings – human, material and psychological – as extra-Valley conquest. Progress was most dramatic to the south and east, most difficult to the north and west: in consequence, the mature Aztec empire was territorially skewed, its capital lying close to fragile northwestern borders, far from its sprawling southern domains. To the north, the Chichimec frontier held few attractions: the scattered, semi-nomadic tribes were too elusive, materially poor and politically indigestible. Like the Spaniards after them, the Aztecs preferred to subjugate existing polities, whose peoples they could profitably subordinate to indirect imperial control.

To the west, Tepanec control of the Valley of Toluca was not successfully emulated until the 1470s.[143] And, beyond, in present-day Michoacan, when the Aztec emperor Axayácatl led an army of some twenty-four thousand against the powerful Tarascan kingdom in 1478, he was sent scuttling back to the Valley of Mexico, bloody and beaten. Twenty thousand Aztec warriors were slain; their whitened

---

[141] Davies, *The Aztecs*, pp. 129–30. Note that the date of Tlatelolco's defeat is open to debate – some would advance it as much as forty years – and the various versions of Tenochtitlán–Tlatelolco relations are 'infuriatingly contradictory': Barry Isaac, 'Notes on Obsidian, the Pochteca, and the Position of Tlatelolco in the Aztec Empire', in Isaac, *Economic Aspects of Prehispanic Highland Mexico*, pp. 338–9. The fact of Tlatelolco's final subjugation to Tenochtitlán is not, however, in doubt.

[142] Offner, *Law and Politics*, pp. 94, 236–7; Conrad and Demarest, *Religion and Empire*, p. 67.

[143] Davies, *The Aztecs*, pp. 139–40.

bones were still to be seen two hundred years later, around Maravatío and Zitácuaro.[144] The Tarascans were redoubtable opponents, whose historical development loosely paralleled that of their Aztec enemies. Northern nomads in origin, they had settled in Michoacan in the twelfth century; by the late fifteenth century they had built a sizeable and powerful kingdom, centred on the city of Tzintzuntzan. Like the Aztecs, they had welded together numerous principalities to form a confederation, which – given the Tarascans' geopolitical location, as a buffer between the Valley of Mexico and the Gran Chichimec – was constantly tried in warfare. The Tarascan kingdom never achieved the level of urbanization and despotic centralization which characterized the Aztecs after the 1420s; Tarascan society was more rural and decentralized, as befitted a people possessed of relatively abundant resources, in terms of arable land, woods and fisheries ('Michoacan' means 'land that has fish').[145] Nevertheless, the Tarascan 'emperor' (or overlord: *cazonci* in the local idiom) exercised an effective authority, exacting tribute and conducting warfare. For want of evidence it is difficult to analyze Tarascan society with any precision (hence, in part, historical analyses of this important topic are wanting). Possibly, its looser, more decentralized nature lent the Tarascan polity certain 'feudal' characteristics: the nobility, pre-eminent in war, enjoyed greater power vis-à-vis the *cazonci* than the Aztec lords did vis-à-vis the *tlatoani*.[146] Though the Tarascans engaged in human sacrifice and cannibalism, these practices apparently did not achieve the levels of grandiose ostentation evident at Tenochtitlán (which, in light of the more ample material base of Tarascan society, may offer some corroboration of the nutritional cannibalism thesis). In one respect, however, the Tarascans outdid the Aztecs: they developed metallurgy to a level unknown in

---

[144] J. Benedict Warren, *The Conquest of Michoacan: The Spanish Domination of the Tarascan Kingdom in Western Mexico, 1521–1530* (Norman, Okla., 1985), p. 11; Pollard, *Taríacuri's Legacy*, pp. 90–2, 169; Brundage, *Rain of Darts*, pp. 195–7. According to one recent – but very dubious – analysis, this was the second most costly military campaign (in terms of casualties per combatant: 87%) in human history: Lawrence H. Keeley, *War before Civilization: The Myth of the Peaceful Savage* (Oxford, 1996), p. 64.

[145] Ulíses Beltrán, 'Estado y sociedad tarascos', in Pedro Carrasco, ed., *La sociedad indigena en el centro y occidente de México* (Zamora, 1986), pp. 46–9, 56–7.

[146] Beltrán, 'Estado y sociedad tarascos', pp. 54–7; though Pollard, *Taríacuri's Legacy*, pp. 60–1, 123–31, depicts a more centralized imperial core, centred on Tzintzuntzan and the Lake Pátzcuaro basin, and a more loosely incorporated, multi-ethnic ('feudal'?) periphery.

Mesoamerica, manufacturing copper tools and weapons. Perhaps this gave them a technological edge when it came to battle; perhaps, too, the 'feudal' character of the Tarascan state lent it a certain military resilience and expertise. If the Aztec-Tarascan wars in fact represented a geopolitical struggle between centralized despotism on the one hand and a more decentralized feudalism on the other, they could be seen as loose Mesoamerican parallels of the medieval crusades.

At any rate, the Tarascans proved to be redoubtable adversaries, and Aztec rulers after Axayácatl chose to contain rather than to challenge Tarascan power. Thus the Tarascan kingdom became an effective buffer, halting the Aztec advance to the west and shielding the city-states of the Jalisco region.[147] Instead, during the 1490s, the Aztecs pushed down into present-day Guerrero, seeking to outflank the Tarascans to the south. Acapulco fell, along with a broad swathe of the Pacific coast, but the rough country of Yopitzingo – populated by 'wild tribesmen', devotees of the 'flayed god' Xipe Totec – remained independent, defying Aztec power.[148] Another enclave was formed within the perforated Aztec empire, one which anticipated the historic resistance of the Guerrero region to central control exercised from the Valley of Mexico in later centuries.

To the northwest, too, dramatic advances were interspersed with cautionary defeats. In the 1460s and 1470s Aztec armies marched against the Huastecs, capturing cities and bringing back droves of yoked captives.[149] A third campaign (1486) provided a haul of prisoners for the hecatomb at the Great Temple. Meanwhile, in a manner reminiscent of the Romans, the Aztecs recruited Huastec auxiliaries to fight against the neighbouring kingdom of Metztitlán. Repeatedly attacked, stripped of its tributary towns and closely hemmed in by Aztec power, Metztitlán nevertheless survived, another hollow in the imperial frontier.

---

[147] Eric Van Young, *Hacienda and Market in Eighteenth-Century Mexico: The Rural Economy of the Guadalajara Region, 1675–1820* (Berkeley, 1981), pp. 16–17. After an armed truce of some 35 years, battle was resumed in 1515, when the Aztecs, under Moctezuma II, were again repulsed: Pollard, *Taríacuri's Legacy*, pp. 169–70. Conrad and Demarest, *Religion and Empire*, p. 55, overlook this, apparently sizeable, Aztec offensive.

[148] Davies, *The Aztecs*, p. 219.

[149] Davies, *The Aztecs*, pp. 105, 146.

To the south and east Aztec arms enjoyed greater sustained success. In part, this was geopolitically determined: from the outset, Tenochtitlán's interests had focused on the southern Valley of Mexico, and subsequent economic incentives pulled Aztec expansion towards the rich lowlands, where coveted luxury goods were abundant and where the inhabitants were neither too primitive to elude conquest nor too powerful to resist it. The Valleys of Puebla and Tlaxcala, the eastern gateways to the Gulf, were first to suffer the aggression of the Aztec triumvirate of the 1420s, who resolved on a 'perpetual war' against the cities of these regions, especially those of Tlaxcala and Huejotzingo.[150] By design or hazard, so it turned out: recurrent campaigns served more to secure prisoners than to win territory. If at the outset these 'flowery wars' gratified Aztec chivalry and bloodlust, it eventually became clear that Tlaxcala constituted a formidable – if embattled – enemy. For while Puebla, including the ancient, now resurgent, city of Cholula, fell under Aztec sway, Tlaxcala and Huejotzingo remained obdurate, resisted, and thus constituted another – close and troublesome – enclave within the expanding empire. By the 1500s the cavalier spirit of the 'flowery wars' had given way to implacable hostility and economic blockade. The Tlaxcalans were denied salt; and they were renowned as 'deadly enemies of the Mexicans'.[151] Politically independent, militarily defiant and geographically located on the route to the Gulf, the highland people of Tlaxcala were well placed to strike an alliance with Cortés's invading Spaniards.

Tlaxcala was poor in resources. Thus it was logical for the Aztec advance to bypass it, letting it survive as a sporting adversary and supplier of prisoners. Beyond lay the richer lands of the Gulf, sources of tropical goods, and the traditional targets of expansionist highland empires. In 1461–2 the Totonac cities of Orizaba and Cotaxtla (then called Ahuilizapan and Cuetlaxtlan) were reduced, not without difficulty; both revolted in the 1470s and were repressed; and resentment against Aztec rule and Aztec tribute collectors still simmered when the Spaniards made contact with the Totonacs in 1519.[152] Successive campaigns riveted Aztec control upon the Gulf coast,

---

[150] Davies, *The Aztecs*, p. 96.
[151] Díaz, *Conquest of New Spain*, p. 134.
[152] Brundage, *Rain of Darts*, pp. 153–4; Díaz, *Conquest of New Spain*, p. 113.

whence valuable tribute of cotton, jade, jewels, feathers and cacao could be extracted.

To the south, the cities of the warm valleys of Morelos – Cuernavaca, Oaxtepec and Tepoztlan – were early victims of Aztec extra-Valley expansion: then as now they afforded pleasant retreats for the elites of the chilly highland metropolis. By the 1440s Aztec armies had taken Taxco – a source of cotton, honey and copal – and crossed the Balsas River into Guerrero. Concurrently, Oaxaca, site of a long-standing Mesoamerican culture, was also incorporated into the empire. Here, the collapse of Monte Albán (c. A.D. 900) and the fragmentation of Zapotec power had left the Mixtecs – 'archetypes of the post-classic militarists' – in control of most of the Valley of Oaxaca, as well as of their old highland kingdom in the sierra (which bears their name) to the northwest. The Mixtecs, who had probably originated in the Puebla-Cholula region, were organized – in typical Mesoamerican fashion – in vigorous city-states; they were skilled in warfare and craftmanship, including metallurgy; and they were led by secular princes who engaged in ceaseless fighting and politicking.[153] In all this they resembled the Postclassic Maya or the feuding cities of the Valley of Mexico prior to the establishment of Aztec hegemony. In the mid-fifteenth century, Mixtec and Aztec came into violent conflict. For neither the first nor the last time, the immediate cause was the murder of Aztec traders, returning from Tabasco to Tenochtitlán via Oaxaca. Moctezuma I sent a punitive expedition which so thoroughly massacred the inhabitants of the city of Oaxaca that (unusually) Aztec colonists had to be sent to repopulate and garrison the site. The cities of the Oaxaca region (Tuxtepec especially) now became important entrepôts in the trading and tributary network which linked the Valley of Mexico to the warm lowlands, yielding 'a veritable flood of luxuries never dreamed of by the [Aztecs'] ancestors'.[154] From their newly established base in Oaxaca, too, the Aztecs could launch expeditions as far south as Soconusco, on the Chiapas coast, which was prized as Mesoamerica's chief centre of cacao production.[155]

---

[153] Whitecotton, *The Zapotecs*, pp. 84, 90, 116; Ronald Spores, *The Mixtec Kings and Their People* (Norman, Okla., 1967), pp. 9–16.
[154] Brundage, *Rain of Darts*, pp. 150–1; Whitecotton, *The Zapotecs*, p. 123.
[155] Davies, *The Aztecs*, p. 107.

Maintaining such long and precarious lines of communication required constant campaigning. The Aztecs sent repeated punitive expeditions into Oaxaca in the 1480s and 1490s, subduing the Zapotec town of Mitla and Mixtec Zaachila and extorting rich hauls of tribute: gold, cochineal, feathers, slaves and cotton cloth.[156] While the Mixtec kingdom of Tototepec, on the Pacific coast of Oaxaca, maintained a belligerent independence, Tehuantepec, the last Zapotec redoubt, soon experienced the familiar sequence of Aztec commercial penetration, local rebellion, and military reprisals leading to military conquest. On this occasion, however, massacres were averted; the local Zapotec lord of Tehuantepec received an Aztec princess in marriage; and Tehuantepec, a privileged dependency, became a vital commercial entrepôt and military pivot of the southern Aztec empire.[157] It was to protect Tehuantepec traders – thus, indirectly, Aztec tribute – that the emperor Ahuítzotl embarked on a gruelling, 800-mile punitive expedition against Soconusco in 1500: an expedition which stretched Aztec morale and logistics to their utmost and brought home to Ahuítzotl and, perhaps, to his perceptive brother and successor, Moctezuma II, the fact that the limits of empire had been reached. Though the attractions of Guatemala, farther south, were seductively depicted by the people of Soconusco (again, we see how 'sub-imperialist' pressures, stemming from local rivalries, could impel the overstretched metropolis into further, far-flung adventures), the lure was resisted. The Aztec empire, reaching its greatest territorial extension to the southeast, came to a halt precisely at the present Mexico-Guatemala border.

In consequence, the great bulk of the Maya south remained independent of Aztec control, though not of Aztec influence. Aztec merchants reached Acalan, a busy commercial zone, known for its canoes and cacao, inland from the Campeche Gulf coast; they established a trading post at Zinacantan, the chief town of the highland Tzotzil Maya; and, participating in the vigorous trade networks which linked the Maya towns of (present-day) southeastern Mexico and Guatemala, they shipped out feathers, pelts, cacao,

---

[156] Davies, *The Aztecs*, pp. 181–2; Whitecotton, *The Zapotecs*, p. 125.
[157] Davies, *The Aztecs*, pp. 183–4, 223–5; Whitecotton, *The Zapotecs*, p. 126.

salt and amber.[158] No conquest ensued, however. The intervening distances were formidable (witness Ahuítzotl's costly expedition to Soconusco), and the Maya were no military pushover. While the Classic Maya collapse had left the Petén depopulated, vigorous communities survived in northern Yucatán, in the Chiapas highlands and in Guatemala. Petty kingdoms, linked by dynastic marriage, were the norm; but in northern Yucatán a powerful confederation, centred on Mayapán, achieved hegemony after its defeat of Chichén Itzá in the thirteenth century. While continuing Chichén's commercial contacts to the west, Mayapán achieved 'a renaissance of native Yucatecan noble lines and traditions': 'foreign' influences abated; foreign nobles were, perhaps, eliminated; Toltec skullracks gave way to traditional Maya *stelae*.[159] Like Chichén, however, Mayapán could not withstand the propensities for feud, rebellion and political decentralization which historically characterized the Maya zone. Around 1450 disaffected nobles rose up, overthrew the ruling dynasty and destroyed the city. Northern Yucatán became a patchwork of petty princedoms, riven by rivalry and war. As such, the region (notable for both its overland and its coastal trade) attracted covetous eyes. Moctezuma flirted with the idea of a Yucatán invasion – a repeat of the tenth-century Toltec expedition – but his scheme never came to fruition. Instead, it was the Spaniard Francisco de Montejo who undertook the formidable task of reducing the fractious Maya to imperial rule.

As this brief resumé suggests, the Aztec empire which Cortés encountered was a recent and, in some respects, ramshackle organization. It was less than a century old in 1519; it faced, to the west, a formidable Tarascan foe; it included, within its broad sweep, many independent enclaves (Tlaxcala, Metztitlán, Yopitzingo, Tototepec). Cities once subjugated displayed a degree of autonomy and a penchant for rebellion. Hence the recurrent, bloody, punitive expeditions

---

[158] John S. Henderson, *The World of the Ancient Maya* (Ithaca, 1981), pp. 64, 69. Conrad and Demarest, *Religion and Empire*, pp. 62–4, attribute the Aztecs' failure to 'incorporate' the Maya lowlands to the latter's 'weak development of markets'. This is not entirely convincing. Maya markets were varied and vigorous (see Farriss, *Maya Society*, pp. 120–1); however, they were remote from the Aztec heartland and scattered among several competing polities – which made military conquest difficult, as the Spaniards later found.

[159] Henderson, *World of the Ancient Maya*, pp. 220–2; Sharer, *The Ancient Maya*, p. 417; Clendinnen, *Ambivalent Conquests*, pp. 149–50.

against Cotaxtla, Orizaba, Oaxaca, Tehuantepec and others. Save in a few cases (such as Oaxaca, or Oztoma and Alahuiztla in modern Guerrero) the Aztecs did not establish permanent garrisons. The Aztec presence was embodied in the ubiquitous *pochteca* ('merchants', of whom more later) and the *calpixtli*, the hated tax-collectors. Many punitive expeditions were despatched – like British gunboats in the days of Lord Palmerston – in response to (alleged) local maltreatment of *pochteca*, and Cortés won over the Totonacs by his brusque manhandling of the resident Aztec *calpixtli*.[160]

The Aztec empire therefore lacked a centralized, bureaucratic structure; it made no attempt to create a uniform imperial administration; it possessed no integrated system of roads or posts; and it was characterized by loose, indirect, rule (sustained by repression) rather than by stable proconsular government. In Mann's terms, it was an 'empire of domination', not a true territorial empire (indeed, the logistical barriers to territorial imperialism, severe enough in the Old World, were even more acute in Mesoamerica, where horses were absent and water communications poor).[161] Thus, as Davies suggests, it resembled less the Roman than the Assyrian empire: a comparison which, in light of the Assyrians' espousal of rapid campaigns, ferocious intimidation and a kind of elite nationalism, seems entirely appropriate.[162] Often, in the outlying provinces as in the Valley of Mexico, local dynasties remained in power, acknowledging Aztec suzerainty, responsible for day-to-day government and tribute collection. The Aztec emperors could guarantee no viable governmental alternative, and they did not relish deposing fellow-princes. Of course, some were deposed (and worse) *pour encourager les autres*: the troublesome rulers of Cotaxtla (who had murdered Aztec envoys by gassing them with chile smoke) were slain and flayed; but others, such as the privileged princes of Tehuantepec, survived and even

---

[160] Díaz, *Conquest of New Spain*, pp. 111–12. Conrad and Demarest, *Religion and Empire*, pp. 65–6, offer a good resumé of the sprawling, sated, hated Aztec empire, c. 1519.

[161] Mann, *Sources of Social Power*, pp. 234–5. The Inca empire, though also of recent creation, was more integrated, boasting an extensive road network, a massive system of obligatory migrant labour, and imperial control of the ancient ecological complimentarities which characterized the Andean 'archipelago': John Murra, 'Andean Societies before 1532', in Bethell, *Cambridge History of Latin America*, vol. 1, pp. 59–90.

[162] Davies, *The Aztecs*, p. 114. Cf. H. W. F. Saggs, *The Might That Was Assyria* (London, 1984), pp. 248–50. Ross Hassig, *Aztec Warfare: Imperial Expansion and Political Control* (Norman, Okla., 1988), pp. 92–3, prefers a Roman parallel, which seems less apt.

enhanced their power through judicious collaboration with Aztec imperialism. In this respect, as in others, the Aztecs broke ground for their Spanish successors, who would similarly rely on collaborating Indian *caciques* for the maintenance of order and government. But the Spaniards – architects of a true territorial empire – also created a centralized bureaucracy and uniform legal system; thus (like the British in Africa) they subtly combined forms of direct and indirect rule. The Aztec empire, an empire of domination, was based largely on indirect rule, tempered by recurrent repression.

V. Aztec Political Economy

The British, we are told, acquired their empire in a fit of absence of mind. The same cannot be said of the Aztecs. On the contrary, the Aztec empire was the product of deliberate policy, dating from the 1420s. But what were the motives of the policy-makers? Were economic, political or religious motives paramount? Or are these very categories inappropriate to the matter in hand? We have already suggested that the Aztec elite, historically conditioned to a martial existence, consolidated their rule on the basis of an inspired 'ideological adaptation', which underwrote continual war and sacrifice.[163] In this sense the empire had to expand to survive. Equally, as Moctezuma II found, stabilization was well-nigh impossible. Expansion did not represent an economically rational response to population pressure: it dissipated energies (literally) and brought in luxury goods rather than staples, to the benefit of the elite rather than the masses. To the extent that conquest followed trade, which it often did, it followed the old, long-distance, luxury trade: hence the emphasis on the Gulf, the Isthmus and the Soconusco cacao route (in which respects the Aztecs, far from developing radical new mercantile methods, continued an ancient tradition, dating back at least to the Olmecs). Aztec tribute lists reveal a clear preference for high-value, low-bulk, trade goods: feathers, cotton textiles, cacao, cochineal, shells, gold, jade.[164] Foodstuffs also figured in tribute lists, but the costs of porterage were counterproductively high and the positive correlation between

---

[163] Conrad and Demarest, *Religion and Empire*, p. 53.
[164] Offner, *Law and Politics*, p. 15; Hassig, *Trade, Tribute and Transportation*, pp. 107–10.

conquests and food imports was weak (hence, in part, the recurrent dearths). Luxury goods also comprised the stock-in-trade of the famous *pochteca*, the professional Aztec merchants whose activities, especially in the southeast, usually preceded military conquest – indeed, whose very presence often afforded the *casus belli*. The flag, in other words, followed trade.

But the *pochteca* were hardly cast in the mould of Cobdenite Quakers. They travelled armed and they spied for the state. In one case – at Ayutla, in present-day Guerrero – they allegedly endured a four-year siege before an Aztec army came to their rescue, only to find that the embattled 'merchants' had donned the quetzal feathers of warriors, sallied forth, and put their enemies to rout.[165] As traders, empire-builders and also important social actors within Tenochtitlán, the *pochteca* played a key role in Aztec society; some historians have cited that role as proof of that society's mercantile, market-oriented, even incipiently capitalist character. Leaving aside the more extreme formulations (Aztec socety was no more capitalist than Inca society was socialist), it is worth evaluating the significance of market activity and attempting a rough evaluation of the Aztec economy (and thus, by implication, of Aztec society as a whole: if it was not incipiently capitalist, may it be called feudal? An example of the Asiatic mode of production? Or none of these?). According to one view, the Postclassic period in Mesoamerica saw a marked growth in market activity and a dramatic reduction of state economic control and income, as compared with the *étatiste*, interventionist economies of the Classic era. With its trade booming and its merchants prospering – both increasingly independent of state control – Mesoamerica came to resemble medieval Europe or China.[166] The Conquest interrupted this dynamic development, but not before it had substantially changed the sociopolitical structures which had characterized Mesoamerica for over two millennia. At the time of the Conquest, 'Mesoamerica was becoming a system of a different order', compared to its traditional past.[167] The Conquest may not have aborted potential capitalist development, but it did arrest a fundamental process of change

---

[165] Davies, *The Aztecs*, pp. 135–6. For a good analysis of the *pochteca*, see Van Zantwijk, *Aztec Arrangement*, ch. 7.
[166] Blanton *et al.*, *Ancient Mesoamerica*, p. 238.
[167] Blanton *et al.*, *Ancient Mesoamerica*, p. 250.

which was transforming Mesoamerican society. According to this argument, the growth of mechant power and associated regional economies at the expense of traditional social status and formal political boundaries was central to this process. Supposedly supportive of this contention is the evidence of vigorous emporia, at Texcoco, Tlatelolco, Coixtlahuaca, Oaxaca and elsewhere. Free markets coexisted with politically controlled tribute at Texcoco, which, Offner argues, displayed a 'mixed' economic system, comprising a 'lively market economy'.[168] The Aztec empire as a whole 'probably depended on trade quite as much as on tribute', suggests Davies.[169] Comparativists, too, have seized upon such contentions, equating Mesoamerican and Middle Eastern economic systems: both, Curtin argues, were permeated by market activities; the notion of administered trade (such as the so-called temple trade of ancient Sumer) is discarded.[170] Reassertion of the power of the market was not, it seems, confined to the realm of government policy in the 1970s and 1980s.

But the matter is not so simple, either theoretically or empirically. Markets and tribute certainly coexisted and interpenetrated: tribute goods, delivered up to Tenochtitlán (or other dominant centres) entered and enlivened market activity (so, too, did some of the by-products of official hecatombs); Aztec rulers 'played the market', in the sense of providing goods for the *pochteca* to dispose of.[171] Given this interpenetration, it is difficult to gauge the relative weight of trade as against tribute (let alone the total production of goods, many of which entered neither network of circulation). Offner, keen to emphasize the importance of trade vis-à-vis tribute, estimates that no more than 10,000 to 20,000 people could have been supported by Texcoco's tribute receipts; Adams, on the other hand, calculates that Moctezuma II's tribute lists involved sufficient foodstuffs to support 360,000 people, which would justify Katz's assertion that 'the whole economy of the city [of Tenochtitlán] rested on tribute'.[172]

---

[168] Offner, *Law and Politics*, pp. 16–17.
[169] Davies, *The Aztecs*, p. 136.
[170] Curtin, *Cross-cultural Trade*, pp. 84–7.
[171] Davies, *The Aztecs*, p. 136.
[172] Offner, *Law and Politics*, p. 16; Wheatley, *Pivot of the Four Quarters*, p. 266; Katz, *Ancient American Civilizations*, pp. 188–9, 198–9.

Rather than swap figures – of dubious accuracy, no doubt – we should try to take in the broad picture and establish the general character of the Aztec economy ('economy' being defined in Polanyi's terms as the 'material-means-provisioning process') and the principles which governed its operation. To this end, we should look for the typical and the essential. A focus on trade *per se* can be misleading. After all, there was plenty of trade, especially long-distance luxury trade, in medieval Europe, coexisting with and not necessarily undermining the dominant feudal structures (an agrarian base, a huge subsistence sector, a basic social polarization of landlords and peasants, a constricted circulation of money, especially in regard to the remuneration of labour). Similarly, we should focus on the Aztec empire and the Mesoamerican heartland. Of course, mercantile activity ranged farther and was particularly evident in the late Postclassic ports of trade like Acalan (Tabasco) and, perhaps, Cozumel (Yucatán), whence massive canoes plied coastal trade routes.[173] But these ports were no more typical of the time than Venice was of feudal Europe; and they did not rival Venice in the scale or sophistication of their trading operations. Rather, they fell within an old tradition of Mesoamerican trading centres, even if they were particularly vigorous representatives of that tradition. Thus, they were neither dramatically innovative, nor typical of their time, nor inherently destructive of what *was* typical of the time.

Concerning the Aztec heartland, two basic points deserve emphasis. The first, which is uncontentious, is that the Aztec empire was an agrarian empire resting upon a massive subordinate peasantry. Carrasco's work on the Yautepec district (of present-day Morelos) reveals a society in which nearly two-thirds of the families possessed their own land and one-third were tenants (of ruler or nobles or other commoners); only 2 per cent of family heads played no part in the cultivation of land.[174] Commoners (*macehuales*) and serfs (*mayeques*) transferred an agricultural surplus, via the tribute system, to state and elite, not only in Tenochtitlán and the Valley of Mexico but also in subject provinces like the Zapotec and Mixtec kingdoms of Oaxaca and in independent principalities like Tlaxcala

---

[173] Blanton *et al.*, *Ancient Mesoamerica*, pp. 216–18; Sharer, *The Ancient Maya*, pp. 348–9.
[174] Cited in Van Zantwijk, *Aztec Arrangement*, pp. 274–5.

and the Tarascan realm. The share accruing to the state (in the form of the prince or emperor) and the landed elite varied from region to region; in the Tecali district (of Puebla) studied by Olivera, the landed elite were apparently stronger and richer than their counterparts in the Valley of Mexico – as was probably true, too, of the Tarascan region.[175] Although such geographical variations existed (they could be theorized in terms of oscillations within Eric Wolf's 'tributary mode'), they do not invalidate the basic point, that the Mesoamerican elites lived upon the surplus extracted from a massive landholding peasantry. The peasants also supplied labour, according to official requirements, and it was this labour which built the causeways, dykes and *chinampas* on which Tenochtitlán depended. Meanwhile, the surplus they rendered in kind was redistributed by the state. The king of Texcoco, for example, doled out tribute goods to judges, captains, officers and heroes every eighty days (tribute was exacted on an eighty-day schedule).[176] At Tenochtitlán, food delivered as tribute was stored, then distributed or sold in the market.[177]

Thus, a tributary relationship underpinned ruling elites throughout civilized Mesoamerica, most lavishly in the Valley of Mexico.[178] In that a subject peasantry maintained a noble class, the system displayed similarities to European feudalism, at least in the broad socioeconomic (not the narrow juridical) sense; and, as we have observed, European feudalism was fully acquainted with trade, especially long-distance luxury trade. But, if such umbrella terms arc to be used (and for the purposes of general comparison they can be

---

[175] Mercedes Olivera, *Pillis y macehuales. Las formaciones sociales y los modos de producción de Tecali del siglo XII al XVI* (Mexico, 1978), pp. 117–19; Beltrán, 'Estado y sociedad tarascos', pp. 49–51.

[176] Offner, *Law and Politics*, p. 16.

[177] Van Zantwijk, *Aztec Arrangement*, p. 285.

[178] Good analyses of Aztec political economy are provided by Hassig, *Trade, Tribute and Transportation*, pp. 103–10; Pedro Carrasco, 'La economía del México prehispánico', in Pedro Carrasco and Johanna Broda, eds., *Economía política e ideología en el México prehispánico* (Mexico, 1978), pp. 13–76; and three key articles by Frances Berdan: 'Distributive Mechanisms in the Aztec Economy', in Halperin and Dow, *Peasant Livelihood*, pp. 91–101; 'Tres formas de intercambio en la economía azteca', in Carrasco and Broda, *Economía política*, pp. 75–94; and 'Enterprise and Empire in Aztec and Early Colonial Mexico', in Isaac, *Economic Aspects of Prehispanic Highland Mexico*, pp. 281–302. 'Berdan's work', as Conrad and Demarest point out (*Religion and Empire*, p. 78, n. 133), 'represents a fundamental shift in thinking on the nature of Aztec economics [in that it] emphasizes the role of tribute in all sectors of Aztec life and the *interdependence* of tribute, market and long-distance trade', these viewed from a 'substantivist' perspective.

useful), it is the concept of the Asiatic mode of production which proves more appropriate. True, this concept (like many of Marxist provenance which deal with non- or pre-capitalist societies) is contentious – 'the most controversial and contested of all the possible modes of production outlined in the works of Marx and Engels'.[179] Weighty authorities deny its theoretical and historical validity.[180] Nevertheless, the broad features of the Islamic empires which afford the diagnostic elements of this mode are reasonably clear and, in this context, helpful. They include: an autocratic regime, part theocratic, part militarist, part bureaucratic; the subordination, above all to the state, of a tax- or tribute-paying peasantry; the relative absence of private property; the relative weakness of an independent landowning aristocracy.

Of course, these elements were not perfectly present in all historical cases, whether Islamic or Mesoamerican. Private property existed in the Aztec empire, but it was hedged about by restrictions; land sales occurred, but there does not appear to have been a recognizable market in land.[181] Private land was dwarfed by that held by the peasantry, which was not subject to sale and alienation.[182] Land grants made to nobles were often conditional, dependent on royal favour and aristocratic merit; in this sense, the Aztec nobility displayed some of the characteristics of a service aristocracy, wedded to the autocracy for its livelihood and legitimation, as in Tsarist Russia; their holdings resembled the 'oriental seigneuries' which, according

---

[179] Barry Hindess and Paul Q. Hirst, *Pre-Capitalist Modes of Production* (London, 1975), p. 178.

[180] Hindess and Hirst, *Pre-Capitalist Modes of Production*, ch. 4; Perry Anderson, *Lineages of the Absolutist State* (London, 1979), pp. 462–549, which concludes with the funereal plea that the Asiatic mode 'be given the decent burial that it deserves' (p. 548). For a more sympathetic evaluation, see Stephen P. Dunn, *The Fall and Rise of the Asiatic Mode of Production* (London, 1982).

[181] Offner, *Law and Politics*, pp. 130, 134; Carrasco, 'La economía del México prehispánico', pp. 27–8.

[182] 'Held', meaning 'occupied' and 'worked', not 'owned'. See Offner, *Law and Politics*, pp. 124–5; Van Zantwijk, *Aztec Arrangement*, p. 273, citing Carrasco; Wayne S. Osborne, 'Indian Land Retention in Colonial Metzitlán', *Hispanic American Historical Review*, 53/2 (1973), p. 220; Olivera, *Pillis y macehuales*, p. 110. Gibson, *Aztecs under Spanish Rule*, pp. 257–9, lists five categories of land: that of the temples, the 'community houses' (roughly, state offices), the king, the nobles and the *calpulleque* ('parishes'); though percentages are not given (and are probably unknown), it seems clear that individual ownership was unusual, and forms of collective usufruct common. Harvey, *Land and Politics*, offers detailed case studies.

to Weber, were prebendal rather than private.[183] The fundamental relationship upon which Aztec society was based – and which, exceptional features notwithstanding, gave that society its fundamental character – was not that of fiefdom or vassalage, with their embodied reciprocal rights, but that of the 'tax-rent couple', whereby 'the surplus product is appropriated in the form of tax...[which] may be paid in labour...[or] in kind'.[184] A landlord class, the beneficiary of peasant labour and produce, certainly existed, but, especially in the politically centralized Aztec heartland, it was less an independent aristocracy, possessed of autonomous wealth, power and status, than an imperial elite, tied to the emperor, who for his part enjoyed a unitary (not parcellized) sovereign authority.[185]

It is worth noting, by way of anticipation, that the Spanish colonial regime inherited from its Aztec predecessor certain key features. Again, a bureaucratic state extracted a surplus from the peasantry via the 'tax-rent couple': namely, tribute paid to the Crown in the form of labour and produce (as well as tithe to the Church). But, in addition, especially after the late sixteenth century, the Crown allowed the formation of an increasingly powerful landlord class, some of its members possessed of formally aristocratic titles and *de facto* political power. The first (tributary) form, most evident in the sixteenth century and, thereafter, in atypical regions like Yucatán, directly reproduced pre-Conquest patterns; it involved the substitution of pre-Conquest political (and clerical) authority by the Spanish Crown and its close ally the Catholic Church; and it required the maintenance of the old Indian community, the organizing unit of royal government and tribute collection. To the extent that the colony replicated this Asiatic mode, it allowed a degree of sociopolitical continuity. The second (landlord/aristocratic) form, in contrast, involved the creation of

---

[183] Cited by Immanuel Wallerstein, *The Modern World-System: Capitalist Agriculture and the Origins of the European World-Economy in the Sixteenth Century* (New York, 1974), p. 58. Carrasco, 'La economía del México prehispánico', p. 25, and Katz, *Ancient American Civilizations*, p. 208, suggest elements of a servitor aristocracy.

[184] Hindess and Hirst, *Pre-Capitalist Modes of Production*, pp. 193–4. Or, within the continuum of Wolf's 'tributary mode', the Aztec model stood closer to the centralized, despotic pole (which roughly corresponds, Wolf says, to the Asiatic mode of production): Eric R. Wolf, *Europe and the People without History* (Berkeley, 1982), pp. 80–1.

[185] Offner, *Law and Politics*, p. 135.

heritable latifundia, worked by dependent peons; the private appropriation of surplus in the form of feudal rent, labour service or incipient wage labour; and the large-scale dispossession of the landowning
Indian community. It developed especially in regions of more intense
market activity (often linked to the new mining industry), and it implied a certain derogation of the power of the central state (namely,
the Spanish Crown and its Atlantic bureaucracy) in favour of provincial landed elites. Again, if umbrella terms are to be used, this approx-
imated to a 'feudal mode'. What deserves emphasis here is the extent
of change, often traumatic change, which this new ('feudal') form implied and which in turn suggests how far pre-Conquest Mesoamerica
had been from constituting a feudal mode itself.

The second basic consideration relates to the role and significance
of the market, a theme which runs through this book. Market activity
appears to have pervaded Postclassic Mesoamerica. But we should
be careful not to impute to these markets anachronistic assumptions
drawn from more modern European examples. Aztec market transactions were governed by prior political and tributary relationships;
genuinely 'free' markets, in which individuals rationally pursued
profit and accumulated capital by the traffic of goods embodying
exchange- (not use-) values, probably did not exist and certainly did
not constitute the pivot of the Mesoamerican economy.[186] Though
'markets' were common, they were not agents of capital accumulation, and they were very likely not expressions of rational profit-
maximization either. At the lowest – but most basic – level, local
markets linked peasant communities, enabling them to exchange
goods according to communal needs and specialities. These, the forerunners of the *tianguis* which continued to abound in colonial and
independent Mexico, operated in the absence of a formal mercantile
class. They were highly localized and dedicated to the acquisition of
use- (not exchange-) values. In other words, peasants attended these
markets in order to acquire their salt, pots, herbs, honey, wax, cacao,
metates; merchants did not come to acquire their profits.

But what of the higher level, long-distance, luxury trade, the
trade of the celebrated *pochteca*? Did this not constitute a genuine

---

[186] A good analysis of use- and exchange-values, and their place within the 'social mode' of
production, is provided by Cohen, *Karl Marx's Theory of History*, pp. 80–1.

profit-maximizing, free market activity, analogous to European market behaviour, corrosive of traditional ways and indicative, perhaps, of radical new socioeconomic developments? Not necessarily. Trade (perhaps the very term is misleading) was embedded in political, tributary, relationships. The simple road system of the Aztec empire reveals, by virtue of its 'dendritic' form, how Tenochtitlán and its Triple Alliance partners monopolized trade and communications, stifling independent commercial activity, funnelling resources to the imperial headquarters and subordinating exchange to the voracious demands of a tribute-hungry political elite who, in consequence, amassed a 'staggering' quantity of goods for consumption or redistribution.[187] The *pochteca*, we have already suggested, were agents of imperial exploitation as much as they were independent merchants. Many of their transactions appear to have taken the form of barter (especially of highland manufactures for lowland raw materials: e.g., textiles for feathers and shells); and, although some goods, such as cacao beans and cotton capes, acquired an exchange-value distinct from their intrinsic use-value (i.e., they became units of exchange, not items of consumption), it does not follow that the exchange which they facilitated followed profit-maximizing market principles. Extensive exchange can be based upon customary rates of exchange, immune to the law of supply and demand: according to Berdan, Aztec long-distance trade operated with prices 'apparently set by administrative policy and exchanges probably took the form of barter'.[188]

This argument, though it cannot be proven by irrefutable evidence, is supported by the absence, within the Aztec economy, of developed forms of monetary exchange. For what is notable is not so much the limited use, as a medium of exchange, of cacao beans or cotton capes as the contrasting absence of any generalized currency of the kind that (even) medieval Europe or (especially) Tang

[187] Robert S. Santley, 'Prehispanic Roadways: Transport Network Geometry and Aztec Politico-Economic Organization in the Valley of Mexico' in Isaac, *Economic Aspects of Prehispanic Highland Mexico*, pp. 231–6; see also Hirth, 'The Analysis of Prehistoric Economic Systems', p. 296, which illustrates how 'primitive' trade, being embedded in customary, religious, magical and political systems, often fails to adhere to 'rational' principles – of profit maximization, risk aversion or energy conservation.

[188] Berdan, 'Distributive Mechanisms in the Aztec Economy', pp. 97–9.

China possessed. The Aztecs found the Spaniards' lust for bullion incomprehensible; Spanish clerics praised the Aztecs' indifference to filthy lucre. 'Blessed money' – Peter Martyr apostrophized the cacao bean – 'which exempts its possessors from avarice since it cannot be hoarded nor hidden under ground'.[189] No system of usury existed, even in the commercial entrepôt of Texcoco.[190] It is not surprising, therefore, that the Spaniards found it difficult to implant notions of profit-maximization among the subjugated Indian masses. 'Far from wishing to grow rich' (as a good *homo economicus* should) 'they [the Indians] had a hard time grasping the idea of earnings and profit' (although it should be added that, in suitably changed circumstances, Mexico's Indians learned fast: their indifference to profit reflected structural conditions, not some inherent psychic inertia).[191] In Yucatán, where the trauma of the Conquest was less severe than in central Mexico, and where the old Asiatic mode survived more vigorously, 'the Spaniards commonly voiced frustration with and bewilderment at the Maya's imperviousness to the blandishments of the market economy' and their 'perverse' reliance on a few simple subsistence goods.[192]

As regards the *pochteca* themselves, their equation with 'merchants' must be queried. The conquering Spaniards gave familiar names to unfamiliar objects. Iguanas were 'Nile crocodiles'; the first town they encountered in Yucatán became the 'Great Cairo'.[193] Today, more diffuse, general equations are still regularly employed: we tend to talk of Aztec priests, emperors, nobles, slaves, serfs and – in this case – merchants, assuming that these terms remain valid when translated from one cultural milieu to another.[194] The

---

[189] Prescott, *Conquest of Mexico*, p. 69. Spanish sources are never, of course, disinterested; Peter Martyr d'Anghera – a Renaissance humanist – was no doubt striving to make a point about materialist, money-grubbing, Europe.

[190] Offner, *Law and Politics*, p. 280.

[191] François Chevalier, *Land and Society in Colonial Mexico: The Great Hacienda* (Berkeley, 1970, first pubd. 1963), pp. 198–9.

[192] Farriss, *Maya Society*, pp. 45, 49.

[193] Díaz, *Conquest of New Spain*, p. 17.

[194] The tendency to assimilate 'merchants' to a standard, modern, market norm, though risky, is common and by no means confined to the Americas: see Karl Bücher's comments on medieval European 'merchants' cited in Wallerstein, *Modern World-System*, p. 19, n. 12. Having cited this salutary reminder, Wallerstein proceeds to assimilate markets and merchants throughout the world.

pochteca were, like European merchants, economic agents operating within a 'material-means-provisioning process'. They channelled goods from the provinces to the imperial headquarters. But so, too, did tribute-collectors (*calpixtli*), whom we would denote as officials rather than merchants. The *pochteca* were intimately associated with state policy, serving as ubiquitous spies and occasional warriors. They enjoyed privileged status, protected by the state. To confer upon them the simple Eurocentric label 'merchants' and then to infer from their historic prominence a marked commercialization and depoliticization of the Aztec economy is to argue in circular and misleading fashion.[195]

Thus, even if genuine markets, governed by principles of supply and demand, existed in pre-Conquest Mexico, it seems likely that they represented exceptions, anomalous enclaves within an economic system based upon barter, tribute, administered 'trade' and official redistribution. These were the hallmarks of the grand 'potlatch state' to which we have already referred. Tlatelolco did not make the Aztec empire a market society any more than the Tennessee Valley Authority made New Deal America socialist. The *pochteca* fitted within the potlatch system and cannot, therefore, be readily equated with a (notional) European model of free enterprise traders. Furthermore, it is not even clear that Aztec society was edging towards a more market-oriented society on the eve of its demise; counterfactual hypotheses of an aborted commercial revolution (or evolution) are unconvincing.[196] The basic organizing principles of the empire remained tributary and redistributive, thus dependent on the extraction of a surplus – goods and labour – from a peasant mass, by a state apparatus, staffed by an elite which combined elements of theocracy, militarism, classic bureaucracy and a prebendal aristocracy.

In the eyes of this elite, we may riskily surmise, the unfettered play of the market was either meaningless or downright dangerous, since it clashed with the basic principles of their sociopolitical hegemony. Meat and circuses were provided by military conquest and political fiat, not by judicious market speculation or shrewd investment.

---

[195] On the *pochteca*, see Van Zantiwjk, *Aztec Arrangement*, ch. 8; Berdan, 'Enterprise and Empire', pp. 283–9.

[196] Blanton *et al*, *Ancient Mesoamerica*, pp. 228, 237–8.

There have been few social groups in history further removed from the *homo economicus* of classical theory than the Aztec *tlatoani*, his belligerent nobles, reverential officials and bloodstained hierarchs. Their concept of the market was exemplified by Tlacaélel, who promoted the bloody and contrived 'flowery wars' as military 'fairs' or 'markets', at which soldiers shopped for the food and drink of their gluttonous gods.[197] Their collective ethic rested upon military prowess, a peculiar sanguinary chivalry and the notion of service (including sacrifice) to state and gods. Status and social mobility were won on the battlefield, in the palace, on the slick steps of the Great Temple. The *pochteca* fitted within this system and no more represented a serious challenge to this elite and its ethic than medieval merchants (who were probably more powerful) posed a threat to Europe's feudal rulers in their medieval heyday. On the contrary, the *pochteca* internalized the prevailing ethic, sought promotion and prestige within the system (e.g., by sacrificial offerings – scarcely the hallmark of market rationality), and, by their efforts, helped shore up the system. Official policy, notably under Moctezuma II, worked to ensure such compliance.[198]

Like the ancient empires of Asia, therefore, that of the Aztecs represented a hugely inflated, militarized and loosely bureaucratized version of the redistributive chiefdoms of an earlier era. The Aztec state organized the redistribution of goods, labour and even human lives on a massive scale, making possible obsessive acquisition and prodigal (but highly inegalitarian) consumption at the centre. As a 'potlatch state', it represented a hypertrophied version of redistributive chiefdoms, in which acquisition, exchange and consumption are fundamental but in which these processes conform to principles of prestige, power and ritual, not to the rationality of the market.

The political consequences of this system were dire. On the eve of the Spanish Conquest the Aztec empire constituted a massive agglomeration of thirty-eight provinces, embracing a range of geographical, cultural and linguistic variations, and an area of territory about half that of modern Mexico. Centrifugal forces, evident

---

[197] Brundage, *Fifth Sun*, p. 207.
[198] Clendinnen, *Aztecs*, pp. 133–40, on *pochteca* ethos and practice; p. 128 on Moctezuma II's 'aristocratic revolution', whereby (state) office became 'at once more finely hierarchical and more fiercely desired'.

in recurrent rebellions, were powerful; countervailing centripetal forces were weak and largely coercive. No device like Roman citizenship bound the discrete parts of the empire together; at best, the Aztecs preserved, manipulated and intermarried with local dynasties. Large chunks of independent territory compromised the empire's cohesion, and, even in the heartland of Anáhuac, Tenochtitlán's overweening power was resented, especially at Texcoco, whose prince, Nezahualpilli, predicted the annihilation of the empire in 1509 and whose people rebelled in 1516.[199] In the heartland, too, population growth, stimulated by 'explosive' immigration, created severe pressures and sporadic famines, during which 'members of the lower classes suffered horribly and died in great numbers', most recently in 1504–6.[200] By then, Tenochtitlán, with a population of perhaps a third of a million, was the biggest city in the world outside Asia. These pressures were aggravated, not alleviated, by the skewed distribution of goods which underlay the imperial political economy. Anáhuac fed off resentful provinces; the elite of Anáhuac were gorged on tribute; the poor periodically starved.

In 1502 the great Aztec generalissimo Ahuítzotl died, either from a blow on the head suffered during the disastrous flood for which he was responsible or from a wasting disease contracted on campaign which left him 'so emaciated he appeared almost fleshless'.[201] Either way, it was a symbolic end: Ahuítzotl paid the price of either botched ecological engineering or excessive warmongering. His successor, Moctezuma Xocoyotzin, was also an experienced general. But Moctezuma possessed a more refined and cerebral nature; he was personally gracious, if politically ruthless; and he was pious to the point of godfearing fatalism. Moctezuma appears to have had some grasp of the empire's structural problems, and he attempted corrective meaures. But the last Aztec *tlatoani*, like the last Romanov Tsar, saw the answer to domestic tensions and external threats in a reassertion of conservative values. His reforms were, therefore, 'aristocratic', representing 'a kind of counterrevolution'.[202] The *pochteca* – commoners whose wealth and status had always

---

[199] Gruzinski, *Man-Gods*, p. 27.
[200] Conrad and Demarest, *Religion and Empire*, p. 55; Offner, *Law and Politics*, p. 147.
[201] Davies, *The Aztecs*, p. 206.
[202] Offner, *Law and Politics*, p. 236; Davies, *The Aztecs*, p. 216.

been precariously dependent on imperial favour – were now more closely regulated; the political preferment of commoners (a feature of Ahuítzotl's turbulent reign) was halted; and many parvenus were purged, even executed. Instead, Moctezuma surrounded himself with blueblooded nobles, versed in courtly prose and etiquette (only pure Nahuatl was to be spoken in the royal presence). The emperor even sought to create a pan-Aztec nobility, transcending local particularism and linking the aristocracies of the Triple Alliance cities (a measure designed, perhaps, to counter the old alliance's fissiparous tendencies). Meanwhile, the power and aura of the *tlatoani* were enhanced by quasi-Oriental ritual and by the effective relegation of the council to a purely advisory role. Moctezuma, in short, reinforced the ascriptive and corporate aspects of Aztec society, while greedily gathering power in his own hands. The social mobility engendered by war and conquest was deliberately curtailed; status barriers were rigidified; the great, shifting glacier of Aztec society was frozen in place. Adherents of the old, military, expansionist regime – clients of the swashbuckling Ahuítzotl – were brushed aside. Moctezuma, as it were, played the Bourbon to Ahuítzotl's Bonaparte.

On the external front, too, Moctezuma retrenched. After decades of 'conquest without consolidation' the new ruler sought to stabilize rather than to extend the empire.[203] But even retrenchment required constant campaigns, especially in (what might be called) the near east and the deep south, and, above all, in mountainous zones populated by 'unconquered peoples, indomitable and aggressive [who] would not easily yield either captives or tribute'.[204] Like later centralizing regimes, Spanish and Mexican, the Aztecs found these serranos to be tough opponents. On the Pacific coast, Tototepec and Yopitzingo held out, harried and circumscribed; the Mixtec principalities of Oaxaca were gradually reduced; a rebellion in far-off Soconusco was put down.[205] The nearest and most troublesome enemy of all, Tlaxcala (ultimately allied to Huejotzingo), was subjected to sustained blockade and aggression. The Tlaxcalans – never possessed of great resources – were denied even salt, which

---

[203] Conrad and Demarest, *Religion and Empire*, p. 53.
[204] Conrad and Demarest, *Religion and Empire*, p. 65.
[205] Davies, *The Aztecs*, pp. 219–22.

they had to extract from the soil. The old dalliance of the 'flowery wars' was forgotten; the struggle between Aztec and Tlaxcalan became a *guerre à outrance*. As successive campaigns between 1504 and 1518 brought more losses than glory, Moctezuma grew peevish, receiving his crestfallen troops with reproaches, punishments and fresh exhortations.[206] The days of spectacular Aztec triumphs, of huge hecatombs of prisoners, were gone. Famine returned in 1505–6; allies, like Texcoco, grew resentful of their costly, compulsory involvement in the Tlaxcala wars; they resented, too, Moctezuma's meddling in their domestic politics, his attempt to assimilate the Texcocan aristocracy. In 1516 the Triple Alliance splintered as Texcoco was convulsed by a succession struggle. Moctezuma installed his chosen candidate, Cacama, and Cacama's rival, Ixtlilxochitl, raised the standard of revolt in the mountain country to the northeast of the Texcocan domains, whence he could not be dislodged.[207] Like the Inca empire (though to a lesser extent), the Aztec empire faced internal dissension on the eve of the Spanish conquest. Ixtlilxochitl and his Texcocan faction would, like the Tlaxcalans, afford vital allies for Cortés's diminutive army.

In short, the empire had now lost the imperial and military momentum which was its *raison d'être*. Successive blitzkrieg victories – swift, glorious and, in their own way, profitable – gave way to grim wars of attrition. The flow of prisoners was staunched; the gods went hungry. Allies grew restive or downright rebellious. The Aztec regime – a regime of 'movement' rather than 'order' – found retrenchment galling, a denial of the ideological base upon which it had been founded a century before. Moctezuma himself grew morose, venting his spleen on his troops, his astrologers, ultimately the gods themselves, who appeared to have deserted him. As the momentous year *Ce Acatl* (1519) approached, portents and prodigies accumulated. Possibly these signalled a form of popular religious revivalism, a broad contestation of the empire, its ruler and its warlike ideology. When Moctezuma persecuted sorcerers and prophets he was not just shooting the messengers who brought bad news; he was, perhaps, trying to stamp out subversive cults, manifestations of a

[206] Davies, *The Aztecs*, pp. 230–1.
[207] Offner, *Law and Politics*, pp. 238–9.

widespread spiritual malaise.[208] Hag-ridden, the emperor yearned to quit the false terrestrial world and skulk in the subterranean caverns of Huemac, king of the dead. He found consolation in penance and fasting. When news came of ships in the Gulf, and of the arrival of bearded strangers from the east, Moctezuma, anxious and perplexed, probably saw in this event the predicted return of the man-god Quetzalcóatl; certainly, he sent lavish gifts which served only to excite Spanish cupidity.[209]

The two sundered branchs of humankind were about to meet, in the form of rival empires, each possessed of military prowess and a sense of imperial mission. But one, whose territory would afford the site of battle, already stood on the brink of internal crisis.

[208] Gruzinski, *Man-Gods*, p. 28.

[209] There is some dispute as to whether Moctezuma really equated Cortés with Quetzalcóatl (or, possibly, Tezcatlipoca, or even Huitzilopochtli); however, the balance of the evidence suggests that he did, at least at the outset. See León-Portilla, *Broken Spears*, pp. vii, 13, 14, 21, 29; Thomas, *Conquest of Mexico*, pp. 185–6, 264.

FOUR. Spain and the Conquest

I. Spain

I t is one of those neat often-noted conjunctures of history that the consummation of the Reconquista – the Catholic kings' subjugation of the last Moslem kingdom of Granada – precisely coincided with Columbus's first voyage and the start of Spanish imperialism in the New World. Indeed, Columbus received his royal commission in the military encampment outside Granada in April 1492. This tidy sequential development was marked by very obvious continuities: the physical and spiritual energies devoted to the now completed Reconquista could be deployed in the Americas; the same methods, the same families, the same terminology (*entradas, capitulaciones*) were at once evident.[1] On this, many scholars agree. The Reconquista 'prepared the rapid conquest and Europeanization of Latin America'; the conquest of Mexico, in particular, represented 'the last of the great medieval conquests'; and the parallel spiritual conquest may be seen as the 'swansong of the Middle Ages'.[2] The product of late

---

[1] *Entradas*, roughly, organized expeditions; *capitulaciones*, contracts between the Crown and individual leaders outlining the terms of exploration, conquest and settlement. Recent examples of the oft-noted conjuncture include: Tzvetan Todorov, *The Conquest of America* (New York, 1992), p. 50; Bernard Lewis, *Cultures in Conflict: Christians, Muslims and Jews in the Age of Discovery* (New York, 1995), p. 8; and Robert Bartlett, *The Making of Europe: Conquest, Colonization and Cultural Change, 950–1350* (London, 1994), p. 313.

[2] Derek W. Lomax, *The Reconquest of Spain* (London, 1978), p. 178, which concludes, with an odd Panglossian flourish, that Spain's triumph in the New World 'spared it (the New World) most of the religious and imperialist wars which would henceforth afflict almost all the rest of mankind'; Chevalier, *Land and Society in Colonial Mexico*, p. 36; John L. Phelan, *The Millennial*

medieval Spain, the Conquest in turn had a dialectical impact on the Spanish metropolis itself, acting as an anchor which secured Spain to its medieval moorings; the 'logical outcome of the traditions and aspirations of an earlier age', the new empire served to 'perpetuate at home and project overseas the ideals, the values, and the institutions of medieval Castile'.[3]

Against this, the continuity thesis, stands an alternative view which stresses change and rupture. Here, the Conquest marks a decisive break, the entrance of new, dynamic historical forces. 'It was in the sixteenth century', Wallerstein writes, 'that there came to be a European world-economy based upon the capitalist mode of production'.[4] In this epochal development, Wallerstein and others concur, the Iberian peninsula took the lead. 'Iberian America', Bagú stresses, 'was born to integrate the cycle of incipient capitalism, not to prolong the languishing feudal cycle'.[5] According to this view, the conquest of Latin America in general and Mexico in particular played a crucial part in the gestation of European capitalism – which first stimulated it and was then, in turn, stimulated by it. Capitalism bred conquest which bred capitalism. Hence the resulting colonization was 'unlike anything that history had previously known'; far from following the feudal precedents of the Reconquista, it served to integrate Mexico 'into the expanding world mercantile capitalist system'.[6]

Feudal or capitalist, old or new, continuity or rupture? Some may dodge the question – or deny its validity – but I do not care for that negative recourse. Those who try to banish offending terms – such as 'capitalism' – from the conceptual kingdom often find that they have sneaked back unbidden, sometimes in disguise.[7] The fact

---

Kingdom of the Franciscans in the New World (Berkeley, 1956), p. 1. The most detailed, erudite, but mildly obsessive, version of the feudal-character-of-the-Conquest thesis is Luis Weckman, *La herencia medieval de México* (Mexico, 1996; first pubd. 1984).

[3] J. H. Elliott, *Imperial Spain, 1469–1716* (Harmondsworth, 1970), p. 45.

[4] Wallerstein, *The Modern World-System*, p. 67; but note the demurral of Fernand Braudel, *Civilization and Capitalism, Fifteenth-Eighteenth Centuries*, vol. 3, *The Perspective of the World* (London, 1985), p. 57.

[5] Quoted in Wallerstein, *Modern World-System*, p. 22; cf. André Gunder Frank, *Capitalism and Underdevelopment in Latin America* (Harmondsworth, 1971), p. 46.

[6] André Gunder Frank, *Mexican Agriculture, 1521–1630* (Cambridge, 1979), p. 5.

[7] Fernand Braudel, *Civilization and Capitalism, Fifteenth-Eighteenth Centuries*, vol. 2, *The Wheels of Commerce* (London, 1982), p. 231; and the same author's *Perspective of the World*, pp. 425–9, which reviews the debate inconclusively. Steve J. Stern, 'Feudalism, Capitalism and the World

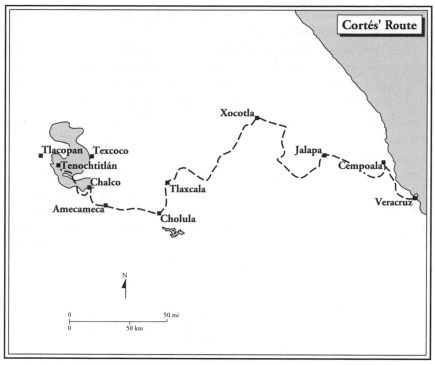

Map 7

is that while for many lesser historical issues these grand terms can be avoided (and, conversely, their invocation at every such instance becomes tiresome and mechanical) they are the best tools we have for making sense of grand processes of historical change – such as the 'expansion of Europe' and the onset of imperialism in the sixteenth century. We will later consider the application of these terms within the context of colonial Mexico and its broad pattern of development from the sixteenth to the eighteenth centuries; here, as we stand at the threshold of that development, it is worth considering its

System in the Perspective of Latin America and the Caribbean', and I. Wallerstein, 'Comments on Stern's Critical Tests', *American Historical Review*, 93/4 (1988), pp. 829–72, 873–85, slug out a few more rounds. For an intelligent recent rebuttal of such Eurocentric terminology – Braudel being, the author says, 'unabashedly Eurocentric' – see Robert W. Patch, *Maya and Spaniard in Yucatán, 1648–1812* (Stanford, 1993), pp. 1–2, 245–9. As will become clear, I am not quite ready to consign these terms to limbo; at least, not until we come up with something better. A good theoretical approach to such questions is provided by Witold Kula, *An Economic Theory of the Feudal System* (London, 1976), pp. 19–27.

European origins, and to confront the feudal/capitalist issue head-on, even if somewhat briefly.

Any discussion of such general but important questions needs some prior conceptual clarification. Rival authorities may 'agree on the facts' – at least to an appreciable degree – but still differ radically as to their interpretation.[8] First, we should stress that 'feudalism' is here treated as a broad socioeconomic system (of which there can be many variants), which is characterized by key features differentiating it from 'capitalism'; these features are political and economic, broad and structural, and cannot be reduced to narrower juridical features typical of classic Western European feudalism (e.g., fealty and vassalage).[9] A 'tight' definition of feudalism might *require* the latter, but such an analytical approach would restrict the category, would inhibit broad comparison and would evade the problem of epochal historical interpretation. It would, instead, imply the existence of numerous, peculiar, sociopolitical systems, each inhabiting its distinct historical universe, each defying comparison and interpretative assimilation. Of course, differences must be recognized. But we are proceeding on the assumption that, for present purposes, narrower juridical differences are not crucial, while broader socioeconomic similarities are. In discussing 'feudalism' or 'capitalism', therefore, we are less concerned with superficial differences than with broad structural similarities. We are discussing modes of production rather than juridical forms.

A basic theoretical difference here exists between definitions of capitalism couched in terms of market relations (these, focussing on relations of *exchange*, whereby commodities *circulate*, can be called 'circulationist') and definitions which focus on relations of production – labour systems and the means by which surplus is extracted from the producers of commodities (peasants, slaves, workers) by non-producers (lords, slave-owners, factory-owners) – which may in turn be called 'productionist'. Circulationists readily classify

---

[8] 'The facts are the same. The theoretical perspective is different': Wallerstein, *Modern World-System*, p. 28, reviewing the Postan-Kosminsky debate.

[9] Kula, *An Economic Theory*, p. 16; compare the narrower definition of F. L. Ganshof, *Feudalism* (London, 1964), on which, see Alain Guerreau, *El feudalismo: Un horizonte teórico* (Barcelona, 1984), pp. 83–6. A useful summary is provided by R. J. Holton, *The Transition from Feudalism to Capitalism*, pp. 18–21, 157–68.

the Spanish colonial empire as capitalist because, they argue, its basic organizing principles were those of market exchange and profit-maximization (we will pass over the 'truth' – the empirical validity – of this argument for the moment; the point is to establish the theoretical premise). Productionists, on the other hand, discern genuine capitalist relations of production only where capital confronts free wage labour. Slave or serf – or 'coerced cash-crop' – agriculture cannot be capitalist, even if it sells its produce in the market, as it often does.[10]

Now, from a strict reading of Marx – to whom most of the rival contenders in this debate defer – it would seem that the productionists are closer to the letter of the original, though this does not stop their circulationist rivals from claiming greater fidelity to the spirit (as we all know, Marx's writings are by no means clear or consistent on some key points).[11] It is not the task of a workaday historian to adjudicate between these warring sects, though I am bound to say that my limited knowledge of Marx and Marxism leads me to prefer the productionist over the circulationist argument, on the grounds that it is both a more faithful – and, better still, a more useful – theoretical perspective. However, a straight choice would be invidious and in some respects unnecessary. The problem arises because Marx's own analysis, on which the theoretical debate hinges, concentrated first on the history and character of capitalism (rather than feudalism) and second on developments in Western Europe, especially England, the cradle of capitalism. Marx offers a clear, if contentious, picture of developed capitalism; but his discussion of the way in which capitalism emerged from a prior feudalism is more partial and strongly Anglocentric; hence it is harder to generalise to other places and epochs.

In analysing England, Marx emphasized the development of 'merchant capital', which – to the delight of later circulationists – he dated in the sixteenth century, which he associated with the rise of overseas empire, and which he saw as leading, logically and progressively, to the triumph of industrial capital some two centuries later.[12]

---

[10] Ernesto Laclau, *Politics and Ideology in Marxist Theory* (London, 1977), pp. 16–50, advances the 'productionist' critique of Wallerstein *et al.*

[11] Wallerstein, *Modern World-System*, p. 126.

[12] Frank, *Capitalism and Underdevelopment*, p. 21.

In the interim, capital accumulated, peasants were dispossessed, a propertyless proletariat was formed, industry developed. The era of merchant capital could legitimately be seen as transitional, linking a dissolving feudalism to a triumphant bourgeois capitalism; and this transition was hurried along by mercantile imperialism overseas. But what works for England (if, indeed, it does) may not work for the rest of Europe, still less for the rest of the world. And the problem lies less in the general theory – which, I repeat, is probably the best we have for such broad historical analyses – than in its specific historical application.

In the case of Europe, Perry Anderson has argued convincingly that the Absolutist state of the early modern era (c. 1500–1800) retained – despite many ambiguities – an 'irreducibly feudal character'. It was controlled by a feudal aristocracy which confronted, came to terms with and successfully dominated 'the nascent mercantile and manufacturing classes'. A commercial bourgeoisie developed under Absolutism – indeed, was vital to the Absolutist project – yet Absolutism 'ended by frustrating and falsifying its promises for capital'.[13] Nowhere was this stultification of capital clearer than in Spain where, Anderson argues, 'the ancien régime preserved its feudal roots . . . to its dying day' – that is, down to the late eighteenth or early nineteenth century.[14] Thus, the supposed era of merchant capital, transitional between feudalism and capitalism, is shown to be a prolongation of feudalism, of feudal rule and feudal forms. These forms are not static: they react and mutate; but they remain dominant down to the early nineteenth century. True to Marx's original schema, Anderson retains the notion of 'transition' ('the rule of the Absolutist state was that of the feudal nobility in the epoch of the transition to capitalism'); but Anderson's transition is mightily stretched.[15] Whereas England – Marx's key case – had clearly debouched into bourgeois capitalism by the time of his writing, other cases to which the same schema is applied had still not arrived at that juncture then, or even a century later.

---

[13] Anderson, *Lineages of the Absolutist State*, pp. 39–42; see also Peter Kriedte, *Feudalismo tardío y capital mercantil* (Barcelona, 1982), pp. 9–28.

[14] Anderson, *Lineages of the Absolutist State*, p. 84.

[15] Anderson, *Lineages of the Absolutist State*, p. 42.

The application of Marx's Anglocentric model to Spain, or to Spanish America, thus impels us towards the unhappy notion of an immensely 'stretched' transition, characterized by a merchant capital which fails to achieve its progressive role (dissolving feudalism and nurturing bourgeois capitalism) or which takes so long about it that the very 'transitional' label starts to seem a misnomer. It is not that long secular changes should be ignored or that impatient historians should set stopwatches for social processes; rather, it is that an excessively stretched 'transition' eventually ceases to look like a transition and begins to look like an era in its own right. After all, capitalism itself is transitional, *sub specie aeternitatis*.

There are three exits from this dilemma. The first, to discard all references to 'feudalism', 'capitalism' and the like, has already been considered and rejected. The second is to denote Spanish America – Mexico included – as a distinct colonial form, divergent from the metropolitan (read: Anglocentric) model by virtue of its dependent, colonial experience. Merchant capital, being colonial and parasitic, could not develop – could not perform its historic 'progressive' function – in the colonies as it had in the European metropolis. Instead, from the sixteenth century on it stunted development (even produced 'underdevelopment'), leaving a legacy that has been liquidated only in rare, recent revolutionary instances.[16] For some, therefore, Spanish America develops as a distinctly dependent, colonial society; its historic fate is determined by external imperialist forces which condemn it to permanent (or, at least, very long-term) structural underdevelopment. This view, which necessarily stresses external determinants, can either be couched in terms of historical specificity (i.e., that's the way it was, the colonial liaison was crucial, and the colony was forced to follow a peculiar path of colonial underdevelopment), or it can be presented as an updated, *dependista* Marxism, a Marxism which takes into account the realities of imperialism in a way that Marx did not.[17] For, not only did Marx repeatedly stress

[16] Such as the Cuban Revolution, according to Frank, *Capitalism and Underdevelopment*, p. 21.

[17] Stern, 'Feudalism, Capitalism and the World System', presents an informed version of the second thesis. Ciro F. S. Cardoso has repudiated the notion of a feudal Latin America, arguing instead for a specifically 'colonial' mode of production: 'Observaciones...', in Charles Parain et al., *El feudalismo* (Madrid, 1992; first pubd. 1972), pp. 97–100, and, with Héctor Pérez Brignoli, *Historia económica de América Latina*, vol. 1, *Sistemas agrarios e historia colonial* (Barcelona, 1979), pp. 187–9. However, Cardoso's argument is much stronger in respect of

that internal relations of production rather than external liaisons of exchange were the crucial determinants of social change, he also tended to view imperialism as a progressive force, opening up peripheral regions to capitalist development (not, as the *dependistas* argue, underdevelopment).[18] Dependency theory offers important insights, but, notwithstanding its professed allegiances, it refutes more than it refines Marx because it emphasizes external constraints over internal dynamics in a way that is antithetical to Marxism and, more important, at odds with the historical evidence.

The third approach, which will roughly be followed here, stresses these internal dynamics and is avowedly 'productionist' in emphasis. It pays more attention to the relations of production prevailing within colonial society than to the external relations of exchange. Its focus is therefore more peripheral than Eurocentric (or 'world-systemic'). It takes Spain's pre-eminent colony – Mexico, or New Spain – as a valid unit of analysis, a 'social formation' in its own right. Of course, New Spain's development was affected by its colonial ties (though decreasingly so for much of the colonial era). Old Spain's development, too, was reciprocally affected by these ties. 'Dependency' was not a one-way street. Nevertheless, the key determinants of Mexican development were to be found within the colony itself, and the character of colonial society was formed, above all, by the economic structures which underpinned it, by the labour systems which it engendered and by the forms whereby surplus was extracted from producers, be they miners or artisans, peasants, peons or slaves. Structures, systems, forms were all varied and mutating. We will examine and categorize them in due course. But the initial point to make is this: if such varied forms are to be given a single, encompassing title, it would be wrong to term them 'capitalist'. Conversely, the only justified umbrella term – to be found within the conventional repertoire – would have to be 'feudal'. Returning to the initial division of scholarly opinion, therefore, we prefer to conceptualize colonial Mexico as a feudal creation of a feudal Spain.[19]

Brazil than Spanish America. Note the critique of Cardoso in Laclau, *Politics and Ideology*, pp. 48–9.

[18] The thesis is developed by Bill Warren, *Imperialism: Pioneer of Capitalism* (London, 1980).

[19] Compare Enrique Semo, *The History of Capitalism in Mexico: Its Origins, 1521–1763* (Austin, 1993), pp. xxiv–xxv, 150–1.

However much scholars may divide according to theoretical perspective, they do reach some consensus concerning the range of motives and preoccupations which impelled Spaniards upon the path of empire.[20] No one suggests a simple, mono-causal explanation. But, as E. H. Carr once argued (if not in quite these terms), to proceed from a mono-causal *open sesame* to a multi-causal shopping list is only a partial advance, worthy of a second-class candidate; a first-class candidate would hazard some hierarchy of explanations (primary, secondary, etc.) and, in addition, would attempt to probe their interrelationship.[21] In considering the origins of the Spanish conquest of America it is possible to discern four broad, portmanteau categories of explanation. These are not watertight, and their contents easily spill over from one to another, as commonly occurs with categories of historical explanation; however, they can help us make sense of this immensely complex and dynamic process. The categories are (1) the economic, (2) the religious, (3) the intellectual and (4) the political. These categories help us arrange primary causes; however, since the Conquest, once under way, quickly acquired a momentum and rationale of its own, new secondary factors soon arose to supplement these and to complicate the picture. Any historical account must therefore also include (5) the 'logic', or 'dialectic', of the Conquest itself.

Economic goals were paramount in the genesis of exploration and conquest. Scarcely a contemporary account exists which does not stress the lure of gold – and, to a lesser extent, other material incentives. Columbus, as he sought a western passage to India, was 'obsessed' by gold; for the three months (October 1492 to January 1493) while he reconnoitred the Caribbean islands, his diary contains over sixty-five references to the yellow metal; and it was his receipt of a barrel of gold at Hispaniola – where he finally found what he was looking for – which shifted the emphasis of the expedition away from the Asian venture in favour of Caribbean conquest and plunder.[22] Balboa's acquisition of a 'considerable haul of gold'

---

[20] For example, Wallerstein, *Modern World-System*, pp. 38–52; Elliott, *Imperial Spain*, pp. 62–6; Thomas, *Conquest of Mexico*, pp. 59–64.

[21] E. H. Carr, *What Is History?* (Harmondsworth, 1964), pp. 89–90.

[22] J. H. Parry, *The Discovery of South America* (London, 1979), p. 61; Pierre Vilar, *A History of Gold and Money* (London, 1984), pp. 63–6; Todorov, *Conquest of America*, pp. 8–12.

(as well as of pearls) on the Isthmus of Panama similarly excited not only his delight but also that of the pious Peter Martyr, who rejoiced that 'Spain need no longer plough up the ground to the depths of the infernal regions . . . in order to draw wealth from the earth. She will find riches on the surface . . . it will suffice merely to sift the earth.'[23] Reports of more easy pickings north of the Isthmus soon spurred voyagers in that direction: Juan de Grijalva's crew sailed post-haste up the Gulf coast because – a crewman recalled – 'we were anxious to push on toward the place where they said there was gold.'[24]

Grijalva's expedition brought back little by way of material returns but plenty of enticing reports of treasure to be won on the Mesoamerican mainland. Grijalva thus earned the reprobation but also excited the 'cupidity' of Diego de Velázquez, governor of Cuba, who at once commissioned Hernán Cortés to lead a larger expedition, its task 'to trade for as much gold as possible and to return with it to the island of Fernandina'.[25] Cortés, avid for conquest and plunder, flouted these orders. But his own itch for gold was no less insistent. Newly acquired gold was rushed back to Spain in 1519 in order to win royal approval of his illicit expedition: this was but a 'sample', Cortés explained, for 'it cannot be doubted that there must be in this land as much (gold) as in that from which Solomon is said to have taken the gold for the temple.'[26] And Moctezuma's envoys, who came bearing gifts of gold, were received with rejoicing and urged to return with more, since Cortés 'wished to know whether the gold of their country was the same as the gold we find in our rivers.'[27]

Thereafter, the conquistadors' lust for gold led them to loot, kill and torture. Luxurious artefacts – feathers, jade, shields – were stripped of their gold and silver, then discarded, burned or given as plunder to Indian allies.[28] The Aztecs themselves, though fond enough of luxury goods, found this obsessive bullionism bizarre: 'the truth is they (the Spaniards) longed and lusted for gold. Their bodies swelled with greed and their hunger was ravenous; they hungered like pigs

[23] Parry, *The Discovery*, pp. 121–2.
[24] Díaz, *Conquest of New Spain*, p. 34.
[25] Fernandina = Cuba. Pagden, *Hernán Cortés*, pp. 5, 24–6.
[26] Pagden, *Hernán Cortés*, p. 29.
[27] Díaz, *Conquest of New Spain*, pp. 91–3.
[28] León-Portilla, *The Broken Spears*, pp. 68, 124.

for that gold'.[29] Greed even bred hallucination: beholding from afar the newly plastered facades of the buildings of Cempoala 'one of the horsemen took the shining whiteness for silver and came galloping back to tell Cortés that our quarters had silver walls'.[30]

This lust for bullion, which the native Americans found incomprehensible, was entirely logical, given the character and conditions of the European economy which had produced the conquistadors. Gold coinage had developed in Europe during the twelfth and thirteenth centuries; growing demand for the metal, however, had been alleviated by the economic crisis and demographic decline of the later fourteenth century. But by the mid-fifteenth century Europe began to suffer a chronic shortage of gold, which was aggravated by the continent's unfavourable trade balance with – hence constant drain of bullion to – the economies of Asia. Spain, in particular, suffered from the fifteenth-century 'flight of gold.'[31] Throughout Europe, prices fell, currencies were debased and a general quest for gold (and, to a lesser extent, silver) agitated the continent. In response, European silver production was boosted, and Portuguese captains – renewing earlier efforts dating back to the gold-hungry thirteenth century – began to scout the West African coast. They sought both centres of gold production and new sea routes to the East, whence they could import bullion as well as those spices which jaded European palates craved during the long months of winter. For the overland route to the East – specifically to India, China and southeast Asia – was barred by expansionist Moslem powers, while Asia's trade itself was largely controlled by Indian and Arab merchants.

By the 1500s the Portuguese had pushed their African voyages as far as the Indian Ocean and begun a successful military campaign to break into the spice trade. Yet this lucrative eastern trade – offering fat pickings to whichever maritime power could usurp Venice's old role as commercial entrepôt between Europe and Asia – further increased the demand for bullion, since Europe produced relatively few trade goods to offer in sophisticated Asian markets. Meanwhile, these emergent economic liaisons meshed closely with national

---

[29] León-Portilla, *The Broken Spears*, p. 51.
[30] Díaz, *Conquest of New Spain*, p. 107.
[31] Vilar, *A History of Gold*, pp. 37, 45; Harry A. Miskimin, *The Economy of Later Renaissance Europe, 1460–1600* (Cambridge, 1977), pp. 23, 28–9.

power politics. Monarchs – like the Catholic kings, Ferdinand and
Isabella – adhered to a crude, unschematic mercantilism and sought
to control profitable trade routes and, thereby, to encourage the flow
of bullion into their domains: 'policy-makers during the sixteenth
century were virtually obsessed with bullion flow.'[32] Insofar as they
could, therefore, monarchs encouraged voyages of discovery, trade
and conquest. Already, following the Portuguese push towards Africa
and the Atlantic islands, the Spaniards had taken the Canaries, where
their rule was ratified by treaty with Portugal in 1475 but only imposed upon the native Guanches by armed force during the 1490s.
No gold was forthcoming here, but the development – as a poor second best – of slave-worked sugar plantations set a vital precedent for
later New World colonial enterprise.[33]

It is clear, therefore, that the quest for luxury goods in general and,
above all, gold in particular, was a primary stimulus for overseas
exploration and conquest, in which kings and conquistadors, merchants and navigators, collaborated according to a perceived common economic interest. It would be wrong, however, to see in this
collective avarice a radical break with the past, brought on by the
birth of capitalism. In other words, the 'circulationist' assumption
that capitalism was conceived in commercial lust, *circa* 1450, and
born, amid the pangs of American conquest, between the 1490s and
1540s, is fundamentally misleading. European expansion certainly
responded to macroeconomic factors at work within Europe. But
these were not radically new. A previous quest for gold, during the
populous thirteenth century, had induced Genoese captains to attempt a circumnavigation of Africa – which failed.[34] The medieval
Genoese were also involved in a form of Mediterranean mercantile
imperialism which offered the closest prototype of later Portuguese
methods in Asia. Continuity – rather than rupture – is also suggested
by the career of the great Portuguese 'imperialist', Henry the Naviga-
tor, a 'staunchly conservative' prince, whose objectives in furthering
African exploration (among others, 'the desire to open profitable new

---

[32] Miskimin, *The Economy of Later Renaissance Europe*, pp. 150–1; see also Elliott, *Imperial Spain*, p. 111, and Pierre Chaunu, *La expansión europea (siglos XII al XV)* (Barcelona, 1982), pp. 60–1.

[33] Elliott, *Imperial Spain*, p. 58; Wallerstein, *Modern World-System*, pp. 88–9.

[34] Vilar, *A History of Gold*, pp. 47–8; Chaunu, *La expansión europea*, p. 38.

trades, presumably with the producers of gold') and whose methods of achieving it were both 'conventionally medieval'.[35] Indeed, as Weber reminds us, with only a touch of hyperbole, Virgil's *'auri sacra fames* (accursed lust for gold) is as old as the history of man'; hence, 'ruthless acquisition', by war, piracy, trade and conquest, or some combination of the four, is no peculiar hallmark of modern capitalism; on the contrary, Weber suggests, it is antithetical to modern capitalism's patient, disciplined, rational pursuit of profit.[36]

Overseas trade could, of course, form part of a broadly 'bourgeois' pattern of capital accumulation, consonant with the theories of Weber or Marx; it did so in England, Marx's paradigmatic case. But here overseas trade conspired with – and, arguably, was dependent upon – far-reaching changes in England's domestic political economy, which provided the real motor of capitalist transition.[37] Late fifteenth-century Spain was another matter. Certainly, important mercantile groups existed: Catalan/Aragonese traders had engaged in Mediterranean commerce and empire-building for centuries, and, along with the Genoese, they helped kit out many of the early voyages of Atlantic exploration; the Castilian woollen interests, too, had more recently developed a thriving trade with northern Europe, shipping through the busy Basque ports. But, within the loose, patrimonial entity we refer to as 'Spain', these were far from being the dominant interests (as, for example, their Dutch counterparts would become by the seventeenth century). The Spanish bourgeoisie – to put it crudely – was too weak to challenge feudal power or to subvert feudal values, both of which underwrote Spanish Absolutism, especially in Castile, the hub of Hispanic imperialism.[38] For Aragon (specifically, Catalonia), where the 'bourgeois' challenge was stronger, was now undergoing political and economic decline

---

[35] J. H. Parry, *Europe and a Wider World, 1415–1715* (London, 1966), pp. 26–7.

[36] Max Weber, *The Protestant Ethic and the Spirit of Capitalism* (London, 1970, first pubd. 1930), pp. 56–7; note also Max Weber, *The Theory of Social and Economic Organization* (New York, 1964), pp. 278–9.

[37] J. Merrington, 'Town and Country in the Transition to Capitalism', *New Left Review*, 93 (1975), pp. 71–95; Robert Brenner, 'Agrarian Class Structure and Economic Development in Pre-Industrial Europe', in T. H. Aston and C. H. E. Philpin, eds., *The Brenner Debate: Agrarian Class Structure and Economic Development in Pre-Industrial Europe* (Cambridge, 1985), pp. 10–63.

[38] Elliott, *Imperial Spain*, pp. 34, 38–9; Miskimin, *The Economy of Later Renaissance Europe*, pp. 107–11.

and would eventually face exclusion from the *carrera de las indias*, the American connection.

Thus, although commercial interests necessarily figured in the process of expansion, they did not control it or determine its basic contours. They were instruments as much as initiators. The thirst for bullion which the merchant class displayed – and which they sought to slake by means of trade – was shared by other powerful groups: mercantilist kings and their entourages; Andalusian grandees (whose classically 'feudal' principles and properties did not debar them from dabbling in colonial ventures); and, above all, the conquistadors themselves. Mexico's conquerors were a mixed bunch. The initial settlers in the Antilles – Simpson writes – 'were the choicest riff-raff ever brought together: ex-soldiers, broken noblemen, adventurers, criminals and convicts'. Cortés, who led such a crew to Mexico, was under no illusions as to their qualities: 'the majority of the Spaniards who come here are of low quality, violent and vicious'. (Bernal Díaz, conquistador and chronicler, stressing the presence of 'persons of quality', probably protested too much.)[39]

When it came to conquest and colonization, of course, the conquistadors displayed the virtues of their defects. Products of a callous, martial society – many hailed from the bleak expanses of Extremadura and most had served a hard apprenticeship in the Antilles before reaching Mexico – they were more adept at conquest than commerce; for them, profit was equated with plunder, and it accrued by means of the sword rather than the double-entry ledger. Nor is this surprising, since they were steeped in the Spanish culture of honour and *hidalguía* (gentility) – a culture which (witness the example of the Andalusian grandee) did not disdain money and commercial profit,

---

[39] Lesley Byrd Simpson, *The Encomienda in New Spain: The Beginnings of Spanish Mexico* (Berkeley, 1982, first pubd. 1950), pp. 7, 60–1; Díaz, *Conquest of New Spain*, pp. 50, 54. Social origins are hard to probe; but, in terms of geographical origin, it is clear that the early conquistadors came principally from Castile, Andalusia and Extremadura: see Thomas, *Conquest of Mexico*, pp. 150–2; Elliott, *Imperial Spain*, p. 63; and, for more detailed analysis, Robert Himmerich y Valencia, *The Encomenderos of New Spain, 1521–1555* (Austin, 1991), pp. 20–1, 28 (which confirms the geographical breakdown and shows that, while one in six *encomenderos* were *hidalgos*, two-thirds were of unknown social origin). Note also Ida Altman, 'A New World in the Old: Local Society and Spanish Emigration to the Indies', in Ida Altman and James Horn, eds., 'To Make America': European Emigration in the Early Modern Period (Berkeley, 1991), pp. 30–58 (a useful case study of Trujillo and Cáceres) and Bernard Grunberg, 'The Origins of the Conquistadores of Mexico City', *Hispanic American Historical Review*, 74/2 (1994), pp. 259–83, which, pp. 282–3, refutes old caricatures more than it presents new conclusions.

but which subordinated profit to older military and seigneurial values and used money to attain status and power (rather than to earn more money in true, accumulative bourgeois fashion). The conquistadors' desire was to eschew ignoble work; their ultimate goal to establish themselves like the *ricos hombres* (grandees) of later northern Mexico: owners of great estates, lords of dependent labourers, captains of retinues, leaders of clienteles, dispensers of charity, champions of the faith, heroes of history and legend.[40] This, therefore, was a culture which set great store by physical courage, chivalry and a certain *macho* arrogance. It scarcely corresponds to the cautious, thrifty, anal bourgeois of Max Weber – or Benjamin Franklin.[41]

This is not to say that some disembodied Iberian 'culture' – or Renaissance *Zeitgeist* – determined the social practice of the Conquest. 'Culture,' as expressed in 'mentalities', reflected preceding social, economic and political conditions. The archetypal conquistador ('proud, ignorant, credulous, unstable, callous to suffering, ambitious of rank, scornful of demeaning labor, and almost invariably hard up') was a classic product of Spanish society, its political and economic arrangements: he was 'the kind of man produced by the nomadic warrior society which inhabited the dry tableland of medieval Castile'.[42] And his preference for swashbuckling adventure over double-entry book-keeping was also the logical consequence of the social milieu in which he lived, seeking his own advantage no less avidly (or even rationally) than a classic capitalist. But advantage in this society was not measured by capitalist criteria or attained by capitalist methods. Rather, as Anderson reminds us, 'war was possibly the most rational and rapid single mode of expansion of surplus extraction available for any ruling class under feudalism.'[43] The ambitions which drew the conquistadors to the Americas were substantially similar to those which had impelled their fathers into North Africa, which had motivated generations of their ancestors during the Reconquista, and which had nurtured 'colonial' enterprises like the medieval kingdoms of Sicily, Jerusalem or Achaia/Morea. Indeed,

---

[40] Chevalier, *Land and Society*, ch. 5.
[41] Weber, *The Protestant Ethic*, pp. 48–59.
[42] Simpson, *The Encomienda*, p. 55; Elliott, *Imperial Spain*, pp. 64–5.
[43] Anderson, *Lineages of the Absolutist State*, p. 31.

we could invoke, as a distant parallel to Cortés, Clovis (d. 511), who 'lived and died a Frankish chieftain, a warrior of the Heroic Age, a man of blood and a seeker after gold.'[44] We will return to the con-quistador 'mentality' later; here, the point to establish is that both mentality and method were old and that the lust for loot which per-vaded the Conquest is poor evidence of an underlying capitalist ethic.

Furthermore, economic motives – whether of 'bourgeois' or 'feu-dal' provenance – mingled with others, in a manner which only ap-pears contradictory (or downright hypocritical) to 'modern' minds, accustomed to familiar, mutually exclusive dichotomies: sacred/secular, God-fearing/self-serving, other-worldly/this-worldly. At the time, Elliott reminds us, 'there was no sharp dividing line between re-ligious and political achievements but, rather, a constant interaction between the two'.[45] For this was still an age of plundering crusaders and warrior-prelates – like the doughty bishop of Zamora, captain of the Comunero rebels, who was gaoled, slew his gaoler while attempt-ing to escape and was finally garrotted by order of Charles V.[46] In-deed, just as fifteenth-century Europe had seen a growth in economic pressures making for overseas expansion, so, too, it had witnessed a revival of crusading fervour, especially in Spain. The Reconquista had never been a smooth, evolutionary process; it had advanced by fits and starts; and in the 1450s a new phase of Christian aggression began which culminated in the conquest of the kingdom of Granada. Nor did it end there: Oran fell in 1509, and massive armadas were launched against Tunis (successfully, 1535) and Algiers (unsuccess-fully, 1541).

This Christian aggression, of course, had little to do with nascent capitalism; on the contrary, it 'entailed the perpetuation of the ar-chaic social organisation of a crusading society'.[47] It also responded to the renewed military and religious challenge of the Ottoman Empire, signalled by the fall of Constantinople (1453) and no less

---

[44] J. M. Wallace-Hadrill, *The Barbarian West, 400–1000* (London, 1952), p. 75; on the Reconquista and Mediterranean colonialism: Bartlett, *The Making of Europe*, pp. 44–5, 48, 93–4, 112.

[45] Elliott, *Imperial Spain*, p. 108.

[46] Elliott, *Imperial Spain*, pp. 157–9, and p. 100 on the 'warrior race' that was the late-medieval Castilian episcopacy.

[47] Elliott, *Imperial Spain*, p. 169; Herbert Frey, *La feudalidad europea y el régimen señorial español* (Mexico, 1988), pp. 15, 116–21, 130–1.

dramatically countered – at least in maritime terms – at Lepanto (1571). Even long-distance exploration had a part to play in this ancient, atavistic conflict, since it held out the prospect of taking the Turks in the rear, by hypothetical alliances with Africa's Prester John or the emperor of Cathay. Crusading also served papal and dynastic interests, as it always had in the past. It provided Spanish kings – who were not overendowed with fiscal resources – with a lever whereby to extract money from their subjects, usually with papal connivance. In addition, the crusade offered a common enterprise whereby to bind Spain's particularist peoples together, to the advantage of their sovereigns; and it justified the Real Patronato – the 'momentous' concession by which the Papacy conferred on the Spanish Crown rights of patronage and presentation to the major ecclesiastical benefices of, first, Granada (1486), then the entire New World (1508).[48]

It cannot be doubted, however, that the spreading of the faith – if necessary by conquest – was a genuine desire as well as a convenient stratagem. 'Affective' and 'instrumental' concerns coincided. Armed proselytisation also tapped a deep well of popular support. Like the Aztecs whom they would soon confront, the Spaniards were a devout imperialist people. The 'Most Catholic Kings' fully deserved the title conferred by the Pope in 1494: Isabella's faith was 'fervent, mystical and intense'; Ferdinand, for all his Aragonese cunning, was – like Cortés – devoted to the cult of the Virgin and attuned to the messianic and reformist currents then agitating Spanish Catholicism.[49] For, during the early sixteenth century, Spain experienced a spiritual recharging, evident in church reform (especially among the Franciscans), in scholarly espousal of the new humanist learning and in a powerful, pervasive mysticism.[50]

All this is easier to describe than to explain. At a time when broad European influences – humanism, Reformation – were brought to bear, Spain was in certain respects uniquely receptive. Spanish 'religious sensibilities had been heightened to almost fever pitch by the miraculous achievements of recent years': the conquest of Granada first, that of the New World second – achievements which

---

[48] Elliott, *Imperial Spain*, pp. 46–7, 101–3, 108.
[49] Elliott, *Imperial Spain*, pp. 103, 105, 108.
[50] Phelan, *Millennial Kingdom*, p. 5; D. A. Brading, *The First America* (Cambridge, 1991), p. 20.

were effects and also reinforcing causes of Spanish crusading zeal. Thus, for all their violence, cupidity and braggadoccio, the conquistadors saw themselves as agents of an active, proselytising faith.[51] They set great store by the conversion of the Indians: Cortés, in particular, had to be restrained by an accompanying friar from his overzealous destruction of Mexican religious idols; and Bernal Díaz, chronicling these events in his matter-of-fact style, sounds almost bored as he recounts Cortés's 'customary exposition of our holy faith and his injunctions [to the Indians] to give up human sacrifice and sodomy.'[52]

Consonant with their beliefs, Cortés's men marched under a banner bearing Constantine's slogan (*in hoc signo vinces*: 'beneath this sign thou shalt conquer'); they charged into battle shouting the old Reconquista war-cry 'Santiago!'; and, on at least one occasion, in the midst of battle, 'the blessed apostles St James and St Peter appeared', lending angelic aid to the embattled Spaniards. (Díaz, while expressing doubts about this story, prudently concedes that 'it may be that . . . those glorious apostles did appear and that I, as a sinner, was unworthy to see them'.) And by their string of victories, many of them hard won, the conquistadors convinced not only themselves but also their enemies that they indeed enjoyed divine favour. As Cortés assured his followers, 'Jesus Christ must be preserving us for some good purpose'.[53] On this basis, the argument for prudential conversion became a staple of the sermons which Cortés preached to Indian audiences, repeatedly and in a manner 'no good theologian could have bettered': accept the faith, his listeners were told, and 'they would then see how well things would go with them and what our God would do for them'; the cross, in particular, 'would always aid them, bring them good harvests and save their souls'.[54]

Given the flexibility and similarly prudential nature of Mesoamerican religion, the Indians were receptive to this kind of appeal. Before long, Cortés's Tlaxcalan allies were fighting with the cry 'Santiago!' on their lips. Moctezuma, meanwhile, even if he soon disabused himself

---

[51]   Elliott, *Imperial Spain*, pp. 46, 53–4, 60–1, 66, 105 ('fever pitch'); see also Weckman, *La herencia medieval*, pp. 118–23.

[52]   Díaz, *Conquest of New Spain*, pp. 120, 137, 177–8. We should recall, however, that Díaz wrote over forty years after the event.

[53]   Díaz, *Conquest of New Spain*, pp. 47, 70, 77, 153.

[54]   Díaz, *Conquest of New Spain*, pp. 96–7.

of the idea that Cortés was the returned god Quetzalcoatl, rational-
ized his incarceration by the Spaniards, Bernal Díaz reports, in these
terms: 'such a thing was only possible because we (the Spaniards)
were wizards and had robbed him of his great strength and courage
with our witchcraft, or because our gods and the great woman of
Castile whom we spoke of as our advocate gave us strength to do
what we liked'. Indeed, the belief that the Spaniards, with their remarkable powers of survival, must be *teules* – gods or wizards –
appears to have been widespread among the Indians and not confined to the brooding Moctezuma.[55]

Religious zeal may, with caution, be distinguished from outright
Realpolitik. It may also be analytically distinguished from other 'intellectual' or 'ideological' preoccupations which were perhaps relevant to Spanish exploration and conquest: innate curiosity, the desire to travel, to learn, to comprehend (preoccupations which, some
suggest, were enhanced by shifts in the European mind of the day).
These factors are, however, conjectural and cannot begin to compete
with the supreme 'ideological' motivation, that of religion, which
has therefore been separately treated. Detached intellectual curiosity
played a minor – perhaps negligible – role in exploration and conquest. Exploration, for example, was instrumental, geared to particular purposes, not free-ranging and open-minded. Pioneers like Prince
Henry, we have noted, were 'staunchly conservative' upholders of old
traditions, not bold Lucretian adventurers.[56] Henry's Spanish counterparts were no less practically minded, seeking to break into the
Portuguese Asian trade by means of a westward passage. And their
chosen agents, the great explorers, were, 'like the rulers and investors
who sent them out . . . , practical men and their purposes were practical'. They sought particular routes and destinations (even if their
search was founded – as Columbus's was – on a 'colossal error'); they
'did not quarter the sea in generalised curiosity to see what they
could find'.[57]

---

55 León-Portilla, *The Broken Spears*, p. 48; Díaz, *Conquest of New Spain*, pp. 177, 203, 223, 262.
56 Parry, *Europe and a Wider World*, pp. 26–7; see also Chaunu, *La expansión europea*, p. 68,
     where Prince Henry is described as 'much more a knight than a sage or a merchant'. In similar
     vein, Weckman, *La herencia medieval*, p. 113, cites an unusually historically percipient Levi-
     Strauss to the effect that 'the Spaniards did not leave their homeland so much to acquire new
     knowledge as to confirm old beliefs'.
57 Parry, *The Discovery*, pp. 23, 76.

The explorers' intellectual equipment, furthermore, was a bizarre mixture of biblical sources, classical geography and practical findings (which were not always mutually compatible). Hence, quests for mythic lands – El Dorado, the Seven Cities of Cíbola – were part and parcel of the (literally) mundane search for a westward passage to Asia. Hence, too, biblical revelation informed concrete discoveries. Columbus identified the mouth of the Orinoco with the Garden of Eden; Cortés put biblical images into the mouth of Moctezuma. The first Spaniards in Yucatán attributed the idols they saw there 'to the Jews who were exiled by Titus and Vespasian and sent overseas' (an explanation which lived on, as both allegory and supposed fact: sixteenth-century friars like Motolinia and Mendieta saw the Mexicans as Israelites being led from bondage by a Spanish Moses, Hernán Cortés; and, three centuries later, the eccentric English peer Lord Kingsborough bankrupted himself and died in a debtors' prison trying to prove that 'the Mexican Indians were descended from the lost ten tribes of Israel').[58]

Scriptural and classical knowledge was thus used to explain new discoveries or to fit them within a broadly traditional cosmogony – which, like some 'Kuhnian' scientific paradigm, proved remarkably resistant to fresh empirical evidence and was only painfully, belatedly, but finally triumphantly overturned in favour of a new cosmogony, grounded upon the discoveries of the era.[59] The Renaissance mind and Renaissance Man (or Woman) did not, therefore, possess unique innovative qualities equipping them for overseas exploration; if anything, Renaissance respect for classical authorities (like Ptolemy) inhibited explorational progress. Conversely, the most important area in which the new learning and and Renaissance 'spirit' found practical expression in the New World was precisely the 'traditional' area of religion, where the enhanced mysticism

[58] Parry, *The Discovery*, p. 75; Pagden, *Hernán Cortés*, p. 467; Díaz, *Conquest of New Spain*, p. 26; D. A. Brading, *Myth and Prophecy in Mexican History* (Cambridge, 1984), p. 15; Nigel Davies, *Voyagers to the New World: Fact or Fantasy* (London, 1979), pp. 4–5.

[59] Thus, while the discoveries did not *derive* from a new European mentality, they certainly helped to *engender* one: for example, by adding to traditional Christian providentialism a new secular teleology ('history as a progressive movement which would culminate in the civilization of all mankind'), which in turn justified European notions of mission and superiority, while confirming the triumph of the 'Moderns' over the 'Ancients': J. H. Elliott, *The Old World and the New, 1492–1650* (Cambridge, 1970), pp. 52–3.

and messianism of the Renaissance Spanish Church made a powerful contribution to the initial 'spiritual conquest' of Mexico, as we shall see.

As for the rank-and-file conquistadors, it is unlikely that humanist learning or a disinterested thirst for knowledge had much bearing on their conduct. True, they sometimes showed a lively curiosity and – especially in the annals of Bernal Díaz – a faithful eye for exotic detail. It was, Díaz recalls, 'our habit to examine and inquire into everything'; but the context of this apparent admission of intellectual curiosity was the discovery – by the alert carpenter Alonso Yáñez – of a concealed doorway in the Spaniards' quarters in Tenochtitlán which led into the treasure-house of Axayácatl.[60] Material acquisition counted for much more than abstract knowledge. To the extent that intellectual factors – of a non-religious kind – figured in conquistador thinking, or that 'Renaissance Man' may be discerned among Cortés's hard-bitten company, it was the cult of honour and heroism, sometimes cloaked in classical or Romance garb, which counted. This, of course, represented only a mutated form of feudal and aristocratic virtues. Díaz, for all his concrete observation, saw the Conquest 'through the haze of romance of chivalry' – the more feeble secular counterpart of the religious messianism which inspired the early Spanish missionaries to the New World.[61]

The city of Tenochtitlán, when first glimpsed by the Spaniards, 'seemed like an enchanted vision from the tale of Amadis' (the celebrated chivalrous epic later lampooned by Cervantes in *Don Quixote*).[62] The Conquest was, in this sense, a thoroughly Quixotic enterprise. And if, back home in Europe, its protagonists were only slowly incorporated into the pantheon of secular heroes (Columbus, Cortés and Pizarro all died in disgrace), they themselves had no doubt about their heroic roles, which placed them on a par with the paladins of old – Cyrus the Great, Alexander, Caesar and Pompey, Scipio and Hannibal. Cortés, an accomplished orator, did not shrink from comparing his own exploits to 'the heroic deeds of the Romans'

---

[60] Díaz, *Conquest of New Spain*, pp. 241–2.
[61] Elliott, *The Old World and the New*, p. 20; Weckman, *La herencia medieval*, pp. 142–59; see also Brading, *First America*, pp. 23–4, who rightly reminds us that 'any sharp contrast between the Middle Ages and the Renaissance is best avoided'.
[62] Díaz, *Conquest of New Spain*, p. 214.

or to those of 'the paladin Roland'; and, when his faint-hearted critics, urging caution, drew upon similar examples ('reminding Cortés
that neither the Romans nor Alexander... had dared destroy their
ships and attack vast populations and huge armies with a small
force'), Cortés neatly capped their argument: 'as for your observation, gentlemen, that the most famous Roman captains never per-
formed deeds equal to ours, you are quite right. If God helps us, far
more will be said in future history books about our exploits than has
ever been said about those of the past'.[63] And, he might have added,
gentlemen in Spain now abed shall think themselves accursed they
were not here...

Needless to say, these are not the quintessential sentiments of merchant capitalism. They represent, rather, the unalloyed metal of a
military and aristocratic ethic, newly burnished by the classical and
vernacular literature of the Renaissance. And, at least as a secondary
factor, this helped both motivate the conquistadors and ensure that,
when 'the two opposite traditions – that of the merchant and that of
the warrior – came into violent conflict', it was the latter which triumphed.[64] The legacy of the Reconquista, in other words, prevailed
over the stirrings of nascent capitalism.

That it did so depended a good deal upon royal policy. As already
mentioned, the Spanish Crown saw numerous advantages in overseas expansion: the acquisition of bullion, the proselytization of the
faith, the outflanking of Islam, the greater glory of the new amalga-
mated dynasty. Given the major civil wars of the period (Catalonia,
1462–72; the Comunero revolt in Castile, 1519–20), and the fragility
of the dynastic union of Castile and Aragon, the imperial enterprise
offered, at least to some, a means to create broader 'Hispanic' sentiments, to restore, even, the 'national' unity of Visigothic or Roman
Spain. Militant Catholicism and stirring nationalism conspired to
give Spaniards – some Spaniards – a sense of heady triumphalism,
even of unique divine destiny. The Spaniards, declared Cortés's chap-
lain, López de Gómara, had pioneered the discovery of America, 'the
greatest event since the creation of the world, apart from the incar-
nation and death of He who created it'; 'never', he went on, 'did a king

---

[63] Díaz, *Conquest of New Spain*, pp. 84, 131, 158–9.
[64] Elliott, *Imperial Spain*, pp. 61–2; note also Frey, *La feudalidad europea*, p. 131.

or people ... subject so much in so short a time as we did'; in light of which, 'the Spaniards are most worthy of praise in all parts of the world'.[65] Specific in its Renaissance and Catholic emphases, this was nevertheless a form of imperial triumphalism, premised on geopolitical expansion, of which history affords many comparable examples: the France of Richelieu and Louis XIV, Victorian Britain, the contemporary United States – even, one should repeat, the fifteenth-century Aztec regime.

Overseas expansion, too, would siphon off some of the superfluous *hidalgos* and aristocratic cadets who were a source of potential instability within the new Spanish state. For this and other reasons, the Crown gave strong – if selective – encouragement to the initial expeditions of exploration and conquest. But royal resources were limited and jealously guarded. Expeditions were organized on the basis of joint public and private financing, with the latter predominating. Explorers and conquistadors therefore had to draw upon their own resources to mount expeditions – as Cortés, for example, did, mortgaging 'his Indians and his estate' in Cuba and securing the support of some rich backers.[66] The Crown might commit its material resources (though in this regard the Spanish Crown was rarely as generous or positive as the Portuguese), but its chief role was political and juridical: it alone could legitimize the achievements of conquistadors, converting lucky strikes into secure titles. Here, Reconquista precedents were crucial: the *capitulación*, the old legal contract of the Reconquista, promised the prospective conquistador rewards (*mercedes*) and sometimes official positions (e.g., that of *adelantado*, or hereditary governor), while reserving to the Crown ultimate jurisdiction and stipulating the beneficiary's obligation to spread the faith.[67]

Given the Crown's ultimate – but always distant and sometimes tenuous – authority, ambitious conquistadors were eager to secure royal legitimation of their conquests, especially in circumstances of inter-Spanish rivalry, which were common enough. This eagerness was sharpened by the pervasive legalism of Spanish society.

[65] Elliott, *Imperial Spain*, p. 19; Elliott, *The Old World and the New*, p. 10; Brading, *Myth and Prophecy*, pp. 10–11.
[66] Díaz, *Conquest of New Spain*, p. 47.
[67] Elliott, *Imperial Spain*, pp. 58–9.

Conquistadors like Cortés (who had studied law at the University of Salamanca) were determined to confer on their conquests not only the benison of religion but also the stamp of legality. Thus the Conquest displayed the apparent paradox of rampant conflict, disorder and violence, conducted according to bizarrely formalistic conventions. *Requerimientos* – ultimata-cum-declarations of war which rehearsed human history from Creation to the Papal donation of America to the Crown of Spain – were solemnly read out to hostile Indian forces on the eve of battle; although interpreters were used, we may doubt whether the Indians heard and comprehended (Las Casas refers to *requerimientos* being 'read to the trees'). By this means, however, the royal conscience was salved, and the Conquest received theological and legal sanction. Similarly, notaries carefully recorded the details as the Tlaxcalans – so Cortés wrote to Charles V – 'offered themselves as vassals of Your Sacred Majesty and swore to remain so always and to serve and assist in all things that Your Highness commanded them'.[68]

As this example suggests, the conquistadors' keenness to secure royal assent to their risky undertakings led them to shameless hyperbole and flattery. The wealth, the extent and – above all – the governability of these new realms were consistently exaggerated, thus – it was hoped – exciting royal pride no less than royal gratitude. The Conquest proceeded with one 'great miracle and divine mystery' following another, Cortés wrote to Charles V; proof, he went on, that 'nothing can be undertaken in Your service which does not end in good'. The Spaniards introduced themselves to the Yucateco Maya as 'subjects of the most powerful monarchs in the world, whom most of the world obey'. And these new realms offered rich pickings. Cholula was rich, irrigated, 'more beautiful than any (city) in Spain'; it was 'fit for Spaniards to live in' and conveniently lacking an 'overlord'.[69]

These general characteristics of Spanish society helped mould the contours of the Conquest, but, once under way, the Conquest soon acquired a momentum of its own. Indeed, momentum was essential,

---

[68]　Pagden, *Hernán Cortés*, pp. 72, 453–54; Brading, no preacher of political correctness, calls the *requerimiento* a 'cynical piece of legal gibberish': *First America*, p. 81; for Stephen Greenblatt, *Marvelous Possessions: The Wonder of the New World* (Oxford, 1991), p. 98, it is 'a strange blend of ritual, cynicism, legal fiction and perverse idealism'.

[69]　Pagden, *Hernán Cortés*, pp. 12, 17, 74–5.

since Cortés's bold advance on and campaign against Tenochitlán had to be carried through to victory if the entire expedition was not to collapse in failure, like some 'childish joke'.[70] The public-private collaboration evident at the outset was therefore subject to constant stress, antagonism and tacit renegotiation (Cortés and Mexico were, in this respect, Balboa and Panama writ large). Aware that it had backed a winner – albeit for a modest stake – the Crown wished to assert control, to maximize revenue and, above all, to prevent over-mighty subjects – so recently tamed in the peninsula itself – from seizing power in the emergent American colonies. Against the 'new transatlantic feudal aristocracy' which the Conquest engendered, the Crown counterposed bureaucratic officialdom and an Erastian church.[71]

The colonies and their native population thus soon became objects of a two-way and sometimes a three-way struggle between Crown, clergy and conquistadors. The conquistadors, who had expended their blood and treasure in the service of the Crown, now expected their just rewards; and, if they could not obtain these by the easy extraction of bullion (a constant hope but a frequent disappointment), then they would have to conquer new lands by way of recompense. Just as the gutting of Hispaniola and Cuba led to the conquest of Anáhuac (central Mexico) so the latter's fall – though a bigger bonanza – soon led to further expeditions, wars and conquests. As the Spanish couplet proclaimed: 'A la espada y compás / y más y más y más y más' [By the compass and the sword / and more and more and more].[72]

Spanish – like Aztec – imperialism recognized no bounds beyond those of necessity. And, when conquest and plunder gave out, as soon they did, alternative means of exploitation had to be devised, consonant with the conquistadors' material ambitions and *hidalgo* morality. The way was thus opened for coerced labour, slavery, cash cropping and stock raising. Mexico would experience the ultimate development of models first devised and more modestly applied during the initial phases of Spanish imperialism in the Atlantic and

---

[70] Díaz, *Conquest of New Spain*, pp. 159–60.
[71] Elliott, *Imperial Spain*, p. 71.
[72] Elliott, *The Old World and the New*, p. 53.

Caribbean islands.[73] Meantime, whatever the original, Eurocentric causes of Spanish exploration and conquest, these were soon refracted through the prism of colonial experience; it was therefore possible for mercantile ambition to create, across the Atlantic, a reconstituted feudalism, part checked and part bolstered by royal bureaucracy.

In seeking to explain the 'why' of exploration and conquest we have left till last the question of 'how'. The latter question, though complex enough, is easier to answer and secondary in importance. Of course, without appropriate means, the ends of conquest could not have been attained. But historians who stress the importance of newly acquired means – who explain the conquest of the New World in terms of the rigging of caravels – forget that powerful motives call forth effective means.[74] In this instance, it is clear that naval and navigational innovations responded to pre-existing demands (indeed, these innovations which, along with those in mining technology, constituted the key technological advances of the day, were alike responses to Europe's bullion famine). The Portuguese, in particular, pioneered naval gunnery and developed the caravel, with its novel three-master rigging, in their quest for African and Asian goods. In the Indian Ocean it was their naval expertise – rather than any commercial edge – which enabled them (partially) to supplant Indian and Arab traders.

But the Portuguese did not use these means to establish a territorial empire; rather, they were content to wrest key points from their victims (Socotra, Goa, Hormuz), leaving the vast hinterland under the control of ancient polities. The Spaniards learned Portuguese methods – and employed Portuguese like Magellan; they capitalized on ship-building skills acquired during previous decades of Spanish maritime trade with northern Europe; and they tapped the cartographical and navigational expertise gained from the

---

[73] Chaunu, *La expansión europea*, pp. 64, 135–6; Wallerstein, *Modern World-System*, pp. 88–9; Elliott, *Imperial Spain*, p. 58.

[74] The Chinese, it should be remembered, had sent fleets across the Indian Ocean in the early fourteenth century; this did not, however, lead to Chinese dominion in East Africa. A good analysis of European maritime technology, culminating in the caravel, is provided by Chaunu, *La expansión europea*, pp. 202–14.

Mediterranean – which Catalan and Balearic captains had sailed for centuries. But, in addition, the Spaniards could draw upon the military experience of both the Reconquista and the recent Italian wars, as well as upon the politico-administrative models developed by the Aragonese Crown in its long history of Mediterranean empire-building. Spain may not have been the only power 'able to conquer, administer, Christianise and Europeanise the populous areas of the New World', but Spain was particularly well suited to pioneer Atlantic exploration – and then to turn exploration into conquest and colonization.[75]

The pace of conquest was fast, and accelerating. Through the first ninety years of the fifteenth century, the acquisition of the Atlantic islands added only 1,500 square miles to Spanish possessions; nearly 20,000 square miles were gained during the 1490s, however, and five times that area between 1502 and 1515.[76] But it was with Cortés's conquest of Mexico and Pizarro's of Peru that the period of grandiose empire-building began. Over three-quarters of a million square miles were added to Spanish – that is, Castilian – possessions between 1520 and 1540; after which, this dizzy rate of acquisition ended. This was not only grandiose empire-building, it was also, very obviously, territorial empire-building, based on the military conquest and assimilation of previous states, chiefly Aztec and Inca. Portugal, we have noted, picked off key ports and fortresses, but Spain conquered entire kingdoms. The comparison points up not only the difference between Portugal's thalassocracy – oriented towards trade, dependent on naval strength and disposed to a certain political and religious toleration – and Spain's empire of crusade and conquest, Christianization and colonization, but also the difference between the Asiatic empires which Portugal harassed and their Indoamerican

---

[75] Lomax, *The Reconquest*, p. 178. On the politico-military significance of the Italian Wars of the 1490s and after, see Charles Tilly, *Coercion, Capital and European States, AD 990–1992* (Cambridge, 1992), pp. 76–9. The significance for the New World lay less in the tactics (mass armies and siege trains played no part in the Conquest) than in the ferocity, ruthlessness and discipline displayed by the conquistadors, who were well aware of the Italian parallel and of the value of having Italian veterans in their midst: see Díaz, *Conquest of New Spain*, p. 289; Thomas, *Conquest of Mexico*, p. 150.

[76] Pierre Chaunu, *Conquête et Exploitation des Nouveaux Mondes (XVIe siècle)* (Paris, 1969), pp. 136–7.

counterparts which Spain destroyed. European parasitism – to return to McNeill's graphic metaphor – could be sustained by Asiatic hosts but proved fatal in the New World.[77]

Between Columbus's American landfall in 1492 and Cortés's arrival in Mexico in 1519 the major islands of the Caribbean were discovered and colonized, and the South American mainland was explored. It was only a matter of time, however, before the continued quest for a western passage to Asia – coupled with the endless search for gold wherever it might be found – revealed the great expanse of Mesoamerica, lying, it should be remembered, over 1,200 miles west of Santiago de Cuba, and 2,500 miles west of the mouth of the Orinoco. As it was, the vagaries of Columbus's voyages – his southern tack from the Bahamas to Cuba, then from Cuba south to the Spanish Main – gave Mesoamerica a brief respite. During this time, as Moctezuma II wrestled with the intractable politics of a swollen empire, the Spaniards were busy organizing and extending their island possessions. The gold they initially found – the product of a millennium of patient placer mining – was soon plundered, and the Indian population, on which the Spaniards depended for food and labour, was decimated by war and disease. Spanish settlers, drawn to the Indies by the promise of plunder, glory and enhanced status, grew increasingly disappointed. Hence the momentum of exploration was maintained, with the islands themselves now serving as centres of 'subimperialism', radiating expeditions of exploration and conquest across the Caribbean. Hispaniola provided the settlers and conquerors of Cuba and Jamaica; and these, in turn, their petty gold stocks exhausted, became the centres of recruitment and the points of departure for expeditions for Mexico.

Meanwhile, methods of conquest and colonization were refined, if that is the right word. In the Caribbean islands, as in the Canaries, the subjugated natives were distributed among Spanish settlers and supplemented by imported African slaves. But when Balboa crossed the Isthmus and beheld the Pacific, he encountered a dense, more developed Indian society. He therefore pioneered methods later to be

---

[77] McNeill, *Plagues and Peoples*, p. 6ff. The comparison with Portuguese thalassocracy is well drawn by C. R. Boxer, *The Portuguese Seaborne Empire, 1415–1825* (Harmondsworth, 1969), p. 52ff.

perfected by Cortés: the manipulation of Indian *caciques*, the striking of alliances, the 'displays of ferocity' which, though recurrent and repulsive, were nevertheless 'economic and calculated' in the best traditions of Renaissance *Realpolitik*.[78] Balboa may have been – in Peter Martyr's words – an 'egregious ruffian', and, like many conquistadors, he eventually perished a victim of Spanish internecine conflict; but he blazed a trail which Cortés, more statesmanlike but no less ruthless, would soon follow.

II. The Conquest of Mexico

Six years after Balboa beheld the Pacific, Cortés made landfall in Yucatán. His was the third voyage in as many years to make the short but often stormy passage across the Gulf from Cuba. But the pioneer voyages of 1517 and 1518, led by Francisco Hernández de Córdoba and Juan de Grijalva, had – to their surprise – met with a hostile response from Indians in both Yucatán and Campeche (perhaps, Parry suggests, because the Indians resented the Spaniards' unthinking depletion of precious fresh water supplies).[79] The Spaniards therefore returned, chastened but optimistic, having learned something of the wealth and complexity of Mesoamerican civilization; in particular, Grijalva had heard from the Totonacs of coastal Veracruz about a great inland empire – 'Culhua' – to which they owed obedience. Even before Grijalva returned with the news, the governor of Cuba, Diego Velázquez, appointed Hernán Cortés commander of a third – and substantially larger – expedition, which included sixteen ships and six hundred men.

Cortés had lived fifteen years in the Indies, having left his native Extremadura in 1504, at the age of nineteen. His background was one of 'modest gentility'; his father had been a soldier and a Knight of the Order of Alcántara; the son's foray into law had been brief and inconclusive, after which – resolving on a military career – he had almost taken ship to join the Italian wars.[80] Sailing westward

---

[78] Parry, *The Discovery*, p. 117.
[79] Parry, *The Discovery*, p. 142. The two expeditions are well described by Inga Clendinnen, *Ambivalent Conquests*, pp. 4–19.
[80] William Weber Johnson, *Cortés* (London, 1977), pp. 4–10; Thomas, *Conquest of Mexico*, pp. 117–25.

instead and settling in Hispaniola, Cortés farmed (i.e., lived off the labour of *encomienda* Indians), prospected unsuccessfully for gold and acquired local political office. But, as the island's short cycle of exploration, settlement and exhaustion proceeded, Cortés was keen to move on, which he did with the opening up of Cuba in 1511. Again, he set up as a prosperous landowner and magistrate. As yet, therefore, his military skill had hardly been put to the test; he was, in Parry's words, 'more of a scrivener than a soldier'.[81] Given this career, and Cortés's record of political and personal disputes with Governor Velázquez, it is odd that Cortés was chosen to lead the Mexican expedition. Indeed, preparations were well advanced (they included not only the provisioning of ships but also the training of troops and testing of weapons – this was no peaceful voyage of discovery) when Velázquez changed his mind and sought to revoke Cortés's commission. In response, Cortés sailed post-haste. Thus he broke with his superior – who was not disposed to forgive this insubordination – and he had to ensure rapid and spectacular success if he were to vindicate his conduct, the more so since the political shifts associated with Charles V's succession to the throne gave Velázquez powerful friends at court. Cortés's best, perhaps only, hope of royal pardon and preferment would be 'if new people were won for the Faith and rich new lands for the Crown'.[82]

In Yucatán and Tabasco, Cortés's forces fared better than had their predecessors: they were more numerous, as well as more circumspect. Making a brief landfall at Cozumel Island, Cortés established good relations with the local Maya *cacique* and had the good luck to encounter and enlist a Spanish castaway, Jerónimo de Aguilar, whose command of the Maya tongue was soon complemented by the Nahuatl spoken by another recruit: Princess Malinche (or Marina) of the Chontal Maya.[83] Cortés thus had the ability to converse directly with the Maya and – indirectly and laboriously – with Nahuatl-speakers too. Diplomacy could not avert sporadic skirmishes with Indian forces; but these were easily survived, and Cortés – drawing

---

[81] Parry, *The Discovery*, p. 144; Thomas, *Conquest of Mexico*, pp. 122–4, notes that Cortés's parents had steered their son – reputedly a sickly only child – towards a legal and classical education.

[82] J. H. Elliott, 'Cortés, Velázquez and Charles V', in Pagden, *Hernán Cortés*, pp. xii–xv.

[83] Thomas, *Conquest of Mexico*, pp. 163, 171–3.

on the experience of the many veterans who sailed with him – followed Grijalva's course up the Gulf to Veracruz. Here, in April, he further infringed Velázquez's authority by founding a city, complete with mayor, magistrates, a town council, a gallows and a pillory. This he did, so he told Charles V, 'so that in this land you might have the same sovereignty as you have in your other kingdoms'.[84] By this smart ploy, Cortés discarded Velázquez's authority in favour of the Crown's, and, to win royal assent, he despatched emissaries directly to Spain. In staging this minor coup, however, Cortés had to counter the influence of a pro-Velázquez faction within his own forces. To this end, he held out the prospect of a profitable and glorious march into the rich interior, and, later, he ordered the scuttling of the expedition's ships, thus ensuring that there would be no easy exit for waverers.[85]

It was at Veracruz, too, that the envoys of Moctezuma – who was closely informed of the Spaniards' arrival in Aztec territory – met Cortés and exchanged gifts: gold, jewels and Aztec artefacts in return for beads and other gew-gaws. Moctezuma's envoys were shown the working of the Spaniards' cannon; they were made drunk on wine; and they observed the wooden cross before which the newcomers made obeisance. In short, they were introduced to the rudiments of European civilization. All this was reported to the troubled *tlatoani*. Cortés, too, was eager for intelligence. He learned more about Aztec material wealth (a request for a helmet full of gold dust was promptly met) as well as about Aztec political problems: the Totonacs, he found out, were disaffected with Aztec rule, as they had been since the 1460s.[86] In the summer of 1519, therefore, Cortés established his headquarters at the chief city of the Totonacs, Cempoala, leaving a garrison of one hundred fifty men to guard the infant municipality of Veracruz. At Cempoala resentment against Aztec demands, conveyed by arrogant tax-collectors, was palpable, and Cortés began his hugely successful policy – a sort of Cortesian version of Stalin's 'salami' tactics – whereby Aztec allies and tributaries were progressively sliced

---

[84] Pagden, *Hernán Cortés*, p. 26; Davies, *The Aztecs*, p. 243; Díaz, *Conquest of New Spain*, p. 102.

[85] Pagden, *Hernán Cortés*, pp. 52–3; Díaz, *Conquest of New Spain*, p. 130; Thomas, *Conquest of Mexico*, pp. 222–3, which notes that Cortés did not, as commonly believed, 'burn his boats'; he grounded and disabled them.

[86] Thomas, *Conquest of Mexico*, pp. 178, 195; Davies, *The Aztecs*, pp. 102–3, on Totonac discontent.

off and politically digested.[87] The Spaniards arrested the Aztec tax-collectors, and the Totonacs – first horrified, then jubilant – necessarily hitched their fortunes to the Spanish cause. No less significantly, Cortés ordered the destruction of Cempoala's idols and the establishment of a Catholic church where a pagan temple had stood.[88] Religious as well as political war was therefore joined; the Totonacs, less keen on religious conversion than political liberation, were taken aback; and the Spaniards – the fervent Cortés above all – signalled their intention of subverting, rather than simply supplementing, the old Mesoamerican pantheon.

From Cempoala the Spaniards headed inland towards the highland state of Tlaxcala, whose resistance to the Aztecs was well known and whose good relations with the Totonacs were long-standing: as the Totonacs put it, the Tlaxcalans 'were their friends and very hated enemies of Moctezuma'.[89] But incorporating the Tlaxcalans into the emergent anti-Aztec coalition was no easy matter. Defiant of the Aztecs, they were also suspicious of the Spaniards; after several debates among themselves, they decided to resist the *teules*; and several fierce battles were fought in the chill Tlaxcalan highlands before the Spaniards forced their opponents to join with them in alliance. Moctezuma's envoys, who regularly intercepted the Spaniards, bearing both gifts and (we shall note) contradictory instructions, were understandably displeased at this turn of events; while Cortés rejoiced, he reports, 'when I saw the discord and animosity between these two peoples . . . for it seemed to further my purpose considerably'.[90]

So it did. Thereafter, the Tlaxcalans proved valuable military allies and vital sources of intelligence. At Cholula, Cortés's next stop, the Tlaxcalans warned of local treachery, inspired by Moctezuma, who was increasingly desperate to halt the Spanish advance on his capital; in the ensuing melee, the Tlaxcalans fought alongside the Spaniards in what became a famous and controversial massacre of the Cholulan forces.[91] Cholula's defeat removed the last major obstacle on the way

---

87 The phrase is Matyas Rakosi's: Robin Okey, *Eastern Europe, 1740–1980* (London, 1982), p. 195.
88 Díaz, *Conquest of New Spain*, pp. 107–14.
89 Davies, *The Aztecs*, p. 103; Pagden, *Hernán Cortés*, p. 57.
90 Pagden, *Hernán Cortés*, p. 69.
91 For different versions: Díaz, *Conquest of New Spain*, pp. 199–200; Davies, *The Aztecs*, pp. 253–4; Thomas, *Conquest of Mexico*, pp. 261–4.

to Tenochtitlán. Avoiding the Chalco road – which Moctezuma had laid with ambushes – the Spaniards and their thousand Tlaxcalan allies crossed the snowy pass since known as the Paso de Cortés and entered the teeming heartland of the Aztec empire. From Ixtapalapa they beheld, with wonder, the lake and the great lacustrine metropolis of Tenochtitlán, which conjured up images of the fabled cities of legend: 'indeed,' Bernal Díaz recalled, 'some of the soldiers asked whether it was not all a dream'.[92]

For Moctezuma, it was all a nightmare. As sombre prophecies were followed by sudden reverses – the Spanish landfall and advance, the Totonac rebellion, the Tlaxcalan defection – the *tlatoani* fretted and vacillated, sending lavish gifts which only whetted the Spanish appetite ('Moctezuma unfailingly sent some gold whenever he sent messengers'), promising to pay tribute to Cortés' emperor, yet also planning ambushes and concocting desperate excuses to stall the Spaniards. 'Your entry into Mexico is forbidden', he declared at one point, 'there is only the narrowest of roads and no food for you there to eat'. The Aztec elite, too, like other native American elites, divided in their attitude to the newcomers. For some, these were gods to be revered, for others, barbarians to be repulsed.[93] Now, in November 1519, *tlatoani* and elite confronted the Spaniards at the gates of Tenochtitlán.

Moctezuma did not resist. He welcomed the Spaniards eloquently and lodged them in the palace of Axayácatl – an unfortunate choice, since it contained a vast cache of treasure which, once the Spaniards had ferreted it out, served to confirm their greedy expectations.[94] The decision to allow the Spanish forces into the city – which has often been retrospectively criticized – was probably sound: Spanish military superiority was diminished, though by no means eliminated, amid the constricted streets, canals and causeways of Tenochtitlán;

---

[92] Díaz, *Conquest of New Spain*, pp. 214, 216.

[93] Díaz, *Conquest of New Spain*, p. 212; Nathan Wachtel, *The Vision of the Vanquished: The Spanish Conquest of Peru through Indian Eyes, 1520–1570* (Hassocks, 1977), p. 19. Thomas, *Conquest of Mexico*, pp. 180–7, reviews the various Mesoamerican interpretations of the Spaniards: (1) dangerous – but human – enemies, (2) emissaries of a distant pacific potentate, (3) new gods, (4) old gods. It is worth noting that, while the Maya plumped for the first (see Farriss, *Maya Society*, p. 22), the Aztecs (and other Central Mexican peoples) oscillated between all four.

[94] Díaz, *Conquest of New Spain*, p. 241.

and, once within the city, the Spaniards were dependent on their hosts for sustenance. What is more, the conquistadors themselves, having reached their objective, now faced a dilemma. They had entered the great city of Tenochtitlán, but they lodged there 'more as guests than victors'.[95] What was to be their next move? How could a force of a few hundred Spaniards subdue a city four times more populous than Seville?

The key to the Spaniards' *coup de main* was Moctezuma himself; their tactics were those of a terrorist hi-jack. Only by seizing the *tlatoani* and exploiting his formidable authority could the Spaniards hope to enforce their will on the Aztecs, some of whose leaders were already beginning to advocate armed resistance. So, when news came that an Aztec tributary *cacique* had attacked Spanish forces on the Gulf, Cortés seized Moctezuma who, while protesting in less than heroic fashion ('I have a son and two legitimate daughters – take them as hostages and spare me this disgrace'), did not dare resist, fearfully aware that resistance would be fatal. And, once captured, the perplexed emperor chose to rationalize his predicament, telling his 'nephews and all the principal Mexican chieftains... that he was spending some days (with the Spaniards) of his own free will and under no constraint'.[96]

Moctezuma's apparently supine attitude, vital to the Spanish strategy, has been the subject of criticism. Was the emperor prudent or merely pusillanimous? Though physical cowardice may have played a part – Moctezuma was surrounded by the 'stern visages and iron forms of the Spaniards', some of whom advocated running him through on the spot – it should also be appreciated that he faced an unenviable dilemma.[97] His initial conviction that Cortés was the returned Quetzalcóatl – if indeed he had ever really entertained it – was now dissipated. The massacre at Cholula, the centre of the Quetzalcóatl cult, could hardly be the work of the god himself. The Spaniards were now known to be mortal, as were their horses; they ate, bled, died and chased women like ordinary mortals; and they snatched gold more like monkeys than deities.[98] For Moctezuma, this

[95] Davies, *The Aztecs*, p. 262; see also Prescott, *History of the Conquest*, pp. 305–6.
[96] Díaz, *Conquest of New Spain*, p. 247.
[97] Prescott, *History of the Conquest*, p. 310.
[98] Wachtel, *Vision of the Vanquished*, pp. 19, 23–4; Díaz, *Conquest of New Spain*, p. 261.

realization removed any pious restraint when it came to tackling the Spaniards, but it did not prevent him still seeing the confrontation in magical and often fatalistic terms.

In this respect he was not alone. By judicious firing of their cannon the Spaniards 'caused great confusion in the city'. It was, an Aztec chronicler observed, as if the people were hallucinating on peyote. Moctezuma himself, accustomed to expect instant obedience and even servile deference, now confronted strangers who, for all their protestations of friendship, defied his authority and threatened his very empire, as the portents had foretold. Months of mounting anxiety had culminated in his sudden arrest and (brief) shackling – at which indignity 'the prince roared with anger'. Thus, Bernal Díaz recounts, was 'the great Moctezuma... tamed'. Indeed, Cortés played on the emperor's hopes and fears like a trained interrogator, alternately berating and cajoling him; after the emperor had been manacled, Cortés 'himself removed the chains and so affectionately did he speak to the prince that his (Moctezuma's) anger soon passed away'.[99] A strange love-hate relationship thus developed between captor and captive – indeed, several of the Spaniards, especially the page Orteguilla, grew fond of their prisoner. Such psychological pressure – as well as Moctezuma's fatalistic mien, which it reinforced – depended, of course, on several practical assets, which more than compensated for the Spaniards' limited numbers and exposed position. Before recounting the dramatic events which led to the overthrow of Tenochtitlán and the Aztec empire, it is worth giving a brief inventory of these assets, which can be summarized under three headings: technology, morale and organization, politics and diplomacy.

By 'technology' we refer to the Spaniards' superior military assets, broadly defined: artillery, arquebuses, steel weapons and armour, horses and dogs. It is striking that Cortés's army, though invariably – and sometimes hugely – outnumbered, won repeated victories and suffered remarkably few casualties. Wounds were frequent but fatalities few. High mortality was reserved for the unique rout of July 1520, when the Spaniards were driven pell-mell from Tenochtitlán (an event which bears out the generalization that it is fleeing armies

---

[99] León-Portilla, *Broken Spears*, pp. 54–5, 66; Díaz, *Conquest of New Spain*, pp. 247, 249, 251.

which suffer heaviest casualties).[100] Conversely, even allowing for conquistador hyperbole, Indian losses were often very heavy.[101] This inequality was in part technologically determined and can be seen to fit within the 'macroparasitic patterns' which McNeill discerns as geopolitical analogues of biological parasitism.[102] Massed Indian armies were vulnerable to gunfire, crossbowfire and cavalry charges, especially in open country. In Tlaxcala, Díaz recalled, 'one thing alone saved our lives: the enemy were so massed that every shot wrought havoc among them'; at Tenochtitlán, 'there was so great a number of them that the artillery had no need to aim but only to point their guns at the Indian forces'.[103] Artillery was thus effective, practically and psychologically; the crossbow, too, proved its worth; and the Spaniards' horses and dogs gave them notable advantages in speed and mobility, while terrifying their opponents (the dogs, 'enormous, with flat ears and long dangling tongues...tireless and very powerful', were adept at 'dogging' and even disembowelling the Indians).[104]

But it was cold steel which counted for most. The Tlaxcalans warned the Cholulans not to 'anger the white men, for they were a very warlike, daring and valiant people, who carried superior weapons made of white metal'.[105] Even at the battle of Otumba – wounded, fleeing, their artillery and powder lost, their horses depleted – the Spaniards were able decisively to defeat a numerically superior army. Steel served principally as an offensive asset. The Spaniards' armour, hot and heavy, was not an unqualified asset (some conquistadors developed a preference for the light quilted cotton armour of the Indians). But steel swords and lances were a different matter. Correctly used, they were superior to the Aztec

---

[100] John Keegan, *The Face of Battle* (London, 1991), p. 71, citing du Picq.

[101] Pagden, *Hernán Cortés*, pp. 131, 174–6 (where Cortés reports the taking of Ixtapalapa, on the southern shore of Lake Texcoco, at the cost of 6,000 Indians killed, and one Spaniard); Díaz, *Conquest of New Spain*, pp. 160, 305, though compare p. 24, on the heavier losses sustained by the Spaniards in their early encounter with the Champoton Maya: the result, it seems, of inexperience and insouciance.

[102] McNeill, *Plagues and People*, pp. 232–3.

[103] Díaz, *Conquest of New Spain*, p. 149; Pagden, *Hernán Cortés*, p. 131.

[104] León-Portilla, *Broken Spears*, pp. 30–1, 45–6, 110; Díaz, *Conquest of New Spain*, p. 137; and note the dedication of Todorov, *Conquest of America*, p. v. In using dogs – probably mastiffs or Irish wolfhounds – the conquistadors were again following contemporary European military practice: Thomas, *Conquest of Mexico*, pp. 153, 180, 228.

[105] León-Portilla, *Broken Spears*, p. 45.

macana, the obsidian-edged axe or 'broadsword.' The latter was a 'dreadful' weapon, capable, it was said, of decapitating a horse at a single blow (though, considering the failings of European executioners, hewing static human necks on the block, this may be another conquistador hyperbole; we do not hear of many decapitated horses in the annals). But the *macana* required a lusty swing, which may not have been feasible in tightly packed battle formations; conversely, the Spaniards' preference for stabbing sword-thrusts was vindicated time and again. Indeed, it may be that Aztec tactics, designed for man-to-man combat with comparable opponents, were inherently ill-suited to warfare against well-drilled blocks of cavalry or infantry.[106] Significantly, the Spaniards' chief concern seems to have been the humble stone which, when thrown, slung or rained down from rooftops, proved troublesome, if rarely fatal: Cortés himself was struck on the head during the disastrous retreat from Tenochtitlán (and again was 'badly wounded in the head' leading an attack on Xochimilco); his skull, preserved in Mexico City, shows evidence of two fractures.[107] The utility of the common stone, however, speaks for the inadequacy of the Indian bow and the famous *atlatl* (spear-thrower), of which little is heard during the battles of the Conquest.[108] The Aztecs confronted the Spaniards, therefore, rather as a numerically superior but ill-organized stone-throwing crowd confronts well-equipped and well-disciplined riot police, complete with shields, batons and rifles – at a distinct disadvantage, numbers notwithstanding.

A confrontation of Stone Age and Iron Age technologies was bound to be unequal. But technology, of course, has to be utilized. Historians have rightly stressed the superior morale and organization of the Spanish forces.[109] In this encounter, the territorial

---

[106] Díaz, *Conquest of New Spain*, pp. 29, 48, 55, 76, 145; on Spanish weaponry, Ross Hassig, *Mexico and the Spanish Conquest* (Harlow, 1994), pp. 37–8; and Aztec tactics, Clendinnen, *Aztecs*, p. 116.

[107] Díaz, *Conquest of New Spain*, pp. 334, 342; Thomas, *Conquest of Mexico*, pp. 399, 424.

[108] Though Díaz, *Conquest of New Spain*, p. 149, refers to sharp 'darts' hurled by the Spaniards' adversaries, Ross Hassig, *War and Society in Ancient Mesoamerica* (Berkeley, 1992), pp. 137–8, suggests that longbows and spear-throwers were known and used effectively by the Aztecs; however, Clendinnen, *Aztecs*, p. 116, refers to the lack of effective 'projectile weapons'.

[109] Davies, *The Aztecs*, p. 251. Todorov, *Conquest of America*, pp. 61-2ff., argues that the Spaniards defeated the Indians 'by means of signs'; because – so the Indian texts tell us – 'the Mayas and the Aztecs lost control of communication'. To the extent that I follow the argument, it reads

imperative worked in reverse: Cortés, we have noted, had to press for victory in order to exploit Moctezuma's indecision and win Charles V's approval; the Spaniards in general – while they sometimes allowed themselves the luxury of debate and dissension – had to adhere to Benjamin Franklin's maxim: 'we must...all hang together or, most assuredly, we shall all hang separately' – or, rather, suffer sacrifice separately. In battle the Spaniards fought tenaciously and with a view to total victory which – since they usually attained it – they confidently attributed to divine favour. Their opponents, too, adhered to a martial religion, but it lacked the fierce exclusivism of crusading Christianity; it was shaken by recurrent defeats, which seemed to presage the end of the old order, even the death of the gods; and, with its mania for sacrifice, it encouraged the taking of live prisoners, which tended to inhibit the Aztecs' tactics in those rare moments when outright victory was within their grasp.[110]

More important was the lack of Aztec military expertise, ostensibly odd in view of the Aztecs' military reputation. The Aztecs, however, possessed no standing army; their wars were fought by knightly elites backed by commoner levies; and their victories (which, when they fought Tlaxcalans or Tarascans, were offset by recurrent defeats) were gained because of superior numbers and morale, not organization. Aztecs, Tlaxcalans, Tarascans, Mixtecs – all adhered to a common pattern of warfare. Hence Mesoamerican battles resembled those medieval European encounters in which chivalrous hosts met in chaotic, man-to-man combat. Indeed, the whole military/ meritocratic ethic – Mesoamerican or medieval – was premised on the notion of individual prowess, proven in individual confrontation.[111] The Spaniards, a good many of them veterans of the Italian wars, fought as organizational units which were trained for combat (weapons and tactics had been practised in Cuba, then perfected in Mexico). They were not averse even to disguising themselves as Aztecs for the sake of military advantage – a tactic anathema to Aztec concepts of warfare and reputation. They also displayed a basic

as a (not uninteresting) semiotic repackaging of older psychological explanations (involving, for example, Spanish *Realpolitik*, Aztec susceptibility to portents and the resulting mutual misunderstanding which favoured the former).

[110] Díaz, *Conquest of New Spain*, pp. 251, 270; Wachtel, *Vision of the Vanquished*, pp. 25, 27–8.
[111] Clendinnen, *Aztecs*, p. 116.

military discipline (Cortés was a stickler for rules) and a functional interdependence of infantry, artillery and cavalry. The organization which would make the Spanish *tercios* the terror of European battlefields was already evident, in embryonic form, in Mexico, deployed against ill-equipped and disorganized Indian hosts. Not surprisingly, the outcome sometimes resembled Kitchener's slaughter of the Sudanese at Omdurman.[112]

Furthermore, the speed of the Conquest was such – a mere two years from initial landfall to final victory – that the Spaniards' opponents had insufficient time to develop countertactics. The onslaught of military macroparasitism was as rapid and devastating as that of biological microparasitism. It is wrong to assert that, when confronted by this new challenge, the Aztecs remained obtusely inert. They began to appropriate Spanish weapons (swords, at least; unlike their Inca counterparts – whose resistance was more protracted – they never acquired arquebuses); they soon fathomed the working of weapons like the Spaniards' improvised catapult; and they developed effective techniques to foil the Spanish cavalry, building barricades, digging pits and boltholes. But time was lacking. Later, of course, more remote and mobile Indians groups familiarized themselves with Spanish military practice and proved to be redoubtable, even if poorly armed, opponents: the ultimate example of such evolutionary adaptation – of learning to live with the Spanish macroparasite – was afforded by the mounted Plains Indians.[113]

Where the northern nomads could flee, survive and learn, the sedentary population of central Mesoamerica had to stand and fight, and had to do so on unequal terms, technologically and organizationally, if not numerically. To these military disadvantages were added certain political factors which proved the most crucial determinants of Aztec defeat. Above all, the Spaniards triumphed because their superior technology, morale and organization were deployed against a state whose mighty aspect concealed serious divisions and weaknesses. Here was another key difference between the great Asiatic

---

[112] León-Portilla, *Broken Spears*, p. 112 (disguise); Díaz, *Conquest of New Spain*, p. 354 (discipline).

[113] Díaz, *Conquest of New Spain*, pp. 193, 364; León-Portilla, *Broken Spears*, pp. 110–11; Pagden, *Hernán Cortés*, p. 135: all illustrate Aztec ingenuity; cf. Davies, *The Aztecs*, pp. 251–2. On the Plains Indians: Farb, *Man's Rise to Civilization*, ch. 8.

empires which the Portuguese nibbled and the Indoamerican civilizations which the Spaniards swallowed whole. Here, too, the territorial imperative worked in reverse: the Spaniards had to push ahead (a loss of momentum could be disastrous), and they pushed ahead into an empire of recent creation, racked by internal feuds and divisions; the ensuing conflict was fought on Aztec territory, where Aztec political failings could be fully exploited. (A far-fetched and literal counterfactual comparison would imagine a powerful Aztec force landing in Castile at the time of the Comunero rebellion; more realistically, we might recall the power politics of the earlier Islamic advance in Spain, when infidel invaders had little difficulty finding useful Christian allies.) Similarly, in Mexico, the Christian invaders formed valuable alliances with the enemies or disaffected tributaries of the Aztec power: Cempoala, Tlaxcala and later, within the Valley of Mexico itself, Texcoco and Chalco. Conversely, Aztec attempts to split the Spaniards – by playing Cortés against Pánfilo de Narváez, for example – were ultimately unsuccessful.

The Tlaxcala alliance in particular provided Cortés with crucial reinforcements, political intelligence, material supplies, labour and a safe haven after the disastrous retreat from Tenochtitlán in July 1520. By then, the Aztecs were feeling the effects not only of military macroparasitism but also of biological microparasitism. Both body and body politic were beginning to succumb to the Spanish onslaught. European diseases – smallpox especially – began to ravage a vulnerable population. It is unlikely that losses were, as yet, so great as to affect Aztec fighting strength (the Aztecs' problem was not that of marshalling men for battle but of using their huge numbers to advantage in the field of battle – where, in fact, numbers could even prove counterproductive). Disease did, however, carry off some key leaders (such as Cuitláhuac, Moctezuma's successor); it probably enhanced feelings of fatalism and surrender; and it depleted the labour force, aggravating the problem of Tenochtitlán's food supply, already disrupted by warfare and a coincidental drought. Thus the Spaniards were finally able to reduce the city by siege, controlling the lake and cutting off incoming food supplies. Tenochtitlán's extreme concentration of population and centralization of political power ultimately made the city – and the entire empire – vulnerable to determined attackers, especially if they were skilled in naval as well as in land warfare. And, once the attackers triumphed, they found they could lay claim not only to Tenochtitlán – a ravaged and depopulated prize – but also to Tenochtitlán's teeming tributaries, who, if they rejoiced at the fall of their old oppressor, soon found that they had exchanged one imperial overlord for another. While scattered, stateless peoples – like the Chichimec of northern Mexico – were less vulnerable to conventional military campaigns, leading to formal political conquest, the Aztec state's very hypertrophy made a concerted, knock-out blow both feasible and effective. Primate cities – Tenochtitlán in 1520–1, Paris in 1870–1 – offered would-be conquerors distinct advantages, short cuts to complete conquest.

But only if the would-be conquerors were bold and accomplished. Cortés was both. In exploiting Aztec weaknesses, while maintaining Spanish morale and discipline, Cortés proved himself not only a skilled general but also a consummate politician. He was, Bernal Díaz recalled, 'very shrewd in all things'.[114] He exhorted, reasoned, gambled, cajoled, tricked, tortured and terrorized. He had no qualms about having his own men flogged (and worse), even for minor offences, nor about razing Indian villages or cutting off the hands or thumbs of Indian 'spies'. He had to be restrained from toppling bloodstained idols wherever he encountered them. At the same time, he sedulously flattered Moctezuma – almost as much as he did Charles V. He also led by tireless example, and he practised constant stratagems: concealing casualties, feigning long-standing knowledge of the Aztec realm, striving to maintain the Spaniards' supernatural reputation. An old, scarred and bearded Basque veteran was despatched as envoy to the Totonacs because, Cortés told him, 'when they see your ugly face they'll certainly take you for one of their idols'.[115] In short, Cortés behaved as Machiavelli had recommended to the princes of the age; and it was to princely status that Cortés probably aspired, and which he finally came close to attaining.

Notwithstanding this string of advantages – mental, military, political – the Conquest was a close-run thing. No doubt, had Cortés's bold confrontation failed, as it nearly did, an alternative Conquest would have ensued, as Spanish power wore down its opponents in

---

[114] Díaz, *Conquest of New Spain*, p. 78.
[115] Díaz, *Conquest of New Spain*, pp. 78, 117, 171.

more piecemeal fashion. In Peru, for example, Inca resistance was protracted – and, partly in consequence, Spanish authority in Peru was never so complete or pervasive as it was in Mexico. In the latter, however, Mexico City soon arose on the rubble of Tenochtitlán, and a new colony – New Spain – effectively supplanted the old Aztec empire. While important social and cultural continuities became apparent (they will be discussed later) the political upheaval of the Conquest was rapid, radical and traumatic.

How did this come about? The apparent stalemate created by the Spaniards' entry into Tenochtitlán and seizure of Moctezuma was broken by a series of dramatic events. On both sides, divisions were opening up. The Aztecs' allegiance to the captive Moctezuma began to falter and an anti-appeasement party formed, including many of the priests as well as key leaders like Cacama, prince of Texcoco, and, later, Moctezuma's own brother, Cuitláhuac.[116] They began to plan resistance. On the Spanish side, meanwhile, news came of the arrival at Veracruz of Pánfilo de Narváez, backed by a sizeable force (eighteen ships and nine hundred men), sent by the governor of Cuba to bring the errant Cortés to heel. Moctezuma's hopes were raised, and he entered into covert negotiations with Narváez. But the Narváez expedition ultimately served Cortés's interests. Leaving Pedro de Alvarado in command in Tenochtitlán, Cortés hurried down to the Gulf, defeated his sluggish rival at Cempoala, and, resorting to the cajolery at which he excelled, persuaded Narváez's men to throw in their lot with him and return to Tenochtitlán: 'he was so persuasive in fact', recalled a comrade, 'that every one of them offered to come with us'.[117]

At Tenochtitlán, however, the inevitable crisis had broken (thus, incidentally, invalidating the rosy picture Cortés had painted for Narváez's men). Handsome but hasty, Pedro de Alvarado – Tonatiuh, 'Child of the Sun,' the Indians called him – grew alarmed at reports of an impending attack, which would coincide with the ceremonial festival of Toxcatl, sacred to Huitzilopochtli. He therefore took advantage of a religious ceremony – which the Spaniards, armed to

---

[116] Davies, *The Aztecs*, p. 268; Thomas, *Conquest of Mexico*, p. 270; Díaz, *Conquest of New Spain*, pp. 260–2.

[117] Pagden, *Hernán Cortés*, pp. 115–26; Díaz, *Conquest of New Spain*, pp. 282, 284.

the teeth, were allowed to attend – to launch a pre-emptive attack. The Spaniards sealed off the temple precincts and massacred the unarmed celebrants within: lords, priests, drummers and dancers. Fresh rivers of blood – shed by Spanish steel rather than by Aztec obsidian – sluiced through the house of Huitzilopochtli. But the Aztecs outside rallied and began to rain spears and arrows upon the Spaniards, now engaged in their customary looting. Alvarado and his men were forced to retreat to their compound, where they remained, effectively besieged within a hostile city.[118]

At this point Cortés returned, bringing some thirteen hundred Spaniards and two thousand Tlaxcalans to reinforce Alvarado's beleaguered garrison of perhaps five hundred. Cortés was livid. Whether he had acted out of fear or fanaticism or simple pre-emptive calculation, Alvarado had precipitated a crisis, of which there could be only a military outcome. Aztec ambivalence had given way to outright hostility; the authority of the captive Moctezuma was spent; the Aztec war party now took control. The Spaniards were deprived of food and water, and fighting within the city grew more severe; an attempted break-out failed, though in the process the Spaniards managed to put Huitzilopochtli's temple to the torch. Veterans of European campaigns averred 'that they had never seen such fierce fighting, not even in Christian wars, or against the French king's artillery, or the Great Turk'. Twenty thousand Hectors and Rolands could not have tipped the balance, Díaz observed.[119] Hugely outnumbered, Cortés decided to seek a truce and attempt a withdrawal. Moctezuma was compelled to appeal to his people from a roof-top in the Spanish compound; he was greeted by a hail of stones and arrows and bundled back to his dungeon, where he later died – the victim of his irate people, the Spaniards claimed, stabbed by the Spaniards, the palace servants (more plausibly) maintained.[120]

---

[118] The massacre, Davies comments, was 'Cholula all over again', complete with the ensuing charges and countercharges: *The Aztecs*, pp. 267–8; see also Díaz, *Conquest of New Spain*, pp. 283, 285, 286; León-Portilla, *Broken Spears*, pp. 74–6, 129–31; Thomas, *Conquest of Mexico*, pp. 384–93, which stresses the Tlaxcalans' – and perhaps the Texcocans' – incitement of the jittery Spaniards.

[119] Díaz, *Conquest of New Spain*, p. 289.

[120] For versions of Moctezuma's death: Díaz, *Conquest of New Spain*, p. 294; Pagden, *Hernán Cortés*, pp. 132, 477–8; León-Portilla, *Broken Spears*, pp. 83, 90; Thomas, *Conquest of Mexico*, pp. 402, 451–2.

With Moctezuma dead, the Spaniards lost their principal hostage –
though a hostage of declining utility – and the Aztecs, led by
Cuitláhuac, pressed home their attacks. 'The war', Cortés reported,
'grew more fierce and pitiless each day'. Evacuation was now essential, but highly hazardous. On the rainy night of 20 July the Spaniards
gathered up their plunder, prepared a wooden platform with which
to bridge gaps in the city's causeways and sallied forth with their
Tlaxcalan allies. They soon came under fierce attack; in their haste
and panic many tumbled into the city's canals, where a heavy bag
of bullion could mean a swift death; in some places the piles of
bodies formed a cadaverous bridge for others to cross. Hundreds
of Spaniards – perhaps as many as a thousand – died on this, the
Noche Triste (Night of Sorrow), and the number might have been
higher had not their pursuers been overconcerned to take prisoners
for sacrifice.[121]

The *Noche Triste* was the stuff of legend. His way barred by a canal,
on which Aztec war canoes plied, Pedro de Alvarado planted his
'long lance' on the bottom and vaulted across: 'an exploit,' Prescott
applauds, 'which rivalled those of the demi-gods of Grecian fable,'
and which gave its name – *Salto de Alvarado* (Alvarado's Leap) – to a
ditch west of the Alameda. 'But', Bernal Díaz interjects in his usual
matter-of-fact way, 'no soldier stopped at the time, I assure you, to
see whether his leap was long or short'. Equally, the story that Cortés
slumped under a cypress at Popotla, witnessing through tear-filled
eyes the retreat of his bedraggled army, may or may not be true,
but it gained later currency from the generations of pilgrims who
visited the ancient *ahuehuete* – Cortés's cypress – where it stood near
Chapultepec.[122]

But Cortés did not lament for long. He force-marched his stricken
army around the northern circumference of the lake, making for
the sanctuary of Tlaxcala to the east. On the plains of Otumba the

[121] Pagden, *Hernán Cortés*, p. 132; Prescott, *Conquest of Mexico*, p. 408; Padden, *Hummingbird
and the Hawk*, p. 208.

[122] Prescott, *Conquest of Mexico*, p. 405; Díaz, *Conquest of New Spain*, p. 300; Johnson, *Cortés*,
p. 152; Thomas, *Conquest of Mexico*, pp. 407–12. Alvarado's leap (now also the name of a
Mexico City metro station) was, of course, favoured by the same geophysical conditions –
rarefied atmosphere and diminished gravity – which helped Bob Beamon set a prodigious
world long-jump record in Mexico City during the 1968 Olympics: Peter J. Brancazio, *Sport
Science* (New York, 1984), p. 356.

Spaniards were again forced to stand and fight; significantly, despite their sad condition (wounded, exhausted, reduced to eating horse-meat), they won a notable victory against the odds.[123] Spanish military organization survived even after defeat; Aztec disorganization was not remedied by victory. The Spaniards thus won passage through to Tlaxcala and – no less important – they ensured that the Tlaxcalan alliance would hold. Though defeated, the Spaniards were not wholly demoralized. For Cortés, this was a strategic withdrawal, and the reduction of Tenochtitlán remained his overriding goal.

To this end, Cortés now methodically planned a siege campaign, combining action by land and water. Fresh troops were recruited – more Tlaxcalans and a force from Chalco, whose old enmity for Tenochtitlán had not abated; supplies were brought up from the Gulf, where Spanish ships had put in; Texcoco, so long a disgruntled junior partner in the Triple Alliance, now split by factional conflicts, provided a contingent and eventually a base for the onslaught on Tenochtitlán. Even before the city fell, therefore, Indians in their thousands fought, laboured and produced for the Spaniards, thus making the Conquest possible. '*Malinchismo*' – collaboration with the Spanish invader – was not the monopoly of a single Chontal Maya princess.[124]

Texcoco, for example, besides providing a fifth column within the heartland of the Aztec empire, also delivered – on demand – fifty thousand copper-tipped arrows. Some ten thousand Indians from Texcoco, Tlaxcala and elsewhere, hauled, dug and logrolled in order to transport thirteen prefabricated brigantines down from the Tlaxcalan highlands to the lakeside, where the vessels could be assembled and launched into battle against the Aztec war canoes.[125] In pursuit of this concerted military strategy, Cortés had to adopt appropriate policies. Seeking Indian recruits, he tempered his religious zeal, even allowing human sacrifice among his Tlaxcalan allies. At the same time such a sustained campaign required extensive

---

[123] Thomas, *Conquest of Mexico*, pp. 424–6, which notes that in this, as in other encounters, 'the great lady of Cortés' army', María de Estrada, played a prominent role, as did the Spaniards' mastiffs.

[124] Díaz, *Conquest of New Spain*, p. 319; Charles Gibson, *Tlaxcala in the Sixteenth Century* (Stanford, 1967; first pubd. 1952), pp. 22, 25.

[125] Díaz, *Conquest of New Spain*, p. 353; Pagden, *Hernán Cortés*, p. 206.

mobilization of labour and systematic intimidation of enemies. Alleged Indian 'rebels' (i.e., allies of the Aztecs) were enslaved, branded, sold or put to work. Collaborating Indian princes, it seems, tolerated the enslavement of their subjects (which was nothing new) more than they did the subversion of their faith (which was).

Gradually, Cortés's reconstituted army – some one thousand Spaniards and ten thousand Indian auxiliaries – closed in on Tenochtitlán. Neighbouring towns were coerced or cajoled into compliance. Those who resisted – like Cuernavaca, to the south – were subdued; Chalco, now committed to the Spanish alliance, successfully beat off an Aztec reprisal. Within Tenochtitlán, smallpox raged (it carried off the new *tlatoani*, Cuitláhuac) and bodies littered the streets. Political divisions also racked the Aztec elite. Then, at the end of June, Cortés launched three detachments across the main causeways leading into the beleaguered city. They made only slow, costly progress. The narrow causeways were unsuitable for cavalry, and the gains the Spaniards made by day were often lost by night as the defenders – still numerically superior – counterattacked, sapping the causeways and destroying their bridges. Though the Spanish brigantines, powered by oars and sail, could scatter the Aztec canoes, they were vulnerable to Aztec countermeasures – such as stakes embedded in the lake bottom – and could not give Cortés the control of the lake which he sought. And so great was the labyrinthine city itself that it swallowed successful attackers into its maw, trapping them in narrow thoroughfares and precincts, subjecting them to the messy street-fighting which most favoured the defenders' cause. Meanwhile, by sudden forays the Aztecs recovered lost ground and captured coveted prisoners, whose bloody sacrifice was witnessed, at a distance, by their horrified comrades, and whose severed limbs were lobbed into the Spanish camp or paraded round the Valley cities in order to display the fallibility of Spanish arms.[126]

This last ploy illustrated one of the many dangers which Cortés's army confronted: an attack in the rear by still-loyal Aztec forces – in particular, those of Toluca – who might, in effect, besiege the besiegers. As these dangers became all the more apparent, as the incessant din of Aztec war-horns and the 'dismal drums' of Huizilopochtli

---

[126] Díaz, *Conquest of New Spain*, pp. 381, 383, 386; Thomas, *Conquest of Mexico*, ch. 33.

deafened their listeners and sapped their resolve, so the Spaniards began to question the feasibility of their bold enterprise, and their Indian auxiliaries began to desert.[127] Now, however, Don Carlos Ahuax Pitzatzin – one of Cortés's Texcocan allies – counselled a different and more patient strategy, advocating a tight economic blockade rather than repeated armed attacks. The defenders, Don Carlos pointed out, 'will suffer worse from hunger than from war'; in response to which, 'Cortés threw his arms around Don Carlos' neck and thanked him', and the strategy of attrition – which implied the progressive destruction of the city, materially and demographically – was adopted.[128]

The tourniquet was tightened: Tenochtitlán was denied water and sustenance; the external Tolucan threat was countered, leaving the Aztec capital bereft of hope. The Spaniards discovered, too, that if their brigantines took sail and bore down on the submerged stakes at full speed they could shatter them without risk of sinking. Thus, the Spaniards won mastery of the lake, the city was sealed off and the ships could support armed attacks along the causeways. It could be said, indeed, that the ultimate overthrow of the great highland empire of the Aztecs was achieved by Spanish naval power, operating in prefabricated boats 7,000 feet above sea level.[129] Within the city, meanwhile, the inhabitants were reduced to scavenging for lizards, or chewing bark and hide, to assuage the pangs of hunger. And they drank brackish water, which further contributed to the rampant morbidity and mortality.

As the fortunes of war again shifted, the Spaniards' opportunistic allies drifted back, ready for the impending assault on the stricken city. Cortés complemented the blockade with attacks designed to destroy Tenochtitlán's defences. Canals were filled in, buildings

---

[127] Díaz, *Conquest of New Spain*, pp. 385, 389.

[128] Díaz, *Conquest of New Spain*, p. 390. Some Spaniards had already suggested laying systematic siege to the city instead of launching costly frontal assaults; but, to begin with, Cortés had been keen for quick results, which would preserve Tenochtitlán largely intact. On the decision to prosecute the campaign even at the price of destroying the city and its inhabitants, see Thomas, *Conquest of Mexico*, pp. 502–3.

[129] Díaz, *Conquest of New Spain*, pp. 395–6; Prescott, *Conquest of Mexico*, pp. 499, 506, where Cortés calls his flotilla 'the key to the war'. The remains of the brigantines were preserved in Mexico City for years thereafter, as 'memorials of the Conquest': Prescott, *Conquest of Mexico*, p. 579.

systematically razed.[130] Gradually, the defenders were driven back into the northeastern corner of the city, where they gathered for a last stand. The advancing Spaniards entered an urban charnel house, bloody, strewn with limbs and bodies, maggot-ridden and shrouded in a foul miasma, which sickened even battle-hardened veterans. At last, resistance ceased. Cuauhtémoc, the last *tlatoani*, beat a retreat across the lake from Tlatelolco but was captured along with his entourage. Cortés's troops now went their different ways. The Tlaxcalan auxiliaries ran riot, burning palaces and cannibalizing prisoners: thus the Aztecs paid for their years of terror and tribute. The Spaniards, jostling to attend Cortés's victory banquet (which, thanks to the timely arrival of a shipment of wine from Veracruz, turned into a bacchanalian revel), now gave vent to their lusts for gold and girls, shamelessly searching the refugees who streamed out of the city, 'thin, sallow, and dirty', seizing 'the pretty women – those of light bodies, the fair[-skinned] ones,' and subjecting the Aztec priests and nobility to torture and interrogation, thereby to discover supposed (in fact largely imaginary) caches of treasure. Cuauhtémoc, who was the object of an unseemly squabble between rival Spaniards, was tortured; other Aztec lords were hanged or savaged by the Spaniards' mastiffs.[131]

The Spaniards' haul was disappointing. Though they did not know it, they had already gutted Tenochtitlán of its accumulated bullion – just as they had destroyed some three-quarters of the city's buildings. Obsessed with gold, they were scarcely content with slaves and concubines. Nor did grumbling against Cortés and his alleged greed (resentful graffiti began to appear on the walls of the commander's whitewashed palace in Coyoacán) assuage conquistador disillusionment and discontent. Great exertions merited greater rewards. It was at once plain that Tenochtitlán's new masters would have to seek further conquests and fresh resources if they were to justify their heroic military efforts and satisfy their high seigneurial expectations.

[130] Padden, *Hummingbird and the Hawk*, p. 219; Thomas, *Conquest of Mexico*, pp. 502–3.
[131] Díaz, *Conquest of New Spain*, p. 405–6, 409–10; Padden, *Hummingbird and the Hawk*, p. 222.

Select Bibliography

Adams, Richard E. W., ed., *The Origns of Maya Civilization* (Albuquerque, 1977).

Altman, Ida, and Horn, James, eds., '*To Make America*': *European Emigration in the Early Modern Period* (Berkeley, 1991).

Anderson, Perry, *Lineages of the Absolutist State* (London, 1979).

Aveni, Anthony F., *Skywatchers of Ancient Mexico* (Austin, 1980).

Benson, E. P., ed., *Dumbarton Oaks Conference on the Olmec* (Washington, 1968).

Benson, Elizabeth P., and Boone, Elizabeth H., eds., *Ritual Human Sacrifice in Mesoamerica* (Washington, 1984).

Berdan, Frances, *The Aztecs of Central Mexico: An Imperial Society* (New York, 1982).

Bernal, Ignacio, *The Olmec World* (Berkeley, 1969).

Blanton, Richard E., Kowalewski, Stephen A., Feinman, Gary, and Appel, Jill, eds., *Ancient Mesoamerica: A Comparison of Change in Three Regions* (Cambridge, 1981).

Brading, D. A., *The First America* (Cambridge, 1991).

Brading, D. A., *Myth and Prophecy in Mexican History* (Cambridge, 1984).

Braudel, Fernand, *Civilization and Capitalism, Fifteenth-Eighteenth Centuries*, vol. 2, *The Wheels of Commerce* (London, 1982).

Braudel, Fernand, *Civilization and Capitalism, Fifteenth-Eighteenth Centuries*, vol. 3, *The Perspective of the World* (London, 1985).

Bray, Warwick, *Everday Life of the Aztecs* (London, 1968).

Brundage, Burr Cartwright, *The Fifth Sun: Aztec Gods, Aztec World* (Austin, 1983).

Brundage, Burr Cartwright, *A Rain of Darts: The Mexica Aztecs* (Austin, 1972).

Carrasco, David, *Religions of Mesoamerica* (San Francisco, 1990).

Carrasco, Pedro, *La sociedad indígena en el centro y occidente de México* (Zamora, 1986).

Carrasco, Pedro, and Broda, Johanna, *Economía política e ideologia en el México prehispánico* (Mexico, 1978).

Chaunu, Pierre, *La expansión europea (siglos XII al XV)* (Barcelona, 1982).

Chevalier, François, *Land and Society in Colonial Mexico: The Great Hacienda* (Berkeley, 1970, first pubd. 1963).

Claessen, Henri J., and Skalnik, Peter, *The Early State* (The Hague, 1978).

Clendinnen, Inga, *Ambivalent Conquest: Maya and Spaniard in Yucatán, 1517–1570* (Cambridge, 1987).

Clendinnen, Inga, *Aztecs* (Cambridge, 1991).

Cohen, Mark Nathan, *La crisis alimentaria de la prehistoria* (Madrid, 1984).

Conrad, Geoffrey W., and Demarest, Arthur A., *Religion and Empire: The Dynamics of Aztec and Inca Expansionism* (Cambridge, 1984).

Culbert, T. Patrick, ed., *The Classic Maya Collapse* (Albuquerque, 1973).

Curtin, Philip D., *Cross-cultural Trade in World History* (Cambridge, 1984).

Davies, Nigel, *The Ancient Kingdoms of Mexico* (Harmondsworth, 1983).

Davies, Nigel, *The Aztecs: A History* (London, 1977).

Davies, Nigel, *The Toltec Heritage* (Norman, Okla., 1980).

Davies, Nigel, *The Toltecs until the Fall of Tula* (Norman, Okla., 1977).

Diamond, Jared, *Guns, Germs, and Steel: A Short History of Everybody for the Last 13,000 Years* (London, 1997).

Díaz, Bernal, *The Conquest of New Spain* (Harmondsworth, 1981; first pubd. 1963).

Diehl, Richard A., *Tula: The Toltec Capital of Ancient Mexico* (London, 1983).

Drennan, Robert D., and Uribe, Carlos A., *Chiefdoms in the Americas* (Lanham, Md., 1987).

Duverger, Christian, *La fleur létale: Economie du sacrifice aztèque* (Paris, 1978).

Elliott, J. H., *Imperial Spain, 1469–1716* (Harmondsworth, 1970).

Elliott, J. H., *The Old World and the New, 1492–1650* (Cambridge, 1970).

Fagen, Brian, *The Great Journey* (London, 1987).

Farb, Peter, *Man's Rise to Civilization as Shown by the Indians of North America from Primeval Time to the Coming of the Industrial State* (New York, 1968).

Farriss, Nancy M., *Maya Society under Colonial Rule: The Collective Enterprise of Survival* (Princeton, 1984).

Fiedel, Stuart J., *Prehistory of the Americas* (Cambridge, 2nd ed., 1992).

Flannery, Kent V., ed., *The Early Mesoamerican Village* (New York, 1976).

Flannery, Kent V., ed., *Maya Subsistance: Essays in Memory of Dennis E. Puleston* (New York, 1982).

Flannery, Kent V., and Marcus, Joyce, *The Cloud People: Divergent Evolution of the Zapotec and Mixtec Civilizations* (New York, 1983).

Frank, André Gunder, *Capitalism and Underdevelopment in Latin America* (Harmondsworth, 1971).

Frank, André Gunder, *Mexican Agriculture, 1521–1630* (Cambridge, 1979).

Gibson, Charles, *The Aztecs under Spanish Rule: A History of the Indians of the Valley of Mexico, 1519–1810* (Stanford, 1964).

Gibson, Charles, *Tlaxcala in the Sixteenth Century* (Stanford, 1967, first pubd. 1952).

Gillespie, Susan D., *The Aztec Kings* (Tucson, 1989).

González Torres, Yolotl, *El sacrificio humano entre los mexicas* (Mexico, 1985).

Gruzinski, Serge, *Man-Gods in the Mexican Highlands, Sixteenth to Eighteenth Century* (Stanford, 1989).

Gutiérrez, Ramón A., *When Jesus Came the Corn Mothers Went Away: Marriage, Sexuality and Power in New Mexico, 1500–1856* (Stanford, 1991).

Hall, Thomas D., *Social Change in the Southwest, 1350–1880* (Lawrence, Kans., 1989).

Hammond, Norman, *Ancient Maya Civilization* (New Brunswick, 1994, first pubd. 1982).

Harris, Marvin, *Cannibals and Kings: The Origins of Cultures* (New York, 1978).

Harris, Marvin, *Cultural Materialism* (New York, 1979).

Harvey, H. R., ed., *Land and Politics in the Valley of Mexico: A Two-Thousand-Year Perspective* (Albuquerque, 1991).

Hassig, Ross, *Aztec Warfare: Imperial Expansion and Social Control* (Norman, Okla., 1988).

Hassig, Ross, *War and Society in Ancient Mesoamerica* (Berkeley, 1992).

Henderson, John S., *The World of the Ancient Maya* (Ithaca, 1981).

Hirth, Kenneth G., ed., *Trade and Exchange in Early Mesoamerica* (Albuquerque, 1984).

Hodge, Mary, and Smith, Michael E., *Economies and Polities in the Aztec Realm* (Albany, 1994).

Isaac, Barry L., ed., *Economic Aspects of Prehispanic Highland Mexico: Research in Economic Anthropology*, Suppl. 2 (Greenwich, Conn., 1986).

Jones, Grant D., and Kautz, Robert R., eds., *The Transition to Statehood in the New World* (Cambridge, 1981).

Jones, Lindsay, *Twin City Tales: A Hermeneutical Reassessment of Tula and Chichén Itzá* (Niwot, Colo., 1995).

Katz, Friedrich, *The Ancient American Civilizations* (London, 1989, first pubd. 1972).

Kriedte, Peter, *Feudalismo tardío y capital mercantil* (Barcelona, 1982).

Kula, Witold, *An Economic Theory of the Feudal System* (London, 1976).

León-Portilla, Miguel, *Aztec Thought and Culture* (Norman, Okla., 1963).

León-Portilla, Miguel, *The Broken Spears: The Aztec Account of the Conquest of Mexico* (Boston, 1990, first pubd. 1962).

Lomax, Derek W., *The Reconquest of Spain* (London, 1978).

López Austin, Alfredo, *The Human Body and Ideology: Concepts of the Ancient Nahuas* (2 vols., Salt Lake City, 1988).

Luckert, Karl W., *Olmec Religion: A Key to Middle America and Beyond* (Norman, Okla., 1976).

McNeill, William, *Plagues and Peoples* (Oxford, 1977).

Mann, Michael, *The Sources of Social Power*, vol. 1, *A History of Power from the Beginning to 1760 AD* (Cambridge, 1986).

Miskimin, Harry A., *The Economy of Later Renaissance Europe, 1460–1600* (Cambridge, 1977).

Montmollin, Olivier de, *The Archaeology of Political Structure: Settlement Analysis in a Classic Maya Polity* (Cambridge, 1989).

Offner, Jerome, *Law and Politics in Aztec Texcoco* (Cambridge, 1983).

Olivera, Mercedes, *Pillis y macehuales. Las formaciones sociales y los modos de producción de Tecali del siglo XII al XVI* (Mexico, 1978).

Ortiz de Montellano, Bernardo R., *Aztec Medicine, Health, and Nutrition* (New Brunswick, 1990).

Padden, R. C., *The Hummingbird and the Hawk: Conquest and Sovereignty in the Valley of Mexico, 1503–1541* (New York, 1970).

Pagden, Anthony, ed., *Hernán Cortés, Letters from Mexico* (New Haven, 1986).

Pasztory, Esther, *The Murals of Tepantitla, Teotihuacan* (New York, 1976).

Patch, Robert W., *Maya and Spaniard in Yucatán, 1648–1812* (Stanford, 1993).

Phelan, John L., *The Millennial Kingdom of the Franciscans in the New World* (Berkeley, 1956).

Pollard, Helen Perlstein, *Taríacuri's Legacy: The Prehispanic Tarascan State* (Norman, Okla., 1993).

Prescott, William, *History of the Conquest of Mexico* (London, 1929, first pubd. 1886).

Sabloff, Jeremy A., ed., *Supplement to the Handbook of Middle American Indians* (Austin. 1981).

Sabloff, Jeremy A., and Andrews, E. Wyllys, eds., *Late Lowland Maya Civilization: Classic to Postclassic* (Albuquerque, 1986).

Sanders, William T., and Price, Barbara J., *Mesoamerica: The Evolution of a Civilization* (1968).

Schele, Linda, and Freidel, David, *A Forest of Kings: The Untold Story of the Ancient Maya* (New York, 1990).

Semo, Enrique, *The History of Capitalism in Mexico: Its Origins, 1521–1763* (Austin, 1993).

Service, Ellman R., *Origins of the State and Civilization: The Process of Cultural Evolution* (New York, 1975).

Sharer, Robert J., *The Ancient Maya* (Stanford, 5th ed., 1995).

Sharer, Robert J., and Grove, David C., eds., *Regional Perspectives on the Olmec* (Cambridge, 1989).

Simpson, Lesley Byrd, *The Encomienda in New Spain: The Beginnings of Spanish Mexico* (Berkeley, 1982, first pubd. 1950).

Spicer, Edward E. *Cycles of Conquest: The Impact of Spain, Mexico and the United States on the Indians of the Southwest, 1553–1960* (Tucson, 1962).

Spores, Ronald, *The Mixtec Kings and Their People* (Norman, Okla., 1967).

Thomas, Hugh. *The Conquest of Mexico* (London, 1993).

Todorov, Tzvetan, *The Conquest of America* (New York, 1992).

Van Zantwijk, Rudolph, *The Aztec Arrangement: The Social History of Pre-Spanish Mexico* (Norman, Okla., 1985).

Vilar, Pierre, *A History of Gold and Money* (London, 1984).

Wachtel, Nathan, *The Vision of the Vanquished: The Spanish Conquest through Indian Eyes, 1520–1570* (Hassocks, 1977).

Wallerstein, Immanuel, *The Modern World-System: Capitalist Agriculture and the Origins of the European World-Economy in the Sixteenth Century* (New York, 1974).

Warren, J. Benedict, *The Conquest of Michoacan: The Spanish Domination of the Tarascan Kingdom in Western Mexico, 1521–1530* (Norman, Okla., 1985).

Weber, Max, *The Theory of Social and Economic Organization* (New York, 1964).

Weckman, Luis, *La herencia medieval de México* (Mexico, 1996, first pubd. 1984).

Wheatley, Paul, *The Pivot of the Four Quarters: A Preliminary Inquiry into the Origins and Character of the Ancient Chinese City* (Edinburgh, 1971).

Whitecotton, Joseph W., *The Zapotecs: Princes, Priests, and Peasants* (Norman, Okla., 1984).

Wittfogel, Karl, *Oriental Despotism* (New Haven, 1957).

Wolf, Eric R., *Europe and the People without History* (Berkeley, 1982).

Wolf, Eric R., *Sons of the Shaking Earth* (Chicago, 1972, first pubd. 1959).

Wolf, Eric R., ed., *The Valley of Mexico: Studies in Prehispanic Ecology and Society* (Albuquerque, 1976).

Index